The Pursuit of Excellence
Through Education

The Educational Psychology Series

Robert J. Sternberg and Wendy M. Williams, Series Editors

The Pursuit of Excellence Through Education

Edited by

Michel Ferrari
University of Toronto

 LAWRENCE ERLBAUM ASSOCIATES, PUBLISHERS
2002   Mahwah, New Jersey   London

Lawrence Erlbaum Associates, Inc., Publishers
10 Industrial Avenue
Mahwah, NJ 07430

Cover design by Marino E. Belich

Library of Congress Cataloging-in-Publication Data

The pursuit of excellence through education / edited by Michel Ferrari.
  p. cm.—(The educational psychology series)
  Includes bibliographical references and index.
  ISBN 0-8058-3187-8 (cloth : alk. paper) — ISBN 0-8058-3188-6 (pbk. : alk. paper)
  1. Education—Aims and objectives. 2. Educational sociology. 3. Excellence.
  I. Ferrari, Michel, Ph. D. II. Series.

  LB14.7 .P87 2001
  370.11—dc21   00-057297
                                                                        CIP

Books published by Lawrence Erlbaum Associates are printed on acid-free paper,
and their bindings are chosen for strength and durability.

Printed in the United States of America
10 9 8 7 6 5 4 3 2 1

Contents

v

Preface

Although the pursuit of excellence is as old as academics itself, the increasing diversity of the student population and limited resources are obliging educators and policymakers to return to the fundamental questions about the nature of excellence at the heart of the educational process. Specific definitions of excellence may change over time; however, few things are considered more important to education than the pursuit of academic excellence. It is almost impossible to imagine an effective educator who does not aim to promote excellent performances in his or her charges.

Nevertheless, there are many different viewpoints on excellence among educational psychologists and those in the other social sciences. One particularly glaring fault line in the debate about how to promote excellence concerns whether excellence is something fostered in individuals—by enhancing their inherent mental abilities, their knowledge, or their personal efforts to excel—or whether excellence is a product of particular institutional practices. Unfortunately, these two perspectives are rarely addressed in a single volume, and there are few chances to jointly consider the arguments for these positions, or for some synthesis of the two.

This volume allows those who emphasize transforming institutions and those who emphasize transforming individual activity to jointly consider how best to promote excellence through education. The point is not to favor either institutional or individual pursuit of excellence; rather, it is to raise the question of the relative responsibilities of each of these two poles to the human dialectic. Stated another way, the point is to consider how these two divergent viewpoints can be reconciled, or simply coordinated, in an effort to benefit both students and society at large. Chapter authors

address the issue of academic excellence, and also explore general principles of excellence that may extrapolate to other domains. Thus, a further
aim of this volume is to give authors a forum within which to discuss general claims about excellence that go beyond any particular individual or
cultural setting.

The main thesis of this volume is that excellence is promoted as much
in particular social and cultural settings as it is through individual activity.
The question then becomes not "Who is gifted or exceptional?", but
"What sort of social and personal conditions promote excellence, and
what sort of actions can educators take to assure that students will learn to
become excellent in ways that both they and society value?" In this view,
excellence can be fostered without sacrificing equity, both of which are
fundamental tenets of a democratic education.[1]

The nine chapters in this volume represent a wide range of viewpoints
on the pursuit of excellence. The chapters in Part I (chaps. 1–4) are
framed in terms of an individual excellence, including how individual differences in abilities, motivation, perceived self-efficacy, and cognitive development affect one's chances of achieving academic excellence.

In the opening chapter, Howard Gardner sets out to answer five questions about how to conceptualize excellence or extraordinariness that
have preoccupied him for much of the last decade. He suggests that any
discussion of excellence must coordinate three vantage points: the individual, the knowledge domain, and the professional field. In essence, he
suggests that extraordinary individuals are those who make a significant
impact on a domain, and he provides a rough taxonomy of different ways
that extraordinary individuals have had such an impact. For example, he
distinguishes between leaders, creators, and experts (which at the limit
may not really be extraordinary) and the particular social and cultural
contexts that allowed them to thrive. Gardner also takes up the rhetorical
challenge that studying exceptionally gifted or excellent individuals is elitist and more appropriate to early modern than to a postmodern psychology, saying that any deep consideration of human psychology must help
explain the emergence of extraordinary individuals. Gardner ends with
some broad lessons that can be learned from the study of such exceptional
individuals.

In chapter 2, Anders Ericsson emphasizes the crucial role of the quality
and amount of critical or deliberate practice in achieving the highest levels of expertise. Ericsson argues that the differences between individuals
acquired through practice far outstrip any innate differences in abilities or
capacity to learn. For example, observed physical differences between ex-

---

[1]A point raised many years ago in an excellent book by J. Gardner (1961). *Excellence: Can
we be equal and excellent too?* New York: Harper & Row.

cellent athletes and the average individual (e.g., exceptional size and endurance of the hearts of excellent runners) can be shown to result from intense physical training and not from inborn differences. Even acknowledged experts—who often appear to need less practice of basic aspects of their domain of expertise, like musical scales—still need to practice new pieces that they agree to perform. Ericsson shows how these extraordinary levels of skill are attained through practice guided by the best teachers and trainers in different knowledge domains. Such training promotes the creation of specialized knowledge structures that mediate performance at expert levels to help them monitor and continue to improve their level of skill.

In chapter 3, Robert Sternberg and his colleagues Elena Grigorenko and Michel Ferrari critically examine several different areas of research that view excellence as expertise. For example, they consider theories that focus on expert knowledge and knowledge organization, and those that focus on expert activities. They attempt to clarify some of the ambiguity that surrounds competing claims by those who argue the essential role of innate differences in mental abilities and those, like Ericsson, who extol the essential role of practice. They describe a small demonstration study that attempts to examine the relative contribution of both abilities and practice to developing expertise. The results of this study suggest that in many ways the current debates may represent a false dichotomy between abilities and practice in developing excellence in particular knowledge domains, as both are shown to be critical to developing expertise.

In chapter 4, Barry Zimmerman shows another direction of further refinement in studying the development of individual excellence. Zimmerman describes several studies that suggest that deliberate practice may be a special case of self-regulation of learning. Specifically, he provides biographic and experimental evidence to support the claim that extraordinary performers use several classic self-regulatory techniques during learning and performance. He also presents a theory of academic self-regulation in which academic excellence results from acquiring expertise at learning through critical attention to practice. In this model, expertise emerges through four levels of increasingly autonomous practice. Zimmerman also discusses motivational influences on effective self-regulation—especially the importance of perceived self-efficacy and causal attributions about academic excellence. Individual excellence is thus shown to depend as much on motivational influences on self-regulation of learning as it does on innate ability or high-quality instruction.

The chapters in Part II (chaps. 5–8) are framed in terms of sociocultural issues, especially how founding or fostering educational institutions and general culturally determined practices can help promote excellence.

In chapter 5, Michael Mascolo, Jin Li, Rosalie Fink, and Kurt Fischer consider how cultural context influences the development of individual excellence. They begin by suggesting that development and education involve both structural changes in specific skills and the fostering of social values about the aims of education. To illustrate their point, they show how American and Chinese educational systems strive toward different educational aims. Furthermore, Mascolo and his colleagues show that there are many paths to excellence within a culture, with individual development resembling a web more than it does a ladder. A wonderful illustration is provided by individuals who are extremely successful in their careers, despite having basic difficulties in decoding text typical of certain "learning disabled" children in school. Another important distinction proposed in the chapter is that of the developmental range of skilled performance, which ranges between optimal and functional contexts for learning and performance; in this light, excellence seems tied to optimal contexts for learning and performance.

In chapter 6, Rosa Pinkus and Ryan Sauder trace the emergence of a new medical subdiscipline, neurosurgery, at the turn of the century. In particular, they show how the emergence of neurosurgery was shaped by the technical and verbal rivalry between two key figures in medicine at that time, Harvey Cushing and his student Walter Dandy. Cushing insisted on publishing his mistakes as well as his successes as an ethical necessity to assure that the profession achieved a high general standard of excellence; Dandy, however, insisted on individual responsibility in determining whether one had the skill to implement specific surgical techniques. Their differences were not only personal, but helped define contemporary practice in neurosurgery. Indeed, their rivalry exemplified an essential tension in any developing profession, specifically, the tension between the need to set universal standards of excellence for an entire profession and the need for extraordinary practitioners to develop new techniques and practices that press at the boundaries of existing professional standards, often infuriating conservative members of the field. For Pinkus and Sauder, this struggle over medical practice emphasizes the intimate connection between ethical considerations and technical skill inherent in any profession, but which is especially prevalent in professions such as neurosurgery that deal in life-and-death decisions.

In chapter 7, Herbert Simon discusses how any consideration of excellence must look beyond the excellence of particular individuals to consider the excellence of organizations, in which individuals live and work. He considers several examples of how specific individuals both created and fostered institutions to accomplish valued goals that they could never have achieved working alone. Through these specific cases, Simon shows the very subtle link between individual excellence and institutional excellence.

Chapter 8 by Michel Ferrari considers the relations between personal and institutional sources of excellence even more broadly in terms of how an individual's personal pursuit of excellence necessarily involves culturally transmitted categories and narratives that frame this pursuit. Furthermore, individuals must negotiate between competing claims about excellence available to (and even imposed on) individual members of a culture—negotiations that require rhetoric and a case-by-case consideration of what constitutes excellence within specific social contexts. It is suggested that most difficult and interesting challenges to claims about excellence involve cases in which one must negotiate between traditions that have different agendas, or that have emerged from historically isolated communities.

Finally, chapter 9 serves as an integration and conclusion in which Michel Ferrari discusses common themes raised in the various chapters. The aim is not to summarize the chapters, but more modestly to tie together some of the key points raised by different authors and to show how views expressed using different terms may reflect common or complimentary concerns.

—*Michel Ferrari*

Part I

THE INDIVIDUAL PURSUIT
OF EXCELLENCE

Chapter 1

Learning From Extraordinary Minds

Howard Gardner
Harvard Graduate School of Education

FIVE QUESTIONS

I have spent much of the last decade studying individuals who would be considered extraordinary by almost any definition. Included in my sample are outstanding scientists (Charles Darwin, Albert Einstein, Sigmund Freud); artists (Pablo Picasso, Wolfgang Amadeus Mozart, Martha Graham) and political and religious leaders (Pope John XXIII, Rev. Martin Luther King, Jr., and Prime Minister Margaret Thatcher; cf. Gardner, 1993a, 1995, 1997, 1999). As a long-time enthusiast of biography and history, I have enjoyed my studies; they are their own reward. Yet any scholar who devotes a substantial part of his career to such an undertaking should be prepared to answer five questions:

1. How do you conceptualize extraordinariness?
2. How do you study it?
3. What discoveries have you made?
4. How do you justify this line of work?
5. What broader lessons might be learned from this work?

CONCEPTUALIZING EXTRAORDINARINESS

There are a number of ways in which one can determine who is extraordinary. One can select individuals on the basis of a quantitative measure, for example, number of home runs hit, number of best sellers. One can rely

3

on the decisions of informed individuals, for example, those who select the winners of the Nobel or Pulitzer Prizes. One can consider a number of different variables (e.g., fame, influence on other persons or on neighboring domains) and make the decision on a weighted multifactorial basis.

My approach grows out of the conceptualization of creativity proposed by Mihaly Csikszentmihalyi (1988, 1996). In Csikszentmihalyi's formulation, one does not ask "Who is creative?" or "What is creativity?" Instead one takes into account three distinct vantage points and the interactions among them. The vantage points are the individual *person*, with his or her talents, interests, ambitions; the *domain* or cultural sphere within which the person works; and the *field* or social system that renders judgment about merit. Only a person working in a domain whose works are considered to be creative by the field—either immediately or in the long run—merits the label "creative."

On the basis of this approach, a convenient measure of extraordinariness emerges. Any person who succeeds in altering a domain in a significant way emerges as extraordinary. Einstein altered physics, Picasso altered painting, Martin Luther King, Jr. altered the practice of protest politics in the United States. Of course, observers may not agree on whether, or to what extent, a domain has been altered; in any systematic study, one wants reasonable consensus that the individual(s) in question has in fact affected the domain. This is particularly important if the individual is controversial; I have restricted my focus to individuals whose effects on the domain would not be questioned by knowledgeable observers.

The concept of domain merits comment. Following Feldman and his colleagues (Feldman, 1986; Feldman, Csikszentmihalyi, & Gardner, 1994), I view a domain as any discipline or craft within a culture where it proves possible to order individuals in terms of expertise. Thus chess, gardening, atomic physics, playing the piano, or writing a scholarly paper are all domains in Western society. Domains typically have a characteristic symbol system (Csikszentmihalyi, 1996; Gardner, 1997). One can define domains narrowly (playing classical music on the piano) or more broadly (musical performance). I have sampled a range of domains in my work: In general individuals fall into the three categories of scientist, artist, and political/religious leader.

As one approaches the phenomenon of extraordinariness, I find it useful to observe the rough-and-ready taxonomy of roles presented here.

Adults

Expert. An expert is an individual who performs at the top level of his/her domain but makes no effort to alter the domain. Strictly speaking, such a person should not be deemed extraordinary.

Creator. A creator is an individual who fashions a new domain or significantly alters the practices or forms of an existing domain.

Genius. A genius is a creative individual who discovers a significant new truth about the world. Scientists typically discover truths about the external world; artists discover truths about the world of human experience.

Direct Leader. A direct leader is an individual who significantly affects the thoughts, feelings, or behaviors of a significant number of individuals. Direct leaders achieve their effects through stories that they tell to their audiences.

Indirect Leader. An indirect leader is an individual who significantly affects others through the creation of some kind of symbolic object, like a scientific theory or a work of art. These symbolic objects ultimately affect work in the domain, as well as the way in which that work is carried out. Creators are typically indirect leaders.

Young Persons

A Talented or Gifted Person. This is an individual who possesses an ability, manifest early in life and possibly inborn, that allows rapid mastery of a domain. Talented individuals may or may not elect to follow the path of creativity.

Prodigy. A prodigy is an individual with a precocious talent or gift.

Note that extraordinary individuals may use their talents for benign, malevolent, or neutral purposes.

THE STUDY OF EXTRAORDINARINESS

Although the study of extraordinariness (or excellence or genius) occupies only a small chapter in the history of psychology, in fact most schools of psychology have devoted some attention to this topic. Psychoanalysts, for example, have emphasized the importance of early family experience and kinds of defenses and sublimations involved in extraordinary output (Freud, 1958; Greenacre, 1959; Rank, 1932). Eschewing internal variables, behaviorists have investigated the patterns of reward for certain kinds of output (Skinner, 1953). Some authorities have argued that extraordinariness is more likely to emerge in certain personalities and temperaments (Eysenck, 1995) or as a result of certain intrinsic motivational states (Amabile, 1996). Cognitivists have questioned whether extraordinary individuals exhibit any special mental processes; in their view, those judged extraordinary are simply able to reorganize universal attentional and problem-solving capacities in particularly effective ways (Perkins, 1981; Simon, 1979).

Given my focus on extraordinary individuals, I have been especially influenced by two contrasting approaches. On the one hand, there is the *nomothetic* approach embraced by Dean Keith Simonton (1990, 1994) and Colin Martindale (1990). This approach features the statement of a hypothesis or the posing of a question about extraordinariness and the securing of quantitative data relevant to that question. So, for example, if one wants to know whether first-born individuals are more likely than their siblings to be extraordinary, one plows exhaustively through the relevant encyclopedias and biographies for information on birth order. In skilled and resourceful hands, the nomothetic approach can secure an approximate answer to a wide range of questions of interest to social scientists. (Note, however, that the methods by which the data are selected and analyzed may still be a subject of controversy.)

The contrasting approach is the *idiographic* approach favored by Howard Gruber (1981) and his colleagues (Wallace & Gruber, 1990). Inspired by humanistic and biographical studies, the researcher in this tradition focuses on a single subject and attempts to secure as much information as possible about the personality, working habits, and mental processes of the subject. The idiographic worker differs from the humanistic scholar in his positing and testing of informal models of how the individual person proceeds in his or her work. (Note, however, that such models do not arise directly from the data; they involve considerable constructive efforts on the part of the investigator.) Among recent examples of work in this tradition are studies by Arnheim (1962), Holmes (1985), Holton (1996), and Miller (1986).

Put succinctly, in my work I begin with the idiographic but proceed toward the nomothetic. That is, I begin with careful case studies of individuals, selected because they are extraordinary in a certain way (e.g., all are 20th-century artists who have contributed to modernism). Poring over autobiographies, biographies, secondary sources, and original manuscripts, I attempt to secure as much information as I can about their personality, developmental history, and manner of working within their chosen domain. Proceeding beyond the practices of the idiographic scholar, I then compare the subjects in my sample. In the manner of a more nomothetically oriented scholar, I search for patterns that apparently characterize all of the subjects (e.g., moving during adolescence to a major city); patterns that characterize some of the subjects (e.g., joining a group of "young Turks"); and those features that seem idiosyncratic to one or two individuals. These emerging patterns can then be tested, against other individuals in the sample, or in the light of data secured about new subjects. So far, my identification of patterns is informal, rather than systematic. However, in recent work, I have laid out the data on which those patterns were identified, so that other researchers can determine whether they discern the same patterns (Gardner, 1995).

To be sure, this method cannot yield the robust generalizations that emerge from a nomothetic study that tracks hundreds or even thousands of data points. Only a concerted program of research, involving many studies, could yield data of that degree of certitude. On the other hand, my modified nomothetic method allows one to gain a better understanding of the ways in which these pattern emerge, as well as detailed insights into apparent exceptions to the generalizations.

PRINCIPAL DISCOVERIES

So far, I have studied about 20 individuals in some depth, another dozen more superficially. Any claim about "findings" or "discoveries" is evidently tentative. Nonetheless, it is useful to step back and to indicate some of the patterns that have thus far emerged.

Nature and Nurture

Without question, some extraordinary individuals manifested unusual talent or gift early in life. It seems reasonable to conclude that these individuals have inherited some kind of skill from their parents or, to express it with more precision, have inherited the potential to master one or more domains with great rapidity. Certainly it is difficult to explain the musicality of Mozart, the graphic skills of Picasso, or the mathematical skills of Gauss in the absence of heritability of relevant traits.

Yet, at most, prodigiousness opens up possibilities. In every case, the prodigy has to work with an adult, usually a parent, who exposes him to material in the appropriate domain and helps him to gain the requisite skills. By most estimates, it takes around 10 years for the gifted individual to attain mastery of a domain; this process involves thousands of hours spent working with the relevant materials, be they patterns of notes, moves on the chess board, or ballet steps (Hayes, 1981). Of course, in cases where the individual begins training in the first few years of life, he may have attained expertise by adolescence.

By no means is extraordinariness restricted to prodigies—individuals who exhibit adult level skills when they are still children (Feldman, 1986). Indeed, most individuals who ultimately alter domains were not prodigies of the seven "creators of the modern world" whom I studied, only one (Picasso) is generally considered to have been a prodigy. And most prodigies, although achieving expertise, do not go on to alter domains, though some of them may seek to do so.

Choosing a Domain

The prodigy and adult creator face contrasting challenges. The prodigy receives his or her domain as part of his or her birthright. Mastering the domain itself is not a great challenge. However, in mastering a domain, the prodigy is exhibiting behaviors that the adult society has already consolidated and that it especially cherishes in the young. To become a creator, the prodigy must ultimately turn his or her back on conventional practice—and this rebellion requires an unorthodox, rather than a compliant personality.

In contrast, the adult creator is typically an individual who, from earlier years, exhibited a strong and somewhat rebellious personality. This person already has the temperament to be creative. What may be lacking is sufficient mastery of a domain. Young adult creators typically select a domain that they must first master and then alter, but they make this selection from a constrained range of options. Thus T. S. Eliot had the option of becoming a scholar or a writer; Igor Stravinsky showed talent in the dramatic, graphic, and musical art forms.

An intriguing question is how an individual comes to intersect with a given domain. Clearly, individuals can only select from among those domains that exist within their society. And, at the outset, individuals have only minimal influence on the course of a domain. Thus, unless one believes (as I do not) that a talented individual could excel in any domain, it is extremely important that the domain be selected carefully. Luck is also involved. Einstein might not have been nearly so successful as a physicist if he had been born a half century earlier or later; and, in all likelihood, Darwin did not have the mathematical and managerial talents that would have allowed him to excel in molecular biology today.

From Master to Creator

Wherever they grow up, future extraordinary individuals move toward the major cosmopolitan areas by the age of 20. Typically, during the early part of the century, these were capitals like Berlin, Paris, or Vienna. In these lively settings, the aspiring creators or leaders meet other young individuals of talent and often strike up meaningful friendships. They are casting about for others with whom they can make common innovative cause.

Yet at the same time, such aspiring creators are mastering a domain, and discovering problems or tensions that lurk within the domain. Although it is tempting to ignore these discrepancies, future creators do not; in fact, they may find them especially intriguing. The more that they become involved with such discrepancies, however, the more they deviate from established career paths. Inevitably, this cognitive marginalization produces a more lonely kind of existence.

The successful creator eventually arrives at a new way of seeing, hearing, thinking, and conceptualizing the domain. Suddenly or gradually, the discrepancies are dealt with as a new vision, captured in an appropriate symbol system, emerges. Such a breakthrough is an exciting experience but it also can be a frightening one. The creator is keenly aware that no one has ever conceptualized issues or patterns in quite the way that he or she has.

At such times, the creator desperately craves support. At a premium is intellectual support—an indication that what was discovered or invented makes sense to another thoughtful person. Equally needed is affective support—an indication that the person is loved, unconditionally, whether or not the creation ultimately stands the test of time. It is remarkable that in a time of great loneliness, nearly all creators seem to need and to benefit from such cognitive and affective support, sometimes from a single individual (composer Louis Horst served as both muse and lover to Martha Graham), sometimes from different sources (Freud received love from his family and intellectual support from his iconoclastic medical colleague Wilhelm Fliess).

By definition, the creator achieves some kind of breakthrough, which is eventually perceived as such by others. My studies indicate that breakthroughs may continue, and typically do so, at approximate 10-year intervals. The first breakthrough is most likely to be the sharpest one; succeeding breakthroughs are more likely to be synthetic, relating the innovations to classical traditions or problems in the domain. Choice of domain affects the possibility of subsequent breakthroughs. Such a series of breakthroughs is less likely in science and mathematics, tightly structured domains that favor the young mind. They are more likely in the arts or in humanistic scholarship, flexible domains where the creator has greater say in the form and content of the breakthroughs.

The Leader's Life

The creator, whom I sometimes term an *indirect leader*, is likely to lead a life that is relatively solitary. Despite the social aspects of late adolescence, much of the creator's time is spent alone or with a small group of individuals, while the creator is reworking the rules and procedures of an artistic or scientific symbol system.

In contrast, the "direct leader" must be a social animal. He or she has to affect other individuals. The principal means of influence available to the leader is the story. Effective leaders tell powerful stories and lead lives that embody the stories that they tell.

Two further points about leaders and their stories. First of all, when leaders are in charge of organizations that already have a strong mission, it is relatively less important that they be articulate. A greater proportion of their leadership can come from a powerful model of embodiment of the consensual mission. Thus, U.S. General George Marshall and Pope John XXIII were both influential leaders of our century; much of their leadership came from the impressive ways in which they led their professional lives, rather than from a new story that they related.

Second, the question arises about whether creators, as indirect leaders, must also be good storytellers. The leadership provided by creators comes from the innovations that they fashion in various symbol systems, which need not be linguistic. Thus Picasso led in the domain of visual arts by the kinds of works that he made. In addition, creators often lead by the ways in which they carry out their work—Picasso's protean style influenced successors like Jackson Pollock and Frank Stella. The styles of working embodied by leading artists and scientists often influence the practices of new members of the domain. Leaders are even less likely than creators to have been prodigies. Often they have struck observers as being youths with considerable as-yet-unchannelled energy that could ultimately be put to various constructive or destructive uses. Creators tend to come from intact bourgeois families, where they imbibe patterns of hard work and dedication. In contrast, leaders more often come from families that have been stressed—very often, the future leaders have lost a parent (usually a father) while they are still young; and have been expected (and have desired) to take on an adult role at a young age.

The Intelligences of Extraordinary Individuals

The study of extraordinariness gives comfort to those who are sympathetic to a pluralistic view of intelligence (Gardner, 1993b, 1993c). Whereas extraordinary individuals doubtless have IQs that are above the average, there is certainly no direct relation between psychometric intelligence and the achievement of extraordinariness (Simonton, 1994). Indeed, the highest IQ group that has been systematically followed—the "geniuses" identified early in the century by Lewis Terman—have gone on to become solid citizens but are not extraordinary in the sense of this chapter (Winner, 1996). It is interesting to note that, so far as we know, neither President Richard Nixon nor Nobel Laureate William Shockley—both younger Californians in the early part of this century—were members of the Terman sample.

My investigation confirms that extraordinary individuals stand out in terms of one or two intelligences, with the intelligences often ones that are uncommon for the domain. Thus, although most scientists are presumably strongest in logical–mathematical intelligence, Einstein displayed spatial intelligence that was particularly remarkable, and Freud stood out in terms of his linguistic and personal intelligences. Most creators also exhibit areas of genuine weakness: Freud was incompetent in the area of music, and Picasso nearly failed school. Given their ultimate accomplishments, Charles Darwin and Winston Churchill were remarkably unremarkable during their school years.

As a group, leaders appear to stand out in terms of at least three intelligences. Gifted in language, they can tell stories well. Sensitive to other human beings, they relate appropriately to other individuals and fashion their stories in terms of audience response. Exhibiting "existential intelligence," they are able to address the fundamental questions of life, questions that ask who are we, where are we coming from, what are we trying to achieve, what are the obstacles, how they might be circumvented (Gardner, 1999). There is, however, no requirement that leaders stand out in terms of other intelligences or have mastered other domains. And indeed, leaders frequently emerge as quite ordinary on many dimensions, including their capacities for logical thinking or economic analysis (Simonton, 1994).

The mix among intelligences no doubt varies across individuals of accomplishment; some leaders are far more gifted in language, some stand out in terms of sensitivity to others, or in their ability to touch on issues of life importance. What is probably important is to have a few strong intelligences, and a high motivation to make the most of them.

Relations to Other Persons

Clearly, leaders must be able to relate directly to other persons, particularly in an era of personal campaigning and the ubiquitous camera. Direct relation to others is much less important for those involved in the standard creative pursuits. As a rough rule of thumb, one could state that leaders spend most of their time with other persons, and need only reflect in a solitary manner for a small proportion of their day. In contrast, creators spend most of their working time in reflection, and need only a small portion of time to interact with others.

To get their work done, all individuals are dependent to some extent on others. Because they tend to become involved in major enterprises, extraordinary individuals are often in a position where they have to rely on the cooperative efforts of many persons. And even if their own work is relatively solitary, they still must be willing to exert effort to bring their work to the attention of others. Even apparently solitary scientists like Newton, Einstein, and Darwin had to direct some of their energies to public relations.

Yet, extraordinary individuals do *not* stand out in terms of their sterling relations to others. Indeed, if they do stand out, it is likely to be because of the poor quality of that relation. Whether creators or leaders, most of the extraordinary individuals whom I have studied turned out to be difficult characters: demanding of others, using others, not hesitant to drop one set of supporters or colleagues when another seemed necessary to get the job done. One British newspaper expressed my finding succinctly: *Einstein = Genius – Niceness.*

To be sure, it is not easy to measure individuals' altruism or sadism. Moreover, we live at a time of pathography, when the flaws of individuals are often put on public display. Still, it is worth considering why extraordinary individuals so often take their toll on those around them.

In my view, the future extraordinary person does not stand out in early life for his or her antisocial nature. The cumulative difficulty that comes to surround the person in later life may result from three related factors. First, the extraordinary person has become involved in huge projects that involve the labors of many persons. It is simply not practical to maintain positive relations with a cast of hundreds. Second, the person has acquired power and prestige; these qualities make him or her attractive to others and he or she is therefore in a position to be self-centered. Finally, the person realizes that life is coming to an end and concludes, therefore, that all must be subjected to the completion of the work. The Romans had a phrase "Libri aut liberi"—books or children. Although they may have children and grandchildren, extraordinary individuals choose to live through their works and, as they age, that life project becomes all-encompassing. A Faustian bargain is struck where all is sacrificed for the work.

These paragraphs give a feeling for some findings and patterns that have emerged from this line of work. I must stress again that all of these findings are decidedly tentative; based on a "small N," they all stand in need of revision and no doubt some will eventually be dropped altogether.

I am not being coy in saying that I crave case studies that apparently challenge the patterns. In such cases one is stimulated to uncover what factors are really at work in the pattern and to determine what, if anything, needs to be revised.

Let me give a few examples of apparent discrepancies. Most creators had a confidante with whom they worked during the time of their greatest breakthrough. But perhaps the greatest scientist of all time, Isaac Newton, apparently did not have one, during his *annus mirabile* of 1665–1666. One could infer that true genius works alone. But one could also pursue two different possibilities. Newton never knew his father and was hardly raised by his mother; thus he had no models of human relations on which to draw (subsequent events in his long and often unhappy life support this hypothesis). It is also possible that the greatest creators depend upon *paragons*—individuals whom they do not know personally but with whom they converse and feel akin. Newton must have had such figures in mind when he famously remarked "If I have seen further, it is by standing on the shoulders of giants."

As noted, most creators are very prickly. Charles Darwin seems an apparent exception; he was noted for kindness to guests and was well loved by his family. But Darwin stood out in at least three ways: (a) He was independently wealthy and could focus completely on his work, he was not dependent on patrons and did not have to spend precious time raising funds; (b) He was, or claimed to be, an invalid, and so was able to avoid social intercourse that he did not desire; (c) For much of his life, he avoided being considered creative, by refusing to publish his iconoclastic findings. Only when Alfred Wallace "forced his hand" by announcing a similar theory did Darwin go public. It is quite possible that Darwin would have gone to his grave as a relatively unknown scholar, only to be discovered posthumously after his notes or drafts were published.

As a final example, the philosopher Ludwig Wittgenstein seems to violate certain generalizations about extraordinariness in our time. Rather than being born in a remote surrounding and moving at adolescence to a cosmopolitan center, his pattern was the opposite. His childhood home was a major intellectual salon in Vienna, and he spent many of his adult years attempting to escape its influence.

Wittgenstein certainly refutes one familiar pattern. However, his case stimulates a reformulation of the pattern: Perhaps extraordinary individuals grow up in one kind of a milieu and, as soon as possible, attempt to move to a sharply contrasting kind of milieu. To escape Vienna, Wittgenstein wandered from rural Austria to far regions of Norway. Yet when it came to carrying out his work, he moved to Cambridge, England, then the center of philosophy, and, confirming a trend found in other young creators, he formed a bond to Bertrand Russell, who for many years served as a mentor and alter ego.

THE RATIONALE FOR SUCH STUDIES

In earlier centuries, the study of genius was considered an appropriate undertaking. Societies were élitist and proudly so; it was considered natural to look for major figures and to try to learn from them and be inspired by them. Plutarch's *Lives*, the medieval lives of saints, Vasari's portraits of artists, and the lengthy biographies by and of Romantic figures all testify to the onetime "political correctness" of this human interest.

Nowadays, however, such scholarly pursuits have come under suspicion. Some humanistic scholars challenge the idea of extraordinariness; either it does not exist at all, or it simply reflects the hegemony of certain centers of power. My samples of subjects are seen as skewed toward men and toward those who have worked in certain domains (high art, science) rather than others (childrearing, folks arts). And even my portrayals of Virginia Woolf or Mahatma Gandhi are often (and revealingly!) seen as studies reflecting the biases of aging Eurocentric White males, perhaps because of the personal identity of the investigating scholar, perhaps just because, despite their apparent marginality, these subjects have somehow managed to become household names.

I readily concede that there is no way to render a value-free judgment of extraordinariness. Any set of criteria is bound to reflect the hegemony of certain values at a given historical moment. Indeed, even at the same moment, different individuals and groups will doubtless place varying priorities on criteria, if not favor different sets of criteria. Nonetheless, I believe that over time these prejudices gradually lose force, and I am impressed by the extent to which certain individuals and accomplishments eventually come to be treasured (or to be deplored) over considerable regions of time and space.

Social and natural scientists are less likely to raise objections to the whole idea of selecting certain persons as extraordinary. They do, however, wonder about the timeliness of investigating single individuals when science is searching for powerful generalizations across a population. They point out the inherent subjectivity in the selection of persons, the securing of "data," and the interpretation of findings. And they note that this line of work is relatively thin with respect to the scientific mainstays of theory and model building, hypothesis testing, coding, and scoring of hard data.

Indeed, one confronts a paradoxical situation. Extraordinary individuals are by definition unusual, if not unique. Science searches for patterns. Perhaps patterns that obtain across highly unusual persons are rare. Gruber (personal communication, June 20, 1998) has urged that we seek the particularity of each subject, rather than worrying about whatever parallels might happen to emerge across a small set of subjects.

I take these objections into account, but I am not convinced by them. First, I do not believe that any area of human behavior and discourse should be ruled "off limits" to investigation. If there are human beings who achieve extraordinary things, they are as deserving of study as the autistic person, the retarded person, or the individual displaying multiple personalities. Perhaps generalizations will prove elusive, but we can only establish that elusiveness after the fact.

Second, I believe that science should be driven in the first instance by phenomena and questions, and not by methods. If an author like Proust or Woolf can accomplish something extraordinary, it is worth trying to unravel her or his achievement. If scholars are interested in how someone like Darwin—an initially indifferent student, a shy person, a person wary of the implications of his work—can become one of the "makers" of our time, that question is worth addressing. Ultimately, of course, one needs appropriate methods for answering those questions in a scientific way. If the past is any guide, such methods will be forthcoming.

In the end we seek a science of human behavior that is comprehensive. Such a scientific picture is inconceivable if it leaves no space for those individuals who have achieved the most, indeed, those whose disciplinary innovations have even made it possible to pose such questions. Some scholars believe that we can eventually explain those persons by building up from our understanding of ordinary persons doing ordinary things. Perhaps so, but I remain skeptical. At any rate, if one wants to understand a phenomenon X, it seems only sensible to me to begin by focusing on that phenomenon X. It makes less sense to hope that it will somehow be illuminated through the investigation of phenomena A or B or C or D, which, though more readily available, may not actually be closely related to phenomenon X.

BROADER LESSONS

In addition to satisfying one's scientific curiosity, there are also important societal reasons for understanding extraordinary individuals. Although certainly not perfect, extraordinary individuals are exemplary in various ways. We need heroes and heroines—if not saints, at least impressive human landmarks—against whom we can judge ourselves, our peers, our children. It is lamentable when young people find no one to admire, or worse, when they cannot even identify *facets* of individuals that they can admire.

We can learn from these individuals. These individuals were not born a species apart; they achieved what they did through hard work, often against great odds. Working with a particular set of intelligences and personality traits, a sense of direction and motivation, such persons fashioned products or sets of beliefs or practices that ultimately influenced many of their fellow human beings.

These last sentences may suggest that I am aligning myself with those who minimize the gaps between the ordinary and the extraordinary. And yet, in my view, what begin as quantitive differences or tendencies ultimately becomes differences of quality, differences in kind. Extraordinary individuals end up leading lives that *are* different: lives that focus on work, creating a network of enterprise, continually taking risks, reflecting on their progress, correcting course as needed. Part onlooker, part agent, they follow the course of that broader enterprise that they have launched as it expands and diversifies and leads to often unexpected conclusions or products.

The costs of a life so focused are not hidden; they make strong demands on the person (so that ordinary desires may be muted) and all too often on those near to the person. The flame may be alluring but the chances that a collaborator or admirer will be singed or even burned are patent. And sometimes the results of this work are not benign; some creators are destructive. Yet the fabric of our world would be less rich—incomparably less rich—were it not for the efforts and achivements of a handful of individuals who have aspired to make a difference.

Still, at the end of the day, it is important to ask whether there are any lessons for those of us who are unlikely ever to alter a domain in any significant way. My own research has pointed to three separate though related "metacognitive" practices, that I have termed *reflecting*, *leveraging*, and *framing* (Gardner, 1997).

In studying the lives of extraordinary individuals, one continually finds evidence that these individuals thought regularly and deeply about the operations of their own minds, the resources available to them, the nature and compatibility of their goals, the need to be flexible in reaching them, and the ways in which to make the most of every experience, be it joyous or painful. These mental activities are particularly important because extraordinary individuals cannot simply model their behaviors on earlier exemplars; they literally have to think through matters themselves.

Extraordinary individuals devote a great deal of time to reflecting. They think about what they want to achieve, how they are doing, when to persevere, when to shift course, when to return, freshly armed, to an earlier course. They may not all keep journals but most of them maintain some kind of record book in a notation that is convenient to them. They use such records as a means of taking stock of their current situation, evaluating their progress, planning their next step.

Extraordinary individuals leverage. They identify their strengths—in intelligence, personality, temperament, resources—and they push these hard. They do not waste precious time worrying much about what they cannot do well—others can (and will) step in and aid. Instead, they try to locate or carve a niche in which their peculiar amalgam of talents is especially needed or desired. And as inveterate reflectors, they are perennially probing the terrain for new niches in which their skills can be freshly leveraged.

Finally, extraordinary individuals frame their experiences. All individuals fail, and being extremely ambitious, extraordinary individuals fail with surprising frequency. But unlike many others, their failures are neither repressed, nor do they cause the creators or leaders to give up or go fishing. Rather, the individuals I have studied ponder their defeats and failures, and ferret out what they can learn from these apparent mishaps. No one expressed this stance more compellingly than the French economist Jean Monnet, justly honored for his role in starting the European Common Market and the European Union. Monnet is said to have remarked, "I regard every defeat as an opportunity."

An appropriate transition is made here from the heights of extraordinariness to the realities of everyday education around the globe. All young people will one day have to find their niche as workers and as citizens. The adults in the culture will have the opportunity, indeed, the obligation, to help children make the transition to these roles. As parents and teachers, what can we do to educate our children effectively? And, in particular, how can we draw on the findings about extraordinary individuals to aid us in accomplishing this responsibility . . . in the most responsible way?

Fortunately, children are very interested in other human beings, and particularly in those who have accomplished something notable. It makes sense to expose young children to examples of individuals whose accomplishments are likely to impress and inspire the child; and it makes special sense to choose those exemplars who are worthy role models in a rounded fashion. Ty Cobb and Mark McGwire may be equally good baseball players, but the latter is much more admirable than the former in terms of human relations.

At a time when nearly everyone is seen as flawed, perhaps all too flawed, those who would introduce heroes to children must proceed in a sensitive manner. (A recent example that comes readily to mind is the ways in which parents had to interpret reports of the transgressions of President Bill Clinton.) If one treats certain individuals as being perfect, one is setting up youngsters for ultimate cynicism. (Only those not made of flesh and blood can be perfect.) Alternatively, if one concentrates too much on the flaws, then the educational potential of the model is likely to be lost. Perhaps it is most important to emphasize that no individual is completely perfect, that we can still learn from those who have flaws, and that the person's achievements need not necessarily be tied to the flaws.

Children can be inspired by examples from literature, history, or the media. But it is much more vivid to encounter individuals first hand. Therefore, it is important, whenever possible, to create situations where children have the opportunity to meet and interact directly with individuals who have accomplished something. Here the individual's effect on the domain need not be dramatic; the very fact that the person has accomplished a feat that the child can admire should suffice.

Role models are a start, but they are no substitute for one's own efficacy in a domain. The most important ensemble of gifts that we can give to children are competence, skill, and flow in one or more domain, or discipline, that is valued by the society. Absent such skill, children may feel that they are proficient but will be unmasked as soon as they attempt to perform publicly. Armed with such skill, children have the chance to earn legitimate recognition from others.

Considered first are skills in domains where an individual can make a living. However, of equal importance are skills in parenting and citizenship, in being a decent human being. These skills will not arise automatically, any more than will skill in playing the piano or writing an essay. Good education, good role models, and constant opportunities to practice these desirable behaviors are vital ingredients.

As youngsters are acquiring skills in these vocational and personal realms, they can again be aided by lessons from those who are extraordinary. In the transition from novice to expert, and then, on occasion, from expert to creator, individuals are aided by the opportunities to reflect, leverage, and frame. Such metacognitive virtues are most unlikely to arise on their own; they come about because children see their elders engage in such activities, have the opportunity to do so themselves, and benefit from practice.

An example may be helpful here. All youngsters who are learning a skill will encounter occasions where they do not perform well. Adults have a variety of responses at their disposal. They can choose to ignore the failure, pretending that it did not happen. They can berate the child. If the situation is competitive, they can criticize the referees, the judges, or the opponents. None of these moves is productive in the long run.

What makes sense? The adult—parent, relative, coach—should sit down with the child and the two should examine what happened and what it means. One can almost always derive lessons from an apparent failure, and often those lessons can be quite helpful to the child the next time around. In asking what can be learned, and then encouraging that learning to take place, the adult and child are "framing." And just as framing has aided many extraordinary individuals to persist in their endeavors, such a positive "construction" of events should prove beneficial to the child in the long run. Indeed, one hopes that eventually the adult's contribution will become superfluous, as the adult's input fades away and the growing youngster learns to frame for herself.

Ultimately, we cannot know in advance who will turn out to be Extraordinary with a capital E, who will demonstrate a modicum of unusualness, and who will simply become a competent adult. There will be false positives, as well as false negatives. Yet there are benefits in treating every individual as if he or she were potentially extraordinary. Following the lines I've sketched out, the person will at least have had exposure to examples of excellence, mastered skills and behaviors that are valued by the culture, and acquired the metacognitive virtues of reflecting, leveraging, and framing. These accomplishments make it likely that the person will realize more of his or her potential. In the process, even if the individuals themselves do not achieve extraordinary feats, the society in which they live may achieve extraordinary results.

ACKNOWLEDGMENTS

The work described in this chapter was supported by generous gifts from The Christian A. Johnson Endeavor Foundation, Thomas H. Lee, the Jesse Phillips Foundation, and the Louise and Claude Rosenberg, Jr. Family Foundation.

REFERENCES

Amabile, T. (1996). *Creativity in context*. Boulder, CO: Westview Press.
Arnheim, R. (1962). *Picasso's Guernica*. Berkeley: University of California Press.
Csikszentmihalyi, M. (1988). Society, culture, and person: A systems view of creativity. In R. Sternberg (Ed.), *The nature of creativity* (pp. 325–329). New York: Cambridge University Press.
Csikszentmihalyi, M. (1996). *Creativity*. New York: HarperCollins.
Eysenck, H. J. (1995). *Genius: The natural history of creativity*. New York: Cambridge University Press.
Feldman, D. H., Csikszentmihalyi, M., & Gardner, H. (1994). *Changing the world*. Westport, CT: Greenwood.
Feldman, D. H. with Goldsmith, L. (1986). *Nature's gambit*. New York: Basic Books.
Freud, S. (1958). *Creativity and the unconscious* (B. Nelson, Ed.). New York: Harper & Row.
Gardner, H. (1993a). *Creating minds: An anatomy of creativity as seen through the lives of Freud, Einstein, Picasso, Stravinsky, Eliot, Graham, and Gandhi*. New York: Basic Books.
Gardner, H. (1993b). *Frames of mind: The theory of multiple intelligences*. New York: Basic Books.
Gardner, H. (1993c). *Multiple intelligences: The theory in practice*. New York: Basic Books.
Gardner, H. (1997). *Extraordinary minds: Portraits of four exceptional individuals and an examination of our own extraordinariness*. New York: Basic Books.
Gardner, H. (1999). Are there additional intelligences? In J. Kane (Ed.), *Education, information, and transformation* (pp. 111–131). Englewood Cliffs, NJ: Prentice-Hall.
Gardner, H. (1999). *The disciplined mind: What all students should understand*. New York: Simon & Schuster.
Gardner, H. with Laskin, E. (1995). *Leading minds: An anatomy of leadership*. New York: Basic Books.
Greenacre, P. (1959). Play in relation to the creative imagination. *Psychoanalytic Study of the Child* (Vol. 14, pp. 61–80). New York: International Universities Press.
Gruber, H. (1981). *Darwin on man*. Chicago: University of Chicago Press.
Hayes, J. R. (1981). *The compleat problem solver*. Philadelphia: Franklin Institute Press.
Holmes, F. L. (1985). *Lavoisier and the chemistry of life*. Madison: University of Wisconsin Press.
Holton, G. (1996). *Einstein, history, and other passions*. New York: Addison-Wesley.
Martindale, C. (1990). *The clockwork muse*. New York: Basic Books.

Miller, A. (1986). *Imagery in scientific thought*. Cambridge, MA: MIT Press.

Perkins, D. N. (1981). *The mind's best work*. Cambridge, MA: Harvard University Press.

Rank, O. (1932). *Art and artist*. New York: Knopf.

Simon, H. (1979). *Models of thought*. New Haven, CT: Yale University Press.

Simonton, D. K. (1990). *Psychology, science, and history*. New Haven, CT: Yale University Press.

Simonton, D. K. (1994). *Greatness*. New York: Guilford Press.

Skinner, B. F. (1953). *The science of behavior*. New York: Macmillan.

Wallace, D., & Gruber, H. (Eds.). (1990). *Creative people at work*. New York: Oxford University Press.

Winner, E. (1996). *Gifted children: Myths and realities*. New York: Basic Books.

Chapter 2

Attaining Excellence Through Deliberate Practice: Insights From the Study of Expert Performance

K. Anders Ericsson
The Florida State University

Almost everyone can remember being awed by the public performances of elite musicians and athletes. All of us have looked at sculptures and paintings and read novels that clearly transcend a level of performance that we and other people in our immediate environment could attain. For a long time it has been considered obvious that some individuals' ability to achieve at a level superior to that of other motivated individuals must reflect an unobtainable difference, some genetically determined, and therefore innate, talent. If there were no immutable inborn limit, why wouldn't every highly motivated individual reach the highest level?

The most obvious approach to determining how individuals excel is to study those who have achieved mastery. As I show by quoting international masters discussing excellence later in this chapter, most masters emphasize the role of motivation, concentration, and the willingness to work hard on improving performance. In contrast to the general population and less accomplished performers, the masters seem to consider inborn capacities and innate talent as relatively unimportant in comparison to their attained abilities and skills. However, most people who have unsuccessfully pursued high excellence in a domain find it very difficult to accept the masters' emphasis on motivation and the continued need to work hard in improving performance. Many of us have worked hard to improve a skill over a period of weeks without catching up or perhaps not even markedly gaining on the individuals who perform at the highest levels. Could it be that the masters were praising motivation and effort due to

21

false modesty? Perhaps they simply do not know the critical factors that lead them toward excellence.

In this chapter, I demonstrate how the masters' descriptions of the critical role played by motivation and willingness to work can be understood as a manifestation of the specially designed training activities that my colleagues and I refer to as deliberate practice (Ericsson, 1996, 1997, 1998; Ericsson & Charness, 1994; Ericsson, Krampe, & Tesch-Römer, 1993; Ericsson & Lehmann, 1996). In the first section, I argue that once we define excellence as consistently superior achievement in the core activities of a domain, an interpretable picture emerges. Even the level of achievement of the most "talented" develops gradually and, with rare exceptions, it takes at least 10 years of active involvement within a domain to reach an international level. However, the vast majority of active individuals in domains such as golf and tennis show minimal performance improvements even after decades of participation. In the second section, I discuss the difference between mere participation in domain-related activities, and activities designed to improve performance—deliberate practice.

THE SCIENTIFIC STUDY OF EXPERT PERFORMANCE

Many of the most dazzling and amazing accomplishments of geniuses, such as those by the famous musician, Paganini, and the famous mathematician, Gauss, refer to events that cannot be independently verified (Ericsson, 1996, 1997, 1998). Our only knowledge about most of these achievements is based on reports in the form of anecdotes about their childhood told by the famous individuals at the end of their career. Under these circumstances it would be reasonable to expect distortions of memory and even exaggerations. To study exceptional achievement scientifically, it is necessary that we disregard questionable anecdotes and focus on the empirical evidence that reflects stable phenomena that can be independently verified, and, ideally, reproduced under controlled circumstances. Once we restrict the research findings to this clearly defined empirical evidence then reviews (Ericsson & Lehmann, 1996; Ericsson & Smith, 1991) show an orderly and consistent body of knowledge even for exceptional achievements and performance.

In most domains of expertise, individuals have been interested in assessing the level of performance under fair and controlled circumstances. In athletic competitions, this has resulted in highly standardized conditions that approach the controlled conditions used to study performance in the laboratory. In a similar manner, musicians, dancers, and chess players perform under controlled conditions during competitions and tournaments. These competitions serve several purposes beyond identifying the best performers and presenting awards. For younger performers, successful performance at competitions is necessary to gain access to the best teachers and training environments, which, in turn, increases the chances of attaining one of the small number of openings as full-time professionals in the domain.

Ericsson and Smith (1991) discussed how one could use similar techniques to measure various types of professional expertise. More recent reviews show that efforts to demonstrate the superior performance of experts are not always successful. For example, highly experienced psychotherapists are not more successful in treatment of patients than novice therapists (Dawes, 1994). More generally, the length of professional experience after completed training has often been found to be a weak predictor of performance in representative professional activities, such as medical diagnosis (Norman, Coblentz, Brooks, & Babcook, 1992; Schmidt, Norman, & Boshuizen, 1990), auditing (Bédard & Chi, 1993; Bonner & Pennington, 1991), text editing (Rosson, 1985), and judgment and decision making (Camerer & Johnson, 1991; Shanteau & Stewart, 1992). If we are interested in understanding the structure and acquisition of excellence in the representative activities that define expertise in a given domain, we need to restrict ourselves to domains in which experts exhibit objectively superior performance.

If expert performers can reliably reproduce their performance in public, it is likely that they could do the same during training, and even under laboratory conditions, a finding confirmed by recent research (Ericsson & Lehmann, 1996). Unfortunately, the conditions of naturally occurring expert performance are quite complex and frequently differ markedly among performers within a domain. For example, musicians are allowed to select their own pieces of music for their performance and the sequence of moves chess players make in a game is never the same. However, most domains of expertise require that experts are able to excel at certain types of representative tasks or else they would not meet the definition of a true expert. Ericsson and Smith (1991) discussed how to identify representative tasks that capture the essence of expert performance in a domain and how to reproduce this performance under controlled laboratory conditions so that investigators could identify the responsible mediating mechanisms.

Figure 2.1 illustrates three types of tasks that have been found to capture the essence of expertise, where the measured performance is closely related to the level of naturally occurring performance. To study chess expertise, players at different skill levels are asked to generate the best move for the same unfamiliar chess positions. Typists are given the same material to type as fast as possible. Musicians are asked to play familiar or unfa-

Domain	Presented Information	Task
Chess	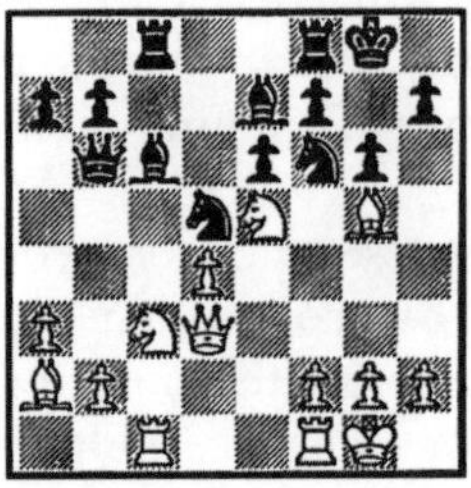	Select the best chess move for this position
Typing	OVERVIEW--NATURE AND NURTURE OF EXPERTISE The central challenge for any account of expertise is to explain how some individuals attain the highest levels of achievement in a domain and why so few reach that level. However, given the continuing struggle in Psychology to explain every day (lower) levels of achievement, it may appear presumptuous to attempt to explain even more advanced levels. Consequently, the accounts of expertise have been focusing on the general characteristics of the mechanisms. In order to be able to achieve at very high (expert) levels in domains of expertise both nature and nurture are necessary. Hence, everyone agrees that experts need to have acquired the necessary domain-specific knowledge and skills (nurture). Furthermore, the expert's performance often looks effortless and their most refined and insightful behavior is generated rapidly and naturally rather than the result of prolonged deliberation. It would thus appear that experts must excel in general basic characteristics, such as intelligence, memory, speed and flexibility, which have been assumed to be impossible to train and thus must be determined to a large degree by genetic factors (nature). Over the last couple of centuries, the arguments of the relative importance of nature versus nurture for expert achievement have been intricately linked to the theories of the actual processes that mediate the achievement of experts and to the conceptions of which aspects of human characteristics could be modified through development and training. Hence, this entry will briefly review the most important conceptions during the last century and then turn to a summary of our current knowledge and in conclusion the implications and connections of expert performance for creativity and genius will be outlined.	Type as much of the presented text as possible within one minute
Music	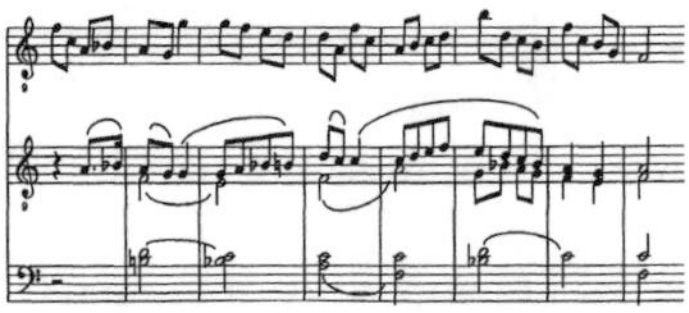	Play the same piece of music twice in same manner

FIG. 2.1. Three examples of laboratory tasks that capture the consistently superior performance of domain experts in chess, typing, and music. From "Expertise," by K. A. Ericsson and Andreas C. Lehmann, 1999, *Encyclopedia of Creativity*. Copyright by Academic Press. Reprinted with permission of the authors.

miliar pieces, then asked to repeat their performance. When musicians are instructed to repeat their original performance, experts can do it with much less deviation than less skilled musicians, thus exhibiting greater control over their performance.

Considering only the superior performance of experts, it is possible to identify several claims about expertise that generalize across domains. First, I review evidence showing that superior expert performance is primarily acquired, and that extensive domain-related experience is necessary but not sufficient for its development. I show that many thousands of hours of deliberate practice and training are necessary to reach the highest levels of performance. Then I describe in depth the cognitive and physiological processes proposed to mediate the development of expert performance and show how deliberate practice optimizes the effect of these processes on performance.

The Necessity of Domain-Specific Experience

Recent reviews (Ericsson, 1996; Ericsson & Lehmann, 1996) show that extended engagement in domain-related activities is necessary to attain expert performance in that domain. What is the process in acquiring expertise? First, longitudinal assessments of performance reveal that performance improves gradually, as illustrated in Fig. 2.2; there is no objective evidence for high initial level of performance without any relevant experience and practice nor for abrupt improvement of reproducible performance when it is regularly tested. Even the performance of child prodigies in music and chess, whose performance is vastly superior to that of their peers, show gradual, steady improvement over time. If elite performance was limited primarily by the functional capacity of the body and brain, one would expect performance to peak around the age of physical maturation: the late teens in industrialized countries. However, experts' best performance is often attained many years, and even decades, later, as illustrated in Fig. 2.2. The age at which performers typically reach their

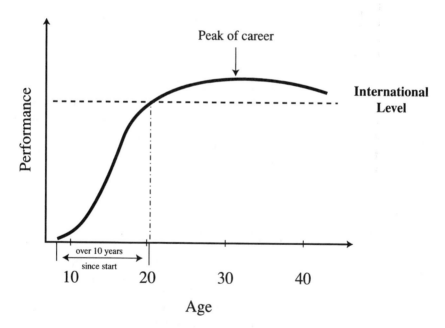

FIG. 2.2. An illustration of the gradual increases in expert performance as a function of age, in domains such as chess. The international level, which is attained after more than around 10 years of involvement in the domain, is indicated by the horizontal dashed line. From "Expertise," by K. A. Ericsson and Andreas C. Lehmann, 1999, *Encyclopedia of Creativity*. Copyright by Academic Press. Reprinted with permission of the authors.

highest level of performance in many vigorous sports is the mid to late 20s; for the arts and science, it is a decade later, in the 30s and 40s (see Simonton, 1997, for a review). Continued, often extended, development of expertise past physical maturity shows that experience is necessary for improving the experts' performance. Finally, the most compelling evidence for the role of vast experience in expertise is that even the most "talented" need around 10 years of intense involvement before they reach an international level, and for most individuals it takes considerably longer.

Simon and Chase (1973) originally proposed the 10-year rule, showing that no modern chess master had reached the international level in less than approximately 10 years of playing. Subsequent reviews show that the 10-year rule extends to music composition, as well as to sports, science, and arts (Ericsson, Krampe, & Tesch-Römer, 1993). In sum, the fact that engagement in specific, domain-related activities is necessary to acquire expertise is well established. Most importantly, given that very few individuals sustain commitment for more than a few months, much less years, most individuals will never know the upper limit of their performance.

Going Beyond Mere Experience: Activities That Mediate Improvements of Performance

Extensive experience and involvement in a domain is necessary for the select group of elite individuals who steadily increase their performance and reach very high levels. In contrast, the vast majority of individuals struggle to reach an acceptable level of performance, and having done so, allow their performance to remain relatively stable for years and even decades. Consider the example of recreational golfers, tennis players, and skiers. The striking difference between elite and average performance seems to result not just from the duration of an individual's activity, but from the particular types of domain-related activities they choose.

From retrospective interviews of international-level performers in many domains, Bloom (1985) showed that elite performers are typically introduced to their future domain in a playful manner. As soon as they enjoy the activity and show promise compared to peers in the neighborhood, they are encouraged to seek out a teacher and initiate regular practice. Bloom and his colleagues showed the importance of access to the best training environments and the most qualified teachers. The parents of the future elite performers spend large sums of money for teachers and equipment, and devote considerable time to escorting their child to training and weekend competitions. In some cases, the performer and their family even relocate to be closer to the teacher and the training facilities. Based on their interviews, Bloom (1985) argued that access to the best training resources was necessary to reach the highest levels.

Given the limited opportunities available to work with the best teachers and training resources, only the most qualified individuals are admitted at each stage. Could it be that the superior training resources do not really enhance the rate of improvement, and the highly selected individuals would improve just as well by themselves? The best single source of evidence for the value of current training methods comes from historical comparisons (Ericsson, Krampe, & Tesch-Römer, 1993; Lehmann & Ericsson, 1998). The most dramatic improvements in the level of performance over historical time are found in sports. In some events, such as the marathon and swimming events, many serious amateurs of today could easily beat the gold medal winners of the early Olympic games. For example, after the IVth Olympic Games in 1908, they almost prohibited the double somersault in dives because they believed that these dives were dangerous and no human would ever be able to control them. Similarly, some music compositions deemed nearly impossible to play in the 19th century have become part of the standard repertoire today. Exceptional levels of performance are originally attained only by a single eminent performer. However, after some time other individuals are able to figure out training methods so they can attain that same level of performance. Eventually, this training becomes part of regular instruction and all elite performers in the domain are expected to attain the new higher standard. In competitive domains, such as baseball, it is sometimes difficult to demonstrate the increased level of today's performers because both the level of the pitcher and the batter has improved concurrently (Gould, 1996).

If the best individuals in a discipline already differ from other individuals at the start of training with master teachers and coaches, how can we explain these differences in performance prior to this advanced level? Can we also explain individual differences in the rate of improvement among individuals in the same training environment? To determine which activities could improve individuals' performance development prior to advanced training, one should first consider activities with conditions beneficial to learning and effective performance improvement. A century of laboratory research has revealed that learning is most effective when it includes focused goals, such as improving a specific aspect of performance; feedback that compares the actual to the desired performance; and opportunities for repetition, so the desired level of performance can be achieved.

Based on interviews with expert violinists at the music academy in Berlin, my colleagues and I (Ericsson, Krampe, & Tesch-Römer, 1993) identified activities for which we could trace the duration of the music students' engagement during the period prior to their entry in the music academy. We were particularly interested in those activities that had been specifically designed to improve performance, which we called *deliberate practice.* A prime example of deliberate practice is the music students' solitary practice in which they work to master specific goals determined by their music teacher at weekly lessons. We were able to compare the time use among several groups of musicians differing in their level of music performance, based on daily diaries and retrospective estimates. Even among these expert groups we were able to find that the most accomplished musicians had spent more time in activities classified as deliberate practice during their development (see Fig. 2.3) and that these differences were reliably observable before their admittance to the academy at around age 18. By the age of 20, the best musicians had spent over 10,000 hours practicing, which is 2,500 and 5,000 hours more than two less accomplished groups of expert musicians, respectively, and 8,000 hours more than amateur pianists of the same age (Krampe & Ericsson, 1996).

Several studies and reviews have found a consistent relation between performance level and the quality and amount of deliberate practice in chess (Charness, Krampe, & Mayr, 1996), sports (Helsen, Starkes, &

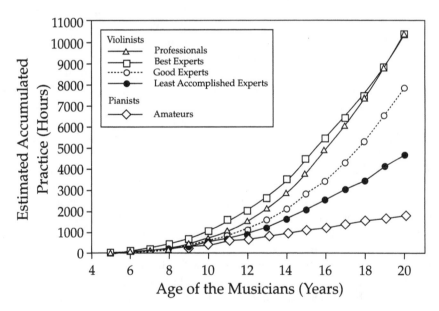

FIG. 2.3.   Estimated amount of time for solitary practice as a function of age for the middle-aged *professional* violinists (triangles), the *best* expert violinists (squares), the *good* expert violinists (empty circles), the *least accomplished* expert violinists (filled circles) and *amateur* pianists (diamonds). From "The Role of Deliberate Practice in the Acquisition of Expert Performance," by K. A. Ericsson, R. Th. Krampe, and C. Tesch-Römer, 1993, *Psychological Review, 100*(3), p. 379 and p. 384. Copyright 1993 by American Psychological Association. Adapted with permission.

Hodges, 1998; Hodges & Starkes, 1996; Starkes, Deakin, Allard, Hodges, & Hayes, 1996), and music (Krampe & Ericsson, 1996; Lehmann & Ericsson, 1996; Sloboda, 1996). The concept of deliberate practice also provides accounts for many earlier findings in other domains, such as medicine, software design, bridge, snooker, typing, and exceptional memory performance (Ericsson & Lehmann, 1996), as well as for the results from the rare longitudinal studies of elite performers (Schneider, 1993).

When most people imagine a child practicing the piano, they tend to think of someone mindlessly repeating the same short piece, while the sound remains unmusical, aversive, and without any noticeable improvement. Nobody in their right mind would argue that poor or mediocre piano students could become outstanding musicians merely by spending more time on this type of mechanical practice. Mindless repetition is the direct opposite of deliberate practice, when individuals concentrate on actively trying to go beyond their current abilities. Consistent with the mental demands of problem solving and other types of learning, deliberate practice is done in limited periods of intense concentration. Diaries of the expert musicians revealed that they only engaged in practice without rest for around an hour and they preferred to practice early in the morning when their minds were fresh (Ericsson, Krampe, & Tesch-Römer, 1993). Even more interesting, the best expert musicians were found to practice, on the average, the same amount every day, including weekends, and the amount of practice never consistently exceeded 4 to 5 hours per day. The experts told us during interviews that it was primarily their ability to sustain the concentration necessary for deliberate practice that limited their hours of practice. And their diaries reveal that the more the experts practiced, the more time they spent resting and sleeping; the increased sleep was primarily in the form of afternoon naps. Our review of other research (Ericsson, Krampe, & Tesch-Römer, 1993) showed that the limit of 4 to 5 hours of daily deliberate practice or similarly demanding activities held true for a wide range of elite performers in different domains, such as writing by famous authors (Cowley, 1959; Plimpton, 1977), as did their increased tendency to take recuperative naps. Furthermore, unless the daily levels of practice were restricted, such that subsequent rest and nighttime sleep allowed the individual to restore their equilibrium, individuals would encounter overtraining injuries, and eventually, incapacitating "burnout."

Do the best performers in a domain also need deliberate practice to perfect their skills, or are they fundamentally different? Fortunately, many of the famous musicians and acclaimed music teachers have been interviewed about the structure of their practice. Their answers are remarkably consistent and are eloquently summarized by one of the best-known violin teachers and virtuosi, Emil Sauer (1913):

One hour of concentrated practice with the mind fresh and the body rested is better than four hours of dissipated practice with the mind stale and the body tired. . . . I find in my own daily practice that it is best for me to practice two hours in the morning and then two hours later in the day. When I am finished with two hours of hard study I am exhausted from close concentration. I have also noted that any time over this period is wasted. (p. 238)

It is clear that the need for specific types of practice, such as etudes and scales, diminishes for musicians who have already attained technical mastery, but not the need for deliberate practice in mastering new pieces: "With the limited time I have to practice nowadays, I apply myself immediately to works that I am preparing," writes Katims (1972, p. 238) and he argues that mastering pieces for upcoming concerts presents the specific challenges that guide deliberate practice. Many elite musicians are able to engage in mental practice: "I have a favorite silent study that I do all of the time, I do it before I start practicing. I do it on the train during my travel, and before I come out on the platform. I do it constantly" (Primrose, 1972, p. 248). With such a generalized definition of practice, even the famous violinist, Fritz Kreisler (1972, p. 98), who claimed to have never "practiced," would have engaged in practice: "How sad it is that in these days the emphasis is on how many hours one practices. When the Elgar concerto was dedicated to me I never put a finger on the fingerboard. Then I saw a passage I thought I could improve, and spent six hours on it."

The necessity of concentration for successful practice is recognized by all adult performers and some of them can even recall when they gained that insight: "For the first five years of musical experience, I simply played the piano. I played everything, sonatas, concertos—everything; large works were absorbed from one lesson to the next. When I was about twelve I began to awake to the necessity for serious study; then I really began to practice in earnest" (Schnitzer, 1915, p. 217). In fact, many of the individual differences among young music students practicing the same amount of time may be attributable to differences in the quality of their practice. The famous violin teacher Ivan Galamian (1972) argued:

If we analyze the development of the well-known artists, we see that in almost every case the success of their entire career was dependent upon the quality of their practicing. In practically each case, the practicing was constantly supervised either by the teacher or an assistant to the teacher. The lesson is not all. Children do not know how to work alone. The teacher must constantly teach the child how to practice. (p. 351)

Recent analyses of famous child prodigies in music showed that all of them had been closely supervised from a young age by skilled musicians (Lehmann, 1997; Lehmann & Ericsson, 1998). The supervising adult could then guide the young child's attention by appropriate activities and also help eliminate mistakes and poor technique. Equally important, the adult could monitor the child's attention and never push the child beyond their ability to sustain concentration. Thus, the training would be restricted to relatively brief periods at the start of systematic training. More generally, Starkes et al. (1996) showed that the duration of daily training given future expert performers was very similar across several domains, such as music and sports. During the first year, the daily level of practice was around 15 to 30 minutes, on average, with steady increases for each additional year, reaching 4 to 5 hours after around a decade. Starkes et al. found an intriguing similarity between increases in the amount of practice for sports when the athletes started practice around age 12, and music, when start of practice is closer to 6 to 7 years of age. If this pattern of results is found consistently across all domains, it would suggest that the level of increased training may require a slow physiological adaptation to the demands of sustained practice, which may be relatively insensitive to chronological age.

It has been shown that the attainment of expert performance requires an extended period of high level deliberate practice, where the duration of practice is limited by the ability to sustain concentration, a capacity that appears to increase as a function of years of practice in the domain. Consequently, a certain amount of deliberate practice may be necessary to reach the highest performance levels, and individual differences, even among experts, may reflect differences in the amount and quality of practice. However, most people would argue that there are distinct limits to the influence of practice, and that inborn capacities and innate talent will play a very important role in determining performance, especially at the highest levels within a domain. It has even been proposed by Sternberg (1996) that individuals with more innate talent would be more successful during practice, and thus more willing to engage in practice—possibly explaining at least part of the relation between amount of deliberate practice and performance.

In the remainder of this chapter, I propose how various types of training activities can, over time, change the body according to well-understood physiological principles, and that expert performance can be viewed as the end product of an extended series of psychological modifications and physiological adaptations. Most proposed individual differences between elite performers that have been attributed to innate talent can more parsimoniously be explained as adaptations to extended, intense practice. Furthermore, I explain how expert performance is mediated by complex memory mechanisms and representations that have been acquired as a result of practice, and how these mechanisms are critical to continued performance improvement.

CHANGE THROUGH DELIBERATE PRACTICE:
SEARCHING FOR THE CAUSAL BIOLOGICAL
AND COGNITIVE MECHANISMS UNDERLYING
THE ACQUISITION OF EXPERT PERFORMANCE

Most people find it inconceivable that the dramatic differences between expert and novice performance can be explained by a series of incremental improvements starting at the novice level. They believe that most of the benefits of learning are attained rapidly within weeks or months as is the case for most everyday skills and leisure activities. They are surprised to hear that it takes years, even decades, of gradual improvements for even the most "talented" to reach the highest levels of performance.

Why is it that everyday performance rapidly reaches a stable level, whereas expert performance continues to improve? The reason appears to be primarily motivational. For example, why don't most of us reach a physical fitness level that we would like? In this case there is ample scientific evidence that increasing the duration and intensity of our daily exercise would eventually get us close. To keep doing what we normally do is easy, but changing our fitness level requires altering our habits. Change is effortful until a new habitual state has been attained. The primary challenge appears not to be maintaining the desired level of activity once it has been reached, but the *process of changing* from one steady state to another. However, to sustain improvements over extended periods, the aspiring expert performer must constantly keep working toward the next higher level of performance.

When considering physical fitness it is well known that merely wanting to be fit is simply not enough to attain fitness. Similarly, daydreaming about how good it would feel to be fit does not do it either. Desire to attain some level of mastery in a domain of expertise is not by itself enough to reach the desired level. Until we can specify the causal mechanisms that link deliberate practice directly to the observed improvements of performance, an account based on deliberate practice is not qualitatively different from one based on prayer or mere intensity of desire. Consequently, we need to show that deliberate practice influences performance in a manner consistent with scientifically well-established mechanisms— not through divine intervention or mere wish fulfillment.

A related obstacle is the common sense conception of the limited malleability of the body and mind as a function of extended activity. Most adults have very limited recent experience of changing their bodies through regular physical exercise or acquiring high levels of mastery in a new domain. Their experience is generally consistent with the view that gradual improvements are possible, but a relatively stable limit is soon reached that is determined by stable characteristics, presumably determined by unmodifiable genetic factors. Because most individuals never achieve very high levels of performance in a domain, they are unacquainted with highly refined, intense deliberate practice and the complex mechanisms mediating expert performance.

Discussions about expert performance and other types of superior achievement have revolved around dichotomies, such as whether this level of performance can be attributed to acquired strategies or basic abilities, hardware or software, environment or genetics. A more promising path toward better understanding of expert performance involves development of explicit models illustrating the mechanisms that mediate expert performance, how training changes these mechanisms, and how these changes alter the body and the nervous system.

Historically, various metaphors and models have been proposed to describe the structure of complex performance. The first proposals described complex activity as the result of an intricate mechanical clock or as a hydraulic system consisting of hoses filled with liquids under pressure. A major breakthrough came when electronic computers made it possible to efficiently program strategies using a small set of basic operations. However, all machine metaphors mislead us about the limits of human modifiability. After all, computer hardware remains fixed until changed by a human operator. Biological systems and animals can change in ways that machines cannot, and these biological comparisons have important implications for human performance. Let me give you one striking example.

As many of you probably know from introductory courses in biology, if a newt (a type of salamander) loses a leg, the leg regenerates. If mammals lose a leg it will not grow back, but some mammalian organs do regenerate. For instance, if a surgeon removes over half of the liver, the remaining tissue will grow back to 70% of its original size. If a kidney is removed during an organ donation, then the remaining kidney will grow as much as 50% in the following week. Most of the internal organs can regenerate lost parts, and, most importantly, many of their characteristics, including size, are adaptively determined by demand. Unlike other mechanical and electric machines that wear out with use, the human body's efficiency increases as a function of the amount of similar activity.

Several types of processes lead to physiological changes, and thereby to changes in performance. The processes that have been most studied in psychology correspond to associative learning, and the acquisition of knowledge, procedures, and skills—in essence, the traditional definition of learning in psychology. These processes result in specific neural changes in the central nervous system. I return to this type of learning later in the chapter. A second major type of process resulting in physiological change that has been studied extensively in exercise physiology involves adaptations at the level of individual cells. Given that, unlike human beings, these cells cannot be told what to do, changes in them occur as reaction to processes that influence their physical and chemical environment.

In the following overview, I focus on the changes in single cells and in the central nervous system, but I recognize the need to consider other types of learning and adaptation that I barely touch on, including learning processes that increase subjects' control over their emotional state, and their metacognitive insights into the long-term development of skill. I first discuss the processes of adaptation of individual cells and then return to processes in the central nervous system involved in the acquisition of skill.

Deliberate Modification of Bodily Systems and Individual Cells

Everyone knows that it is possible to improve many kinds of performance by training and exercise. Virtually all adults have increased their performance in some activity such as running or doing push-ups. To improve, individuals typically engage in the activity, but this is not enough. In addition, it is essential to push the limits of current capacity, applying the overload principle, to get into the aversive zone of "No strain, no gain." Research on aerobic fitness has found that young healthy adults have to maintain a heart rate above 70% of the maximal heart rate (over 140 to 150 for most adults) for an extended time on a regular basis (around three times a week) in order to attain measurable improvement in fitness. By inducing this strain or overload for an extended time, a chain reaction of metabolic processes and chemical changes is initiated to counteract deviations from equilibrium, triggering additional control processes and their chemical by-products. When sufficient strain is attained, chemical changes activate the processes responsible for regeneration and growth of the affected tissue. Of course, the level of intensity should not be so great to cause permanent damage to tissue. In fact, the intensity, duration, and frequency of practice has to be set at a level such that the body is given enough opportunity to recuperate between practice sessions, otherwise there is eventual risk for over-use injuries or even burn-out (Ericsson, Krampe, & Tesch-Römer, 1993). Finding the appropriate balance between strain and rest is one of the major challenges for individuals pursuing their limits of performance.

Most improvements in fitness occur following activity, when the body has a chance to recuperate. Through a delicate process of alternating strain and regeneration/growth, the body slowly adapts to the demands of the increased regular physical activity. As expected, large-scale studies (Bouchard, Shephard, & Stephens, 1994) have found a close relation between the amount and intensity of habitual physical activity for individuals and their physical fitness, as illustrated in Fig. 2.4.

Fitness: Adaptation to Activity

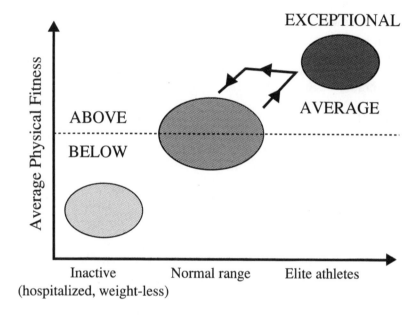

FIG. 2.4. A schematic illustration of the relation between the level of habitual activity and current fitness level.

When the level of habitual physical activity changes, the body adapts to the new situation. For example, the fitness of well-trained individuals is rapidly reduced when they cannot engage in demanding physical activity due to various conditions, such as weightless astronauts in space or injured athletes confined to bed rest. Fitness level also increases with the duration and intensity of daily training. It is important to note that the duration of weekly training necessary to improve fitness is often several times greater than the duration required to merely maintain an existing level, as is illustrated by the arrows in Fig. 2.4.

When intense daily training is sustained for months or years, the observable results are often dramatic. There is documented evidence of practice-related anatomical changes in elite athletes (see Ericsson, 1996; Ericsson & Lehmann, 1996; Robergs & Roberts, 1997, for reviews). For example, after years of intense practice, adaptive processes can increase the size and endurance of athletes' hearts so more oxygen-rich blood is pumped through the muscles. Even bones have been shown to change in response to training. The arm with which an elite tennis player holds the racquet not only has bigger muscles, but thicker, wider bones. It has been recognized for years that the mechanical vibration of the bones due to intense activity stimulates bone growth in the direction orthogonal to the plane of the vibrations.

One interesting hypothesis for controlling these adaptive processes suggests that when cell walls are deformed due to the mechanical vibration, molecules are torn off, which, in turn, stimulate the growth to counteract the effects on cell walls from future mechanical vibrations. This mechanism can also explain why only the thickness and width of bones are affected rather than their length. The inability of increasing the length of bones through physical activity means that height cannot be increased by practice. Height thus appears to be one of a very small number of innately determined factors that have been clearly shown to influence some types of sports performance, such as basketball (favorably) and gymnastics (unfavorably), that cannot be modified by physical training.

The most compelling evidence for physiological adaptation is provided by longitudinal studies showing that critical performance characteristics change favorably as a function of training, then revert back to the normal range when training is discontinued. Elite swimmers who stopped training in early adulthood were shown to lack any benefits of prior training compared to an age-matched control group when they tried to reacquire their fitness years later. The primary benefit of training for long-term fitness maintenance is that it requires much less effort to maintain already acquired adaptation than it took to acquire it originally. Recent research shows that many types of adaptations can be maintained with shorter periods of intermittent practice as long as the intensity of training activity is preserved. Perhaps the sustained intense effort leads to production of metabolic waste products, such as lactic acid, that stimulate chemical processes preserving the new state of equilibrium.

There are good reasons to believe that many of the mechanisms regulating adaptation to training are also involved in normal physiological development of children and adolescents (see Ericsson & Lehmann, 1996, for a brief review). Hence, training during certain periods of development appear to yield especially large adaptive responses. For example, recent research has shown that average children between 3 and 5 years of age can acquire perfect pitch, the ability to name individual tones when presented in isolation, given appropriate training. Differences in brain structure may be observed in individuals with perfect pitch compared to that of other musicians (Schlaug, Jäncke, Huang, & Steinmetz, 1995). These differences can be explained by early childhood activities that lead to different patterns of neurological development. Numerous animal studies show that training influences neurological development through the growth of blood supply, the density of synapses, and even by restricting development of certain structures. For musicians who play stringed instruments, the size and elaboration of cortical mapping for the fingers, especially the little finger on the left hand, is correlated with the onset of music training (Elbert, Pantev, Wienbruch, Rockstroh, & Taub, 1995). Other performance-related physiological characteristics, such as the metabolic characteristics of muscle fibers, and the range of motion for classical ballet dancers, may be relatively easily influenced during development, but are much harder to influence through training in adolescence and adulthood.

These cellular and physiological characteristics will only result in performance change if they are integrated with skilled actions and movements. The next section discusses the acquisition of skilled and expert performance.

Everyday Skills and Expert Performance: The Acquisition of Integrated Appropriate Actions

Everyday skills and expert performance require that individuals efficiently generate appropriate actions when needed. A comprehensive theory needs to describe both the similarities and differences in the acquisition of everyday skills and expert performance. How individuals are able to acquire everyday life skills, such as typing, playing tennis, or driving a car, is extensively researched and well understood. It is therefore easiest to briefly review theories of everyday skill acquisition, then describe how the acquisition of expert performance differs.

The traditional theories of skill acquisition (Anderson, 1982, 1987; Fitts & Posner, 1967) propose that during the initial "cognitive" phase (see Fig. 2.5) individuals learn the underlying structure of the activity and what aspects they must attend to. In the early stages of learning the activity, they get clear feedback about their misunderstandings as they make mistakes. Gradually they become able to avoid gross errors, and eventually, during the second "associative" phase, they can attain an acceptable level of performance. During the third and final "autonomous" phase, their goal is typically to achieve effortless performance as rapidly as possible. After some limited period of training and experience, frequently less than 50 hours for most recreational activities, such as skiing, tennis and driving a car, an acceptable standard of performance can be generated without much need for effortful attention. At this point, execution of the everyday activity has attained many characteristics of automated performance (Anderson, 1982, 1987; Fitts & Posner, 1967; Shiffrin & Schneider, 1977) and requires only minimal effort.

Figure 2.5 illustrates the transition from the first stage, when everyday performance initially improves as individuals expend effort to reach an acceptable level, to adaptation as their performance becomes automatized, and the performance level fixated, as individuals lose conscious con-

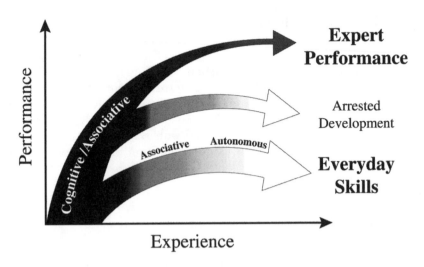

FIG. 2.5. An illustration of the qualitative difference between the course of improvement of expert performance and of everyday activities. The goal for everyday activities is to reach as rapidly as possible a satisfactory level that is stable and "autonomous." After individuals pass through the "cognitive" and "associative" phases they can generate their performance virtually automatically with a minimal amount of effort (see the gray/white plateau at the bottom of the graph). In contrast, expert performers counteract automaticity by developing increasingly complex mental representations to attain higher levels of control of their performance and will therefore remain within the cognitive and associative phases. Some experts will at some point in their career give up their commitment to seeking excellence and thus terminate regular engagement in deliberate practice to further improve performance, which results in premature automation of their performance. Adapted from "The Scientific Study of Expert Levels of Performance: General implications for optimal learning and creativity" by K. A. Ericsson, 1998, *High Ability Studies, 9*, p. 90. Copyright 1998 by European Council for High Ability. Adapted with permission.

trol over intentionally modifying and changing it. Everyone can easily recall from their childhood and adolescence how many hours of rote memorization of the alphabet, the multiplication tables, and foreign vocabulary items are necessary for direct retrieval from memory. Once this occurs, increased experience will not be associated with increased accuracy. Within this simple view of skill acquisition, it is inevitable that the major improvements are limited to the first phases, but then performance reaches a stable automatic level determined by factors that are believed to be outside the individuals' control. Individual differences are thus believed to reflect stable immutable differences, such as innate capacities and neural speed.

This popular conception of how everyday skills are acquired has little in common with our view of the acquisition of expert performance through deliberate practice. In contrast to the rapid automatization of everyday skills and the emergence of a stable asymptote for performance, expert performance continues to improve as a function of increased experience and deliberate practice, as illustrated in Fig. 2.5. One of the most crucial challenges for aspiring expert performers is to avoid the arrested development associated with generalized automaticity of performance and to acquire cognitive skills to support continued learning and improvement. Expert performers counteract the arrested development associated with automaticity by deliberately acquiring and refining cognitive mechanisms to support continued learning and improvement. These mechanisms increase experts' control and ability to monitor performance. The expert has to continue to design training situations where the goal is to attain a level beyond their current performance in order to keep improving. There are many methods for discovering new and higher levels of performance (Ericsson, 1996). One common method involves comparing one's performance to that of more proficient individuals in their domain of expertise. One can then identify differences and then attempt to reduce them gradually through extended deliberate practice.

In the next section I show that expert performance is not fully automated. I first briefly summarize empirical evidence demonstrating that experts retain cognitive control over detailed aspects of their performance at the highest levels and that experts rely on acquired representations to support planning and reasoning (Ericsson & Delaney, 1999). These cognitive representations allow the experts to generate internal images of a desired performance without having experienced it before and to design plans for producing a similar performance without having previously done so. In a second subsection I then discuss how future experts acquire representations, and how these representations allow them to identify new goals so that they can continue improving their performance. These representations form the foundation for continued learning without teachers, and ultimately allow for the very best of them to make innovative creative contributions to their domain of expertise.

The Cognitive Mediation of Expert Performance.   An everyday skill like driving one's car to work is typically viewed as a means to an end, where the goals of the activity concern safety and minimization of effort. These goals differ completely from those for expert-performance version of that activity, such as professionals driving race cars. Like other expert performers, race car drivers have to maintain full concentration as they try to push the limits of their best performance during training and competition without unduly increasing the risks for accidents.

To reach their highest possible level of performance, expert performers make adjustments appropriate to specific opponents or performance situations. For example, experts routinely make extensive adjustments to accommodate situational factors, such as weather and new equipment. A concert pianist will familiarize themselves with the piano and the acoustics of a concert hall. An expert billiard player will carefully examine any peculiarities of the billiard table before competing on it. Expert performers often study and prepare for competition against particular opponents, identifying their weaknesses to gain competitive advantage. As part of their expertise they are able to make fast, fluent adjustments to changes in their opponents' strategies. None of these adjustments would be possible if expert performance were fully automated. Furthermore, expert performers are well known for having accurate, detailed memories of their performance long after the competitions, which would be impossible if their performance during those events had been automated.

The most compelling scientific evidence for preserved cognitive control of expert performance comes from laboratory studies where experts reproduce their superior performance with representative tasks that capture the essence of expertise in their domain (Ericsson & Smith, 1991). In his pioneering work on expertise, de Groot (1946/1978) instructed good and world-class chess players to think aloud while selecting the best move to a set of unfamiliar chess positions. He found that the quality of selected moves was closely associated with the performers' chess skill. From verbal reports, he found that the chess players first perceived, then interpreted the chess position, and rapidly retrieved potential moves from memory. The moves were then evaluated by planning where the consequences of each move were explored by generating sequences of plausible counter moves using a mental representation of a chess board. During the course of this evaluation even the world-class players would discover better moves. Consequently, experts' defining ability to generate better moves for chess positions than less skilled players (see Fig. 2.1) depends to a large extent on deliberate planning and reasoning, as well as on careful evaluation, in order to reduce the frequency of mistakes.

In sum, Ericsson and Lehmann (1996) found that experts' think-aloud protocols revealed how superior performance was mediated by deliberate preparation, planning, reasoning, and evaluation in a wide range of domains, such as medicine, computer programming, sports, and games. Therefore, the performance of experts cannot be completely automated, but remains mediated by complex control processes.

Recent reviews (Ericsson, 1996; Ericsson & Kintsch, 1995) show that individuals who perform at higher levels utilize specific kinds of memory processes. They have acquired refined mental representations to maintain access to relevant information and support more extensive, flexible reasoning about encountered tasks or situations. In most domains, better performers are able to rapidly encode, store, and manipulate relevant information for representative tasks in memory (Ericsson & Lehmann, 1996). To illustrate this ability, I describe a couple of examples from two different domains. With increased skill, chess players are able to do deep planning, to mentally generate longer sequences of chess moves and evaluate their consequences (Charness, 1981). Chess masters are even able to hold the image of the chess position in mind so accurately that they can play blind-fold chess—play without perceptually available chessboards.

Similar evidence for mental representations has been shown for motor-skill experts, such as snooker players and musicians. In recent studies, Lehmann and Ericsson (1995, 1997) had expert pianists memorize a short piece of music. The pianists were then given an unexpected series of tasks in which they were asked to reproduce the piece at the same tempo under changed conditions, such as playing every other measure, and play-ing notes with only one hand. Although reliable individual differences were observed, accuracy was uniformly very high. Many subjects were even able to accurately transpose the music into a different key at regular tempo when unexpectedly asked to do so. During accurate transposition performance, the pianists pressed different piano keys with new finger combinations, which demonstrates mediation of a flexible memory repre-sentation of the music. In sum, the essence of expert performance is a gen-eralized skill at successfully meeting the demands of new situations and rapidly adapting to changing conditions.

Even expert performance in activities where superior speed is the crite-rion, such as typing (see Fig. 2.1), appears to depend primarily on mediat-ing representations rather than faster basic speed of neurons and muscles. The superior speed of expert typists is related to how far they look ahead in the text beyond the word that they are currently typing, as illustrated in Fig. 2.6. With increased acquired skill, expert typists can look further ahead in the text so they can prepare future keystrokes in advance, mov-ing relevant fingers toward their desired locations on the keyboard. The importance of anticipatory processing has been confirmed by analysis of high-speed films of expert typists and experimental studies where expert typists have been restricted from looking ahead. Furthermore, the further someone looks ahead in a text when asked to read aloud rapidly, the higher their ability to read and the faster their silent reading speed (Levin & Addis, 1979).

Similarly, the rapid reactions of athletes, such as hockey goalies, tennis players, and hitters in baseball, have been found to reflect skills acquired primarily to avoid time stress by successfully anticipating future events (Abernethy, 1991). This evidence supports the hypothesis that expert ath-letes have a learned, rather than a biological, speed advantage over their less accomplished peers. For example, when skilled tennis players are pre-paring to return a serve, they study the movements of the opponent lead-

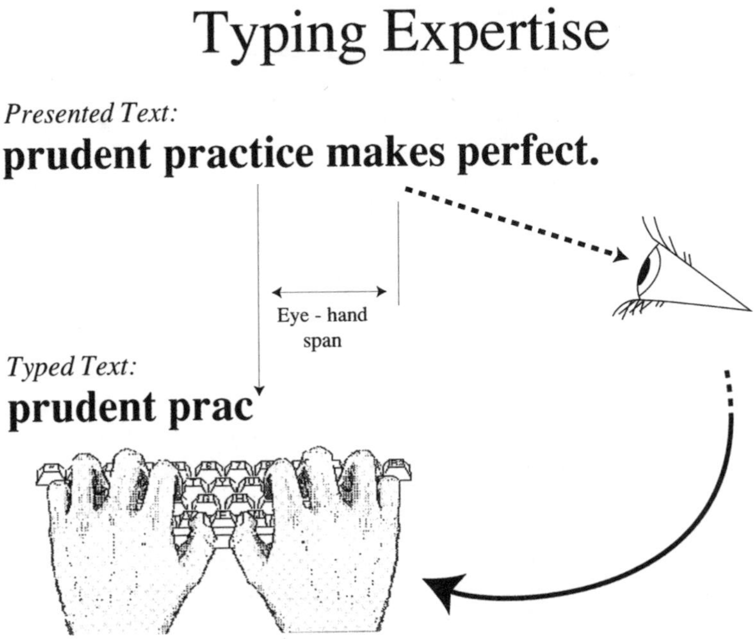

Typing Expertise

Presented Text:
prudent practice makes perfect.

Eye - hand
span

Typed Text:
prudent prac

FIG. 2.6.   An illustration of how the eyes of expert typists fixate material in the text well in advance of the currently typed text in order to gain advantages by advance preparation. Copyright 1999 by K. Anders Ericsson. Reprinted with permission.

ing up to contact between the ball and the racquet to identify the type of spin and the general direction. Given the ballistic nature of a serve, it is often possible for skilled players to accurately anticipate the consequences of these movements. It is important to note that novice tennis players use an entirely different strategy, and usually initiate their preparations to return the ball once it is sufficiently close to see where it will bounce. If the cues that immediately precede ball contact had become fully automated to guide the hitting of the ball, anticipatory perceptual skills would never develop. The anticipatory use of predictive cues must have been acquired later at a more advanced level of skill. The superior anticipation of the ball trajectory has frequently been misinterpreted as evidence for superior basic perceptual capacity. It is a common misconception that elite athletes have more accurate vision that allows them to see the balls better, when, in fact, their performance reflects a highly specialized perceptual skill. Consistent with this hypothesis, elite athletes are not consistently superior on standard vision tests compared to less accomplished performers and other control groups.

The increasingly refined representations allow expert performers to attain more control of relevant aspects of performance and greater ability to anticipate, plan, and reason about alternative courses of action. In addition to providing better control, these mental representations play an essential role in helping individuals continue improving their performance: setting new goals for improvement, monitoring their performance, and refining skills necessary to maintaining the integrity and fluency of their current level of superior performance during continued learning. How are these representations acquired during development? Are there special training activities that allow individuals to refine them?

The Acquisition of Representations That Mediate the Attainment of Expert Performance. The most important differences between autonomous everyday skills and expert performance are related to the experts' representations that allow them to keep controlling and monitoring their behavior. In an earlier section I showed that there is a natural tendency toward developing effortless automatized performance in which conscious access to mediating representations is not acquired. Fluent repeated performance appears to become highly automated unless the individual actively resists. I argue that experts and aspiring experts rely on deliberate practice to counteract complete automatization and to promote the development and refinement of representations. First, I briefly discuss how the mediating representations are acquired from the start of supervised practice to the attainment domain expertise. Then I discuss a few specific examples of how deliberate practice refines these representations and the associated mechanisms that improve the integrated performance.

In many domains of expertise, individuals are introduced into the domain as children and after short period of playful interaction the future expert performers start working with a teacher (see Fig. 2.7), illustrating the three stages proposed by Bloom (1985)). The playful interaction will not stop but it will be augmented by deliberate practice. When beginners are initially introduced to practice in a domain, the teacher instructs them using very simple objectives and tasks and will explicitly guide the beginners' attention to specific aspects of the training situations as part of the instruction. The beginner, often aided by a parent, must learn to regenerate the goals of the training activity and sustain focus on attaining them through repeated attempts.

The assigned goal of the training activity also provides the beginners with a means to generate feedback about the correctness of their performance, which would imply some mental representation although not necessarily a sophisticated one. During development, teachers often help their students identify errors and make necessary changes and specific corrections. As the student's performance improves, they acquire more complex representations to monitor and control the aspects of performance targeted by the teacher for correction during solitary practice. As the com-

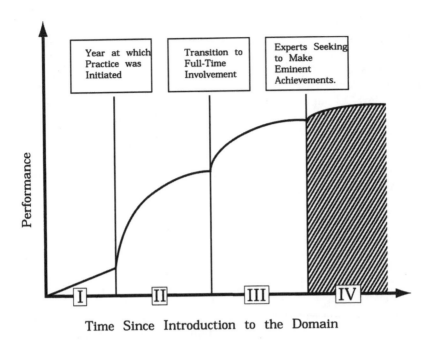

FIG. 2.7.   Three phases of acquisition of expert performance, followed by a
qualitatively different fourth phase when, in order to make a creative contribution, experts attempt to go beyond the available knowledge in the domain. From "Can We Create Gifted People?" by K. A. Ericsson, R. Th.
Krampe, and S. Heizmann in G. R. Bock and K. Ackrill (Eds.), *The Origins
and Development of High Ability* (pp. 222–249), 1993, Chichester, England:
Wiley. Copyright 1993 by CIBA Foundation. Adapted with permission.

plexity of the acquired performance level increases, so does the complexity of practice goals and the associated training activities. At higher levels,
the teacher will provide primarily general instructions and feedback,
which requires the students to monitor their own performance, to actively
engage in problem solving as errors occur, and to make appropriate adjustments to their performance. Hence, parallel to improvement of their
performance, students develop complex mental representations of the desired performance so that they can monitor their concurrent performance
to identify discrepancies between their desired and actual performance
(Ericsson, 1996; Glaser, 1996). As students reach high levels of achievement, they will have acquired the knowledge of their teachers and have
mental representations that enable them to independently monitor and
improve their performance. They may also augment the training methods
of their teachers by studying the performance and achievements of current and past masters in their domain (Ericsson, 1996, 1997). When indi-

viduals have mastered all the knowledge and techniques of their domain (see the fourth phase in Fig. 2.7), they are uniquely positioned to have a chance to make major creative contributions by adding something genuinely new, whether it is a new idea, a new training method, or a new interpretation of past achievements. This type of creative expansion of the space of conceivable achievements and accumulated knowledge in a specific domain represents the supreme level of achievement in any domain.

There is still an incomplete understanding of representations: how they are acquired and refined, and their close connection to performance, but I illustrate their involvement in deliberate practice with a few examples from chess, copying, and music.

Deliberate Practice in Chess: Planning and Anticipating the Consequences of an Opponents' Actions. Once an individual has reached a level of proficiency in a domain, when they are better than everyone else in the chess club, for example, how can they be challenged to find increasingly better chess moves? Expert chess players have been shown to collect books and magazines with the recorded games of chess masters (Charness et al., 1996). They can play through the games to see if their selected moves correspond to those originally selected by the masters. If the chess master's move differed from their own, it would imply that they must have missed something in their planning and evaluation. Through careful, extended analysis the chess expert is generally able to discover the reasons for the chess master's move. Similarly, the chess player can read published analyses of various opening combinations and supplement their own knowledge by examining the consequences of new variations of these openings. Serious chess players spend as much as 4 hours every day engaged in this type of solitary study (Charness et al., 1996; Ericsson, Krampe, & Tesch-Römer, 1993).

Deliberate Practice in Typing: A Focus on Improving Copying Speed. Once an individual has reached a stable typing speed, how can it be increased? During normal typing activities it is important to minimize errors and maintain a typing speed that can be sustained. On the other hand, typists can for short intervals sustain higher speeds with full concentration, at least 10 to 30% above normal rates. Consequently, the recommended practice to improve speed is setting aside time daily to type selected materials at the faster rate without concern about accuracy. Initially typists seem only to be able to sustain the concentration necessary to type 10 to 20% faster than normal speed for 10 to 15 minutes per day. After adaptation to this kind of regular practice, the duration of the training sessions can be increased (cf. the earlier discussion of the development of weekly practice time). When typists push themselves beyond the comfortable range of reliable typing, they will encounter key-stroke combinations that slow them down, causing hesitations or awkward motor movements. By eliminating the specific problems through better anticipation or coordination of motor behavior, these problems can be corrected. Typists can then iteratively confront remaining typing combinations that limit typing speed. The recommended training to improve speed in other perceptual motor activities shares many of these same methods of progressive improvement.

Deliberate Practice in Expert Music Performance: The Importance of Mental Representations for Monitoring Performance. Now consider the different types of mental representations that are necessary for advanced music performers. For example, musicians must be able to internally represent many aspects involved in mastering the interpretation of a new piece of music. Three of them are illustrated in Fig. 2.8: the performer's image of how they want a given performance to sound to the audience, their plan of how the instrument should be played to achieve this goal, and their capacity to monitor the produced sound as they practice to produce the desired performance (Ericsson, 1997).

The importance of these representations and, in particular, the key role of critical listening to one's music performance, have been recognized and

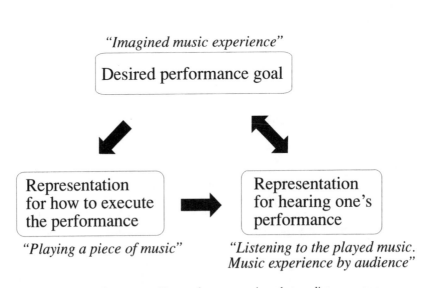

FIG. 2.8. Three types of internal representations that mediate expert music performance and its continued improvement during practice. From "The Scientific Study of Expert Levels of Performance: General Implications for Optimal Learning and Creativity," by K. A. Ericsson in *High Ability Studies, 9,* p. 92. Copyright 1998 by European Council for High Ability. Reprinted with permission.

articulated by master teachers. "One of the greatest difficulties which stand in the way of progress is the failure to hear what one is doing at the piano. . . . When the moment comes that the pupil actually hears what he is doing, consciousness is awakened and the progress begins" (Buhlig, 1917, p. 218). Critical listening remains equally important at advanced levels. "In his practicing, the real art is for the pupil to acquire the uncanny ability to listen to his own work, to discover his own minute failing" (Szigeti, 1972, p. 205). Even experts must be wary of the risk of reducing the level of concentration and lowering their performance criteria. "The habit of not listening becomes worse and worse, and in a short time the player is unconscious of the slight inaccuracies in pitch. There is listening, and listening *intently*" (Tertis, 1972, p. 267). Expert musicians actively try to counteract the threat of automaticity and reliance of habitual performance. The famous cellist Pablo Casals carefully prepared and studied even very familiar music pieces before playing them in public. "To play it perfectly every piece should be studied with the constant idea of improvement in mind, and it is seldom, working in this way, that I do not find that I can improve some one or another detail" (Casals, 1923, p. 234). Working out the intended music experience in detail allows the musician to carefully monitor their performance. "I try to form an ideal conception of the piece, work this out in every detail, then always endeavor to render it as closely like the ideal as possible" (Lerner, 1915, p. 46). And perfection is never permanently attained. "I never neglect an opportunity to improve, no matter how perfect a previous interpretation may have seemed to me. In fact, I often go directly home from a concert and practice for hours upon the very pieces that I have been playing, because during the concert certain new ideas have come to me" (Busoni, 1913, p. 106)

Individual differences in the acquired representations responsible for musical abilities, such as sight-reading, rapid memorization of music, and improvisation, are frequently attributed to musical talent, perhaps because it has been difficult to understand how such abilities are acquired (Bamberger, 1991). However, there are several theoretically and empirically supported accounts of how they are acquired through practice-related activities (Lehmann & Ericsson, 1993, 1995, 1996; Sudnow, 1978).

In sum, the superficial characteristics of deliberate practice are unimportant and differ greatly across as well as within domains, but the defining common feature of deliberate practice refers to its ability to change and improve performance and will therefore depend on the desired changes in achievement. Once upon a time all effective methods for deliberate practice must have been discovered by individuals who experimented with different methods for practice. Today students do not need to rediscover these training techniques but they are passed along by their teachers and coaches. Recent accounts (Ericsson, 1996; Zimmerman, 1994) of the development of past and current masters describe how these individuals were able to invent techniques to increase their mastery of skilled activities with minimal instruction and external support. This type of extended self-guided search for effective practice methods in a domain is likely to foster the development of representations that benefit subsequent development of expertise supervised by skilled teachers.

Expert Performers' Learning: Generalizable Aspects and Specific Implementations

For anyone interested in general mechanisms mediating learning, the most striking findings from the study of expert performance concern its domain specificity and diversity. Not only does deliberate practice differ between domains, but the particular training that would be optimal for individual experts within a domain will differ and depend on the individual's strengths and weaknesses. For this reason, training in most domains is designed to develop independent performers so they can find their own path toward expertise through reflective self-evaluation and problem solving. In fact, individual differences and diversity are encouraged at the highest levels to prepare elite performers to go beyond the accumulated knowledge in their domain and extend its boundaries through major innovations.

Is it possible to extract some generalizable principles for experts' learning in light of this striking variability and diversity? Many significant efforts have been made to extract concepts, mechanisms, and characteristics of effective learning in the fields of education and professional development. Many of those findings capture several generalizable characteristics of experts' learning and deliberate practice: Changes in behavior and performance are facilitated by setting specific attainable goals (Locke & Latham, 1984), effective students optimize improvement by designing and monitoring their learning activities (Schunk & Zimmerman, 1994), and learning should be mindful and reflective, striving toward genuine understanding, rather than mindless memorization (Langer, 1997). These three abstract characteristics reveal important higher level differences between how experts and amateurs tend to learn, and focus on necessary characteristics of effective learning and thus explain why the learning of the amateurs tends to be limited. How much of the experts' efficient learning is explained by these characteristics? Would it be possible to induce effective learning by merely instructing the amateurs to change the methods for learning? If not, which conditions and prerequisites are necessary for efficient types of learning?

The study of the acquisition of expert performance gives us insight into these issues. The more we learn about the development of expert performance in specific domains, the better our understanding of prerequisites for effective learning. First, before reflective monitoring of behavior and learning in a domain can occur, the individuals have to have acquired appropriate knowledge and domain-specific representations. Use of reflective analysis and self-regulation is feasible only after prerequisite representations have been sufficiently developed at more advanced levels of performance. Given that these domain-specific representations are acquired to meet specific demands of reasoning in the domain, their transfer across domains seem to be quite limited (cf. Ericsson & Lehmann, 1996). To become an effective learner within a domain would appear to require a sustained commitment to acquiring the necessary representations and relevant knowledge.

Second, acquisition of complex representations for monitoring and evaluation (self-regulation) have to be closely intertwined with the acquisition of task-specific performance. Consequently, it may not be reasonable to try to distinguish these representations and associated learning activities from the structure of domain-specific performance (Ericsson & Kintsch, 1995). In complex skills it may be necessary that the same representations mediate the generation of the desired performance as well as the subsequent reflective analysis and modification of the actual performance. It is essential that structural changes made to improve performance during learning will not have any undesirable side effects on other aspects of performance. By using the same representation to monitor their performance during deliberate practice as the expert performers use to control the final public performance, it is possible to make incremental adjustments without interfering with the integrity of the skill.

Finally, the research on deliberate practice has shown that concentration is necessary for optimal learning. Because most individuals seem to prefer less effortful activities that satisfy short-term learning goals, they must be motivated to attain high achievement in a domain before they will engage in sustained deliberate practice. Motivation is then an essential part of interventions to initiate acquisition of knowledge and representations that are necessary for effective learning. In sum, I believe that the study of expert performers will provide us with insights into the detailed structure of the complex, extended interactions required for the sustained efficient learning leading to mastery and expert performance.

CONCLUDING REMARKS ON THE GRADUAL ATTAINMENT OF EXCELLENCE THROUGH DELIBERATE PRACTICE

The general "law" of least effort predicts that activities are carried out with the minimum expenditure of effort. For this reason, the nervous system automates behavior whenever possible, and activities tend to be performed with the simplest possible mediating mechanisms. Individuals usually reach a satisfactory level of performance in most types of habitual everyday activities. At this level of achievement, repeating a similar series of actions doesn't change the structure of performance, it merely reduces the effort required for their execution. Any successful attempt to improve performance beyond this stable level thus requires active effort, changing the goal of performance, as well as designing new activities for training and improvement—deliberate practice. Depending on the domain, deliberate practice can range from simple repetitive activity aimed at increasing endurance or flexibility, to reflective analysis focused on identifying and improving aspects of skilled complex performance. Consequently, the specific activity of deliberate practice may differ dramatically across domains, but it always involves efforts to stretch performance toward higher, yet attainable, goals.

The emphasis on the sustained striving for improvement by expert performers may sound reminiscent of the arguments traditionally associated with motivational speakers advocating self-improvement. Both approaches agree that individuals tend to underestimate their achievement potential and that the first step in initiating change through training and practice requires that individuals are convinced that they are capable of attaining their new goals. Beyond that, the resemblance is superficial. For example, where motivational speakers tend to be rather general about which attributes can be improved, accounts in terms of deliberate practice are limited to domains of expertise with reproducible superior performance. From laboratory analyses of the experts' superior performance, scientists have consistently found evidence for the acquired mediating mechanisms discussed previously: very complex skills, highly refined representations, and large physiological adaptations. The complexity of these acquired mechanisms is consistent with the finding that not even the most "talented" can reach an international level of performance in less than a decade of dedicated practice. In this chapter I have shown how the acquisition of expert performance in several domains is closely related to engagement in deliberate practice. In particular I have focused on how well-understood mechanisms of skill acquisition and physiological adaptation can provide causal accounts of changes in the body and the nervous system that produce the desired improvements in performance.

The complex integrated structure of expert performance raises many issues about how these structures can be gradually acquired and perfected over time. It appears that teachers start guiding skill development from a child's initial introduction to training. The teacher knows the appropriate sequencing of skills and can provide training assignments of a challenging, yet attainable, difficulty level. Equally important, the teacher knows the future challenges at the highest levels and can therefore insist on mastery of the fundamentals during development to avoid the need for re-learning at advanced levels. However, the best teachers in the world can never successfully train students without their full cooperation and active participation in the learning process. At all levels of performance, students who have representations supporting their planning, reasoning, and evaluation of the actual and intended performance will be better able to make appropriate adjustments to their complex skill. This advantage becomes absolutely essential at higher levels of achievement. Given that deliberate practice involves mastering tasks that students could not initially attain, or only attain imperfectly or unreliably, it is likely that more successful students acquire representations to support problem solving and learning through planning and analysis. Consequently, the faster learning of "talented" students might be explained by individual differences in acquired representations supporting effective learning.

Why would so many individuals engage in the strenuous, concentration-demanding activities of deliberate practice regularly over years and decades, when the research shows that the relaxed comfort zone provides the mood-enhancing effects of exercise and the states of high enjoyment associated with "flow" or the "runners' high"? An important part of the answer lies in their instrumentality: They offer the means to attaining superior performance with its many associated rewards and benefits, such as social recognition, relationships with teachers, playful interactions with like-minded peers, travel, scholarships and occupational opportunities, and the other benefits associated with improved performance. The myth that hard work at the start will enable one to coast into future success is not supported by the evidence, and it most likely reflects confusion between merely maintaining a performance at a high level and continued further improvement of performance. In fact, as an individual's performance level improves, the demand for effort to further improve performance remains high. In support of this claim, the rated level of effort during training is greater, not less, for elite athletes than it is for amateurs.

From the perspective of deliberate practice, the rarity of excellence is primarily attributable to the environmental conditions necessary for its slow emergence, and to the years required to develop the complex mediating mechanisms that support expertise. Even individuals considered to have natural gifts gradually attain their elite performance by engaging in extended amounts of designed deliberate practice over many years. Until ordinary individuals recognize that sustained effort is required to reach expert performance, they will continue to misattribute lesser achievement to lack of natural gifts, and thus will fail to reach their own potential.

The scientific study of expert performance and deliberate practice will increase our knowledge about how experts optimize their learning through the level of daily effort that they can sustain for days, months, and years. This knowledge should be relevant to any motivated individual aspiring to excel in any one of a wide range of professional activities. It is unlikely that we will ever be able to fully understand how excellence is acquired. Even if we were able to specify the exact path of development for the highest levels of performance at some point in time, such as today, excellence is protean, not static, and by the time we discovered that description expert performers will have reached even higher levels of performance. The highest levels of expertise and creativity will remain at the threshold of understanding, even for the masters dedicated to redefining the meaning of excellence in their domains.

ACKNOWLEDGMENTS

This research was supported by the FSCW/Conradi Endowment Fund of Florida State University Foundation. The author thanks Elizabeth Kirk for her most valuable comments on several earlier drafts of this chapter. Furthermore, Peter Delaney's and Len Hill's helpful comments on the final draft are gratefully acknowledged.

REFERENCES

Abernethy, B. (1991). Visual search strategies and decision-making in sport. *International Journal of Sport Psychology, 22,* 189–210.

Anderson, J. R. (1982). Acquisition of cognitive skill. *Psychological Review, 89,* 369–406.

Anderson, J. R. (1987). Skill acquisition: Compilation of weak-method problem situations. *Psychological Review, 94*(2), 192–210.

Bamberger, J. (1991). *The mind behind the musical ear: How children develop musical intelligence.* Cambridge, MA: Harvard University Press.

Bédard, J., & Chi, M. T. H. (1993). Expertise in auditing. *Auditing, 12*(Suppl.), 1–25.

Bloom, B. S. (1985). Generalizations about talent development. In B. S. Bloom (Ed.), *Developing talent in young people* (pp. 507–549). New York: Ballantine.

Bonner, S. E., & Pennington, N. (1991). Cognitive processes and knowledge as determinants of auditor expertise. *Journal of Accounting Literature, 10,* 1–50.

Bouchard, C., Shephard, R. J., & Stephens, T. (Eds.). (1994). *Physical activity, fitness, and health: International proceedings and consensus statement.* Champaign, IL: Human Kinetics.

Buhlig, R. (1917). The value of learning to hear. In H. Brower (Ed.), *Piano mastery, second series: Talks with master pianists and teachers* (pp. 215–223). New York: Frederick A. Stokes.

Busoni, F. B. (1913). Important details in piano study. In J. F. Cooke (Ed.), *Great pianists on piano playing: Study talks with foremost virtuosos* (pp. 97–107). Philadelphia: Theo Presser.

Camerer, C. F., & Johnson, E. J. (1991). The process-performance paradox in expert judgment: How can the experts know so much and predict so badly? In K. A. Ericsson & J. Smith (Eds.), *Towards a general theory of expertise: Prospects and limits* (pp. 195–217). Cambridge: Cambridge University Press.

Casals, P. (1923). The newer cello technique. In F. H Martens (Ed.), *String mastery: Talks with master violinists, viola players and violoncellists* (pp. 225–235). New York: Frederick A. Stokes.

Charness, N. (1981). Search in chess: Age and skill differences. *Journal of Experimental Psychology: Human Perception and Performance, 7*, 467–476.

Charness, N., Krampe, R. Th., & Mayr, U. (1996). The role of practice and coaching in entrepreneurial skill domains: An international comparison of life-span chess skill acquisition. In K. A. Ericsson (Ed.), *The road to excellence: The acquisition of expert performance in the arts and sciences, sports, and games* (pp. 51–80). Mahwah, NJ: Lawrence Erlbaum Associates.

Cowley, M. (Ed.). (1959). *Writers at work: The Paris Review interviews.* New York: Viking.

Dawes, R. M. (1994). *House of cards: Psychology and psychotherapy built on myth.* New York: Free Press.

de Groot, A. (1978). *Thought and choice and chess.* The Hague: Mouton. (Original work published 1946)

Elbert, T., Pantev, C., Wienbruch, C., Rockstroh, B., & Taub, E. (1995). Increased cortical representation of the fingers of the left hand in string players. *Science, 270*, 305–307.

Ericsson, K. A. (1996). The acquisition of expert performance: An introduction to some of the issues. In K. A. Ericsson (Ed.), *The road to excellence: The acquisition of expert performance in the arts and sciences, sports, and games* (pp. 1–50). Mahwah, NJ: Lawrence Erlbaum Associates.

Ericsson, K. A. (1997). Deliberate practice and the acquisition of expert performance: An overview. In H. Jorgensen & A. C. Lehmann (Eds.), *Does practice make perfect? Current theory and research on instrumental music practice* (NMH-publikasjoner 1997:1). Oslo, Norway: Norges musikkhögskole.

Ericsson, K. A. (1998). The scientific study of expert levels of performance: General implications for optimal learning and creativity. *High Ability Studies, 9*, 75–100.

Ericsson, K. A., & Charness, N. (1994). Expert performance: Its structure and acquisition. *American Psychologist, 49*, 725–747.

Ericsson, K. A., & Delaney, P. F. (1999). Long-term working memory as an alternative to capacity models of working memory in everyday skilled performance. In A. Miyake & P. Shah (Eds.), *Models of working memory: Mechanisms of active maintenance and executive control* (pp. 257–297). Cambridge, England: Cambridge University Press.

Ericsson, K. A., & Kintsch, W. (1995). Long-term working memory. *Psychological Review, 102*, 211–245.

Ericsson, K. A., Krampe, R. Th., & Heizmann, S. (1993). Can we create gifted people? In G. R. Bock & K. Ackrill (Eds.), *CIBA Foundation Symposium 178. The origin and development of high ability* (pp. 222–249). Chichester, England: Wiley.

Ericsson, K. A., Krampe, R. Th., & Tesch-Römer, C. (1993). The role of deliberate practice in the acquisition of expert performance. *Psychological Review, 100*, 363–406.

Ericsson, K. A., & Lehmann, A. C. (1996). Expert and exceptional performance: Evidence on maximal adaptations on task constraints. *Annual Review of Psychology, 47*, 273–305.

Ericsson, K. A., & Lehmann, A. C. (1999). Expertise. In M. A. Runco & S. Pritzer (Eds.), *Encyclopedia of creativity* (Vol. 1, pp. 695–707). San Diego, CA: Academic Press.

Ericsson, K. A., & Smith, J. (1991). Prospects and limits in the empirical study of expertise: An introduction. In K. A. Ericsson & J. Smith (Eds.), *Toward a general theory of expertise: Prospects and limits* (pp. 1–38). Cambridge, England: Cambridge University Press.

Fitts, P., & Posner, M. I. (1967). *Human performance.* Belmont, CA: Brooks/Cole.

Galamian, I. (1972). Ivan Galamian. In S. Applebaum & S. Applebaum (Eds.), *The way they play: Book I* (pp. 240–351). Neptune City, NJ: Paganiniana.

Glaser, R. (1996). Changing the agency for learning: Acquiring expert performance. In K. A. Ericsson (Ed.), *The road to excellence: The acquisition of expert performance in the arts and sciences, sports, and games* (pp. 1–50). Mahwah, NJ: Lawrence Erlbaum Associates.

Gould, S. J. (1996). *Full house: The spread of excellence from Plato to Darwin.* New York: Harmony.

Helsen, W. F., Starkes, J. L., & Hodges, N. J. (1998). Team sports and the theory of deliberate practice. *Journal of Sport and Exercise Psychology, 20,* 12–34.

Hodges, N. J., & Starkes, J. L. (1996). Wrestling with the nature of expertise: A sport specific test of Ericsson, Krampe and Tesch-Römer's (1993) theory of "Deliberate Practice." *International Journal of Sport Psychology,* 1–25.

Katims, M. (1972). Milton Katims. In S. Applebaum & S. Applebaum (Eds.), *The way they play: Book I* (pp. 233–242). Neptune City, NJ: Paganiniana.

Krampe, R. Th., & Ericsson, K. A. (1996). Maintaining excellence: Deliberate practice and elite performance in young and older pianists. *Journal of Experimental Psychology: General, 125,* 331–359.

Kreisler, F. (1972). Fritz Kreisler. In S. Applebaum & S. Applebaum (Eds.), *The way they play: Book I* (pp. 95–109). Neptune City, NJ: Paganiniana.

Langer, E. J. (1997). *The power of mindful learning.* Reading, MA: Addison-Wesley.

Lehmann, A. C. (1997). Acquisition of expertise in music: Efficiency of deliberate practice as a moderating variable in accounting for sub-expert performance. In I. Deliege & J. A. Sloboda (Eds.), *Perception and cognition of music* (pp. 165–191). Mahwah, NJ: Lawrence Erlbaum Associates.

Lehmann, A. C., & Ericsson, K. A. (1993). Sight-reading ability of expert pianists in the context of piano accompanying. *Psychomusicology, 12,* 182–195.

Lehmann, A. C., & Ericsson, K. A. (1995, November). *Expert pianists' mental representation of memorized music.* Poster session presented at the 36th annual meeting of the Psychonomic Society, Los Angeles, CA.

Lehmann, A. C., & Ericsson, K. A. (1996). Music performance without preparation: Structure and acquisition of expert sight-reading. *Psychomusicology, 15,* 1–29.

Lehmann, A. C., & Ericsson K. A. (1997). Expert pianists' mental representations: Evidence from successful adaptation to unexpected performance demands. *Proceedings of the Third Triennial ESCOM Conference,* 165–169. Uppsala, Sweden: SLU Service/Reproenheten.

Lehmann, A. C., & Ericsson K. A. (1998). The historical development of domains of expertise: Performance standards and innovations in music. In A. Steptoe (Ed.), *Genius and the mind* (pp. 67–94). Oxford, England: Oxford University Press.

Lerner, T. (1915). An audience is the best teacher. In H. Brower (Ed.), *Piano mastery: Talks with master pianists and teachers* (pp. 38–46). New York: Frederick A. Stokes.

Levin, H., & Addis, A. B. (1979). *The eye-voice span.* Cambridge, MA: MIT Press.

Locke, E. A., & Latham, G. P. (1984). *Goal setting: A motivational technique that works!* Englewood Cliffs, NJ: Prentice-Hall.

Norman, D. A., Coblentz, C. L., Brooks, L. R., & Babcook, C. J. (1992). Expertise in visual diagnosis: A review of the literature. *Academic Medicine Rime Supplement, 67,* 78–83.

Plimpton, G. (Ed.). (1977). Interviews, second series. In *Writers at work: The Paris Review.* New York: Penguin.

Primrose, W. (1972). William Primrose. In S. Applebaum & S. Applebaum (Eds.), *The way they play: Book I* (pp. 243–261). Neptune City, NJ: Paganiniana.

Robergs, R. A., & Roberts, S. O. (1997). *Exercise physiology: Exercise, performance, and clinical applications.* St. Louis, MO: Mosby-Year Book.

Rosson, M. B. (1985). The role of experience in editing. *Proceedings of INTERACT '84 IFIP Conference on Human–Computer Interaction,* 45–50.

Sauer, E. (1913). The training of the virtuoso. In J. F. Cooke (Ed.), *Great pianists on piano playing: Study talks with foremost virtuosos* (pp. 236–250). Philadelphia: Theo Presser.

Schlaug, G., Jäncke, L., Huang Y., & Steinmetz, H. (1995). In vivo evidence of structural brain asymmetry in musicians. *Science, 267,* 699–701.

Schmidt, H. G., Norman, G. R., & Boshuizen, H. P. A. (1990). A cognitive perspective on medical expertise: Theory and implications. *Academic Medicine, 65,* 611–621.

Schneider, W. (1993). Acquiring expertise: Determinants of exceptional performance. In K. A. Heller, J. Mönks, & H. Passow (Eds.), *International handbook of research and development of giftedness and talent* (pp. 311–324). Oxford, England: Pergamon Press.

Schnitzer, G. (1915). Modern methods in piano study. In H. Brower (Ed.), *Piano mastery: Talks with master pianists and teachers* (pp. 215–224). New York: Frederick A. Stokes.

Schunk, D. H., & Zimmerman, B. J. (Eds.). (1994). *Self-regulation of learning and performance: Issues and educational applications* (pp. 1–21). Hillsdale, NJ: Lawrence Erlbaum Associates.

Shanteau, J., & Stewart, T. R. (1992). Why study expert decision making? Some historical perspectives and comments. *Organizational Behaviour and Human Decision Processes, 53,* 95–106.

Shiffrin, R. M., & Schneider, W. (1977). Controlled and automatic human information processing: II. Perceptual learning, automatic attending and a general theory. *Psychological Review, 84,* 127–189.

Simon, H. A., & Chase, W. G. (1973). Skill in chess. *American Scientist, 61,* 394–403.

Simonton, D. K. (1997). Creative productivity: A predictive and explanatory model of career trajectories and landmarks. *Psychological Review, 104,* 66–89.

Sloboda, J. A. (1996). The acquisition of musical performance expertise: Deconstructing the "talent" account of individual differences in musical expressivity. In K. A. Ericsson (Ed.), *The road to excellence: The acquisition of expert performance in the arts and sciences, sports, and games* (pp. 107–126). Mahwah, NJ: Lawrence Erlbaum Associates.

Starkes, J. L., Deakin, J., Allard, F., Hodges, N. J., & Hayes, A. (1996). Deliberate practice in sports: What is it anyway? In K. A. Ericsson (Ed.), *The road to excellence: The acquisition of expert performance in the arts and sciences, sports, and games* (pp. 81–106). Mahwah, NJ: Lawrence Erlbaum Associates.

Sternberg, R. J. (1996). Costs of expertise. In K. A. Ericsson (Ed.), *The road to excellence: The acquisition of expert performance in the arts and sciences, sports, and games* (pp. 347–354). Mahwah, NJ: Lawrence Erlbaum Associates.

Sudnow, D. (1978). *Ways of the hand: The organization of improvised conduct.* Cambridge, MA: Harvard University Press.

Szigeti, J. (1972). Joseph Szigeti. In S. Applebaum & S. Applebaum (Eds.), *The way they play: Book I* (pp. 95–109). Neptune City, NJ: Paganiniana.

Tertis, L. (1972). Lionel Tertis. In S. Applebaum & S. Applebaum (Eds.), *The way they play: Book I* (pp. 262–270). Neptune City, NJ: Paganiniana.

Zimmerman, B. J. (1994). Dimensions of academic self-regulations: A conceptual framework for education. In D. H. Schunk & B. J. Zimmerman (Eds.), *Self-regulation of learning and performance: Issues and educational applications* (pp. 1–21). Hillsdale, NJ: Lawrence Erlbaum Associates.

Chapter 3

Fostering Intellectual Excellence Through Developing Expertise

Robert J. Sternberg
Yale University

Elena L. Grigorenko
Yale University

Michel Ferrari
University of Toronto

What made Dostoyevsky a world-class novelist, Einstein a world-class physicist, Disraeli a world-class diplomat, or Mozart a world-class musician? We suggest that what made such world-class leaders excellent is that they were experts in their areas of skill. To explore this possibility, we first consider alternative views of the nature of expertise and of how expertise develops. We then present a demonstration study that argues for our own preferred point of view about how developing expertise translates into excellence.

We begin by making a strong claim: A key aspect of intellectual excellence is expertise. The advantage of referring to excellence instead of merely speaking about expertise is that expertise essentially refers to a high level of skill, whereas excellence has a broader meaning that allows one to ascribe a positive value to that expertise. In other words, whereas one can be an expert criminal, it is less common to refer to an excellent criminal (except in a sense one speaks of a "good" criminal).

WHAT IS EXCELLENCE AS EXPERTISE?

Granting then that we are considering excellence to reflect socially valued expertise, an obvious question becomes: What makes someone excellent? The answer is far from straightforward. Sometimes the question of "What is excellence?" is not squarely addressed in the literature on expertise, making it hard to say whether individuals studied as experts truly are excellent, or even expert. There are several different conceptions of what would constitute an expert (Sternberg, 1994) and which conception one adopts will determine, in large part, what one studies when one seeks to understand excellence as individual expertise.

Expertise as Knowledge

One conception of expertise is *knowledge-based*. On this view, an expert is someone who knows a lot about a given area of endeavor. Knowledge is certainly a necessary condition for expertise: No one would want to go to a doctor, lawyer, or psychotherapist who lacked knowledge of his or her field. One probably would not wish to pay a lot for a ticket to listen to musicians who knew little or nothing about their musical instruments or the music they were playing. However, although knowledge seems to be a necessary condition for expertise, it does not seem to be a sufficient condition. Memorizing vast volumes of medical or legal references would not make one an expert doctor or lawyer. Expert musicians have gone far beyond memorizing the pieces they play.

Theories focusing on the role of the knowledge base and its organization often stress the role of stored information in long-term memory as a key to understanding expertise (Ericsson & Smith, 1991). These theories generally have their origins in the work of de Groot (1946/1978) and of Chase and Simon (1973). Because this work often is considered the seminal work in the study of expertise, we consider it in somewhat more detail.

De Groot (1946/1978) asked chess players of differing levels of expertise to think aloud while they contemplated the next moves they would make from several different presented chess positions. In most cases, grand masters and chess experts below the grand-master level evaluated moves similarly. Participants at both levels of expertise considered a similar number of moves. (Both groups considered somewhat more than 30 possible moves.) But grand masters arrived at the best move earlier in their consideration of moves than did the more typical experts. De Groot concluded that the grand masters must rely on a more extensive knowledge base than the more typical chess experts; they recognized the presented position as similar or identical to one they had seen before and hence were able to zero in rapidly on the optimal move. Knowledge acquired through experience rather than any special kind of information processing seemed to be what distinguished the chess experts.

Furthermore, de Groot asked both the grand masters and the experts to recall a middle-game position shown to them for just short amounts of time. The grand masters were able to recall the positions of 63% to 94% of chess pieces, whereas the experts were able to recall with only 50% to 70% accuracy. Why the difference? De Groot again attributed it to differences in knowledge base. The grand masters were recalling a configuration they had seen before. They were able to *integrate* all of what they were seeing into a single whole. The experts, in contrast, either had not seen the position or had not seen it as often. Hence they were not able to integrate it into a single whole or as easily encode it so they could retrieve it easily.

Chase and Simon (1973) recognized a flaw in the design of de Groot's study. Perhaps the grand masters simply had better memories than did the more common experts. Perhaps the greater knowledge base of the grand masters was due to their exceptional generalized memory skills. Chase and Simon tested this hypothesis by presenting grand masters and experts with chess configurations for 5 seconds and then asking the two groups to recall them. The critical difference was that Chase and Simon included both configurations of pieces from real games and random configurations of pieces. If the grand masters simply had better memories for pieces than the experts, then their recall should have been better for all chess board configurations, regardless of whether they were real or not. The same applied for experts versus novices. The results were clear: level of chess expertise influenced recall only of sensible (real-game) configurations of chess pieces. It had no influence on recall for random chess positions. In other words, what distinguished the experts from the novices and the grand masters from the experts was not overall superior recall abilities, but rather the extent and organization of their knowledge base.

Chase and Simon (1973) took things one step further by observing how individuals at various levels of expertise produced their recall. The investigators noted that recall did not happen in a smooth ordered progression but rather in bursts. In other words, some chess pieces would be rapidly placed on the board, then there would be a pause, then more chess pieces would be rapidly placed on the board, and so on. The sets of pieces placed in a single burst were viewed as chunks, in the sense described by Miller (1956). Miller had concluded that people were able to hold in their available short-term memory about 7 ± 2 chunks of information, where chunks were groupings of information encoded by individuals trying to recall the information. A critical feature of Miller's analysis, and of Chase and Simon's as well, was that chunks could vary in size, depending on how the information was encoded. Chase and Simon found that the chunk size of more expert players was larger than the chunk size of less expert players, including novices. In other words, the more expert players were able to use their knowledge base to retrieve large amounts of information in each burst of recall of chess pieces.

Exactly how many chunks of information did people at various levels of expertise have? Simon and Gilmartin (1973) showed via computer simulation that one could reproduce the performance of chess experts with just 1,000 chunks stored in memory. But they estimated that experts had stored in memory anywhere from 10,000 to 30,000 chunks. Thus experts were drawing on huge knowledge bases unavailable to novices in doing the chess-related tasks. These knowledge bases may be organized into problem schemas, or organized bodies of knowledge on which people can draw in order to help them represent and then solve a problem.

If Chase and Simon's findings applied only to chess, they would be of only modest interest. But the same basic finding regarding the role of the knowledge base has been replicated in a number of other domains, such as the game of Go (Reitman, 1976), electronic circuit diagrams (Egan & Schwartz, 1979), and bridge (Charness, 1979; Engle & Bukstel, 1978). Thus, the importance of a vast and organized knowledge base and the problem schemas that come with it seem to be fundamental to many different kinds of expertise. Such schemas and the information within them are not rapidly acquired. Simon and Chase (1973) estimated that it would take about 3,000 hours of play to become a chess expert and 30,000 hours to become a chess master.

Adaptive Expertise

Curiously, some research has shown that there are costs as well as benefits to expertise (e.g., Adelson, 1984; Frensch & Sternberg, 1989; Hecht & Proffitt, 1995; Luchins, 1942; Sternberg & Lubart, 1995). One such cost is the potential for increased rigidity: The expert can become so entrenched in a point of view or a way of doing things that it becomes hard to see things differently.

In fact, knowledge can interfere with expertise, at least the flexible kind of expertise that is needed for success in many pursuits (Adelson, 1984; Frensch & Sternberg, 1989). For example, Frensch and Sternberg (1989) compared the performance of expert and novice bridge players when playing bridge against a computer. Predictably, the experts played better than the novices when the game was played in the usual way; however, Frensch and Sternberg also modified the game in two ways. One modification (which they viewed as a surface-structural modification) varied the game only in the names of the suits. Instead of using the terms *clubs*, *diamonds*, *hearts*, and *spades*, the experimenters used different names (neologisms) for the four suits. Both the experts and the novices were initially hurt in their playing but quickly recovered.

A second modification was viewed as a deep-structural modification, in which a basic rule of the game was changed. Typically, in bridge, the high player on a given round opens the next round of play. In this version of the game, however, the player putting out the low card led off. This change, because it affects the basic way the game is played, disrupts fundamental strategies experts develop. But novices are less likely to have any fundamental strategies and so are less likely to be disrupted. This result is exactly what the investigators discovered. Experts were actually disrupted more than novices in their playing, although only initially. Eventually they recovered and once again started playing better than the novices.

This result makes a potentially important point about flexible expertise. A risk of expertise is entrenchment, or a kind of comfort with old ways of doing things. A danger in acquiring expertise can be that knowledge interferes with, rather than facilitates, new ways of looking at things. Flexible experts constantly have to be on guard against letting their knowledge of a domain interfere with their work. Clearly, something more is needed to be an expert than just knowledge.

Indeed, expertise seems to require not just knowledge, but the flexible application of knowledge. Thus, the most effective experts are adaptive experts (Ferrari, 1996; Gott, Hall, Pokorny, Dibble, & Glaser, 1993). Adaptive experts (a) use knowledge critically, (b) adapt prior knowledge to the specific case at hand, and (c) have high motivation and perceived competence. Studies of air force technicians (Gott et al., 1993) and experts in motor skills (Ferrari, 1996) have shown that adaptive experts tailor their knowledge based on a critical consideration of the existing circumstances. Such experts are in the best position to profit from their knowledge while adapting to the specifics of the problem at hand, leading to further development of their expertise.

Three Critical Aspects of Expert Performance

In any case, no matter what the field of endeavor or the degree of flexibility demonstrated by particular experts, analytical, creative, and practical skills all seem important to expertise (Sternberg, 1994).

Experts need to *analyze* problems that are presented to them. Thus, doctors must analyze reports of symptoms and themselves look for diagnostic signs of various illnesses. Musicians must analyze the pieces they play in order to meet their technical requirements. Chess players must analyze the challenges of each chess game they play. Artists must analyze the attributes of the persons, scenes, or whatever else they decide to paint or otherwise represent.

Analytical thinking is needed for expertise, but like knowledge, it too is not enough. For one thing, some people can analyze and criticize the work of others without themselves being capable of outstanding work. Furthermore, there seems to be quite a difference between criticizing ideas and coming up with one's own ideas. For example, an art critic might critique an artistic exhibition, or a music critic might critique a work of music or a concert, but these critics might not be able to—nor would they claim to be able to—produce their own expert artistic or musical work.

Coming up with one's own ideas and how to implement them requires *creative* thinking. The doctor dealing with a difficult case may soon find him or herself in uncharted waters, having to synthesize information that does not fall into any routine pattern previously encountered. Lawyers devise creative legal strategies to free their clients from legal jeopardy. Musicians not only play musical notes, but create unique interpretations of the music they play. Chess players make moves that go beyond any exact situations they have encountered before. And of course, scientists create new theories and experiments to chart the unknown.

But creative and analytical thinking are still not enough. An expert needs to know how to get people to pay attention to and then accept his or her creative ideas. Such efforts require *practical thinking* on the part of the expert. Successful doctors need "patient skills"—ways to reach, comfort, and reassure patients that they are getting expert care. Lawyers need to convince their clients to tell them the truth so that they can adequately represent them. Scientists need to convince a frequently skeptical public— scientific or otherwise—that their ideas reflect the scientific truth, not just some hare-brained blend of fact and fiction. Musicians and artists need to reach out to potential audiences so that they will appreciate the professionals' performances or art works.

Expertise as a Label

If performers have knowledge and the analytic, creative, and practical skills needed to use that knowledge effectively, then their audiences may label them *experts*. Thus, in some sense, expertise is a labeling phenomenon whereby some group of people declares a person an expert. Without that declaration, the person may have difficulty in exercising his or her expertise. For example, an individual trained in medicine cannot practice without a license; an individual trained in the law cannot represent clients without having passed the bar. A scientist can do science without academic credentials, but may have difficulty obtaining an academic job or research funding without those credentials. In chess, expertise is often recognized in terms of a person's numerical rating according to a system of evaluation (discussed later) of how well the person plays chess. So labeling seems to play some role in expertise, or at least in its recognition. On this view, expertise is not just as an attribute of a person, but of the way the person is perceived by others. It reflects an interaction between a person and a situation.

If one thing should be clear by now, it would be that there is no simple definition of excellence as expertise that will suffice. Expertise does not seem to be a "classical concept" with a clearly delineated set of defining features. Expertise is perhaps a prototypically defined construct where it is quite difficult to specify any one set of characteristics, each of which is singly necessary and all of which are jointly sufficient for a person in any field to be labeled an expert. Or perhaps there are multiple exemplars that serve as bases for our recognizing expertise. But what is clear is that in studying excellence as expertise, we cannot simply take for granted that a given person or group of persons is an expert.

THEORIES OF EXPERTISE

Having considered definitional issues surrounding the notion of excellence as expertise, we now consider some of the major theories that address the issue of excellence.

Map Models of Expertise

One view of what constitutes excellence is a traditional view that inborn or largely innate capacities develop into expertise over time. In modern times, this point of view has taken the form of a *psychometric* or "geographic" approach to abilities (Sternberg, 1990). The geographic metaphor of expertise presupposes a theory of intelligence as a map of the mind in which individual differences in expertise can be mapped through appropriate tests of mental abilities. The psychologist studying intelligence was both an explorer and a cartographer, seeking to chart the innermost regions of the mind. According to this approach, people differ in abilities at birth, and these differences remain fairly stable throughout the course of their lives. Thus, people like Dostoyevsky, Einstein, Disraeli, and Mozart had the good fortune to be born with high levels of these abilities and this is why they later became excellent in their areas of expertise.

This view may have originated with Plato, but in modern psychology, it extends back at least to Gall, perhaps the most famous of phrenologists (see Boring, 1950). Gall implemented the metaphor of a map in a literal way: He investigated the topography of the head, looking (and feeling) for the hills and valleys in each specific region of the head that would tell him a person's pattern of abilities. The measure of intelligence, according to Gall, resides in a person's pattern of cranial bumps.

During the first half of the 20th century, the metaphor of intelligence as something to be mapped dominated theory and research. However, the metaphor of the map became more abstract, and less literal, than it had been for Gall. Visual inspection and touching just would not do; instead, the indispensable map-making tool appeared to be the statistical method of factor analysis.

Factor analysis was invented by Charles Spearman, and so to understand its origins one needs some understanding of Spearman's work. Spearman was nothing if not contentious. He criticized Wundt and other experimental psychologists of the late 19th century on two grounds. Spearman (1923) argued that the methods of early experimental psychology were insignificant and trivial; in words that he might still apply if he were alive today to some contemporary researchers in basic information processing, he "regarded as an infatuation to pass life in measuring the exact average time required to press a button or in ascertaining the precise distance apart where two simultaneous pin pricks cannot anymore be distinguished from one another" (p. 203). Furthermore, Spearman believed that there had come to be a "yawning gulf" between science and reality and that this gulf was the result of experimental psychology's use of trivial methods to solve trivial problems.

Spearman dismissed the work of Galton and his disciples, then in decline (the approach of Binet had not yet gained momentum). He criticized much of the experimental work, and thereby paved the way for his own correlational psychology, the fullest expression of which was in his 1927 book, *The Abilities of Man*, which presents the major statement of his "two-factor" theory of intelligence. Note that the name of the theory is something of a misnomer. Spearman did not claim that there are two factors of intelligence, but rather two kinds of factors: general and specific. The general factor is indeed a single one, but there are as many different specific factors as there are tests to measure mental abilities, and each specific factor is uncorrelated with every other.

Spearman got the idea that a general factor underlies all tests of human intelligence by noticing what is sometimes called the "positive manifold," or g, namely, the tendency for different tests of intellectual abilities to correlate positively with each other. What is this g, or general factor? Spearman considered a number of alternative explanations, such as attention, will, plasticity of the nervous system, and the state of the blood, but his preferred explanation was that of "mental energy." Spearman's theory thus remains one of the most durable in all of psychology. His specific interpretation of g as a general factor is not undisputed and the notion of g is still popular today; in fact, *The g Factor* serves as the title of two recent volumes on intelligence (Brand, 1996; Jensen, 1998).

In contrast to Spearman, Louis Thurstone proposed a theory of primary mental abilities that remains popular today. In general, Thurstone believed that Spearman's general factor was obtained only because Spearman failed to rotate his factorial axes upon obtaining an initial solution. Thurstone was a major contributor to the literature on factor analysis and proposed a form of rotation—simple structure—that is still widely used today. Because Thurstone believed that simple-structure rotation is in some sense psychologically natural, he believed his theory to be more valid than Spearman's.

However, the argument between Spearman and Thurstone was not soluble in the terms in which these scientists presented it. Mathematically, either rotation is correct, and it is of course arguable which is psychologically more valid. There exist today mathematical algorithms for rotations that approximate simple structure and that yield orthogonal factorial axes. However, factor scores on primary mental abilities are almost invariably intercorrelated (and not simply due to error of estimation of the factor scores). The result, of course, is that if one factor analyzes the factor scores, one can end up with a general second-order factor. Thus g reappears in another form.

The fact that g reappears when the factors are themselves analyzed led to the formation by some theorists of *hierarchical theories*. A number of hierarchical theories of intelligence have been proposed, but perhaps the most sophisticated hierarchical model is the three-tiered model proposed by John Carroll (1993). The first tier includes minor group factors, the second tier, major group factors, and the third tier, general ability. This theory is unique in that it is based on a reanalysis of hundreds of data sets taken from previous psychometric work. A similar model has been proposed by Horn (1994; Horn & Hofer, 1992), which builds on the earlier model of Cattell (1971).

However, despite the widespread notion of individual excellence as reflecting a mental map, this notion and the factor-analytic methods used to create the maps became increasingly unpopular in the second half of the 20th century, for three main reasons.

First, the mental maps have little, if anything, to say about mental processes. Yet two individuals could receive the same score on a mental-ability test through very different processes, and indeed, by getting completely different items correct (Horn & Knapp, 1973; Sternberg, 1977).

Second, it proved to be extremely difficult to test factor-analytic models against each other, or even to falsify them at all (Sternberg, 1977), a difficulty that stems largely from the problem of deciding how best to rotate factorial axes. The fit of different mathematical models to the data does not change as a function of orientation of axes, and each orientation is equally acceptable mathematically. But different factorial theories proved to differ as much in terms of the orientations of factorial axes for a given solution as in terms of anything else, so that model fitting did not prove to be useful in distinguishing among theories (Sternberg, 1977). Thus, psychometricians resorted to arguing about the psychological plausibility of the various rotations; but such arguments were inconclusive as theorists in each camp thought their rotations to be the most psychologically plausible. Modern, confirmatory methods of factor analysis yield solutions with nonarbitrary axes (Joreskog & Sorbom, 1978), and such methods are now gaining widespread use among those wedded to a psychometric approach to intelligence and other psychological constructs (Whitely, 1980).

Third, the whole notion of trying to understand intelligence primarily on the basis of individual-differences data came under attack. McNemar (1964) asked whether two identical twins, stranded on a desert island and growing up together, would ever generate the notion of intelligence if they never encountered individual differences in their mental abilities. Psychologists were coming to answer "yes" and to believe that they should not depend upon substantial individual differences in isolating abilities. Because factor analysis, as it was typically used, critically depended on such differences, psychologists either had to find a new model, a new method, or both. Most psychologists opted for both, and in recent years, much research on intellectual excellence has neither followed the map model nor used the factor-analytic method.

Theories Focusing on Mental Processing

Some early theories of intellectual excellence emphasized the role of planning, problem solving, and reasoning processes (Ericsson & Smith, 1991). Adriaan de Groot (1946/1978), mentioned earlier as a pioneer in the study of expertise in chess, found no reliable differences in the depth to which experts versus novices planned in advance. However, Neil Charness (1981; see also Charness, 1991; Charness, Krampe, & Mayr, 1996) found that chess players at higher levels of skill tend to plan possible move sequences to greater depths. That is, more skilled players plan further in advance than do less skilled players.

One possible reconciliation of these conflicting findings might be that Charness detected differences that de Groot, with weaker methods, was unable to detect. Or it may be that the differences are so small that they are detectable but of no practical importance. Charness (1989) suggested, however, that the difference are real, but nonlinear. In other words, perhaps depth of search may increase up to a certain level of expertise, after which it stops increasing and other factors become more important in distinguishing who will or will not succeed in games of chess.

But whatever the depth to which expert chess players *plan* in advance, it is clear that they and other experts need to engage in highly sophisticated *information processing*. For example, they need to be able to engage not only in the cognitive processing that underlies successful performance, but in what Sternberg (1985) called metacomponential processing. Metacomponential processing involves planning, monitoring, and evaluating one's problem solving and decision making. Thus, experts need to be able to define problems and redefine them as further information arrives. Medical doctors, for instance, need to revise the way they view information as further information is presented (Lesgold et al., 1985; Patel & Groen, 1991).

Experts also set up strategies and monitor their performance in sophisticated ways. For example, several teams of investigators have studied expert versus novice physicists as they solve problems or sort them into categories (Chi, Feltovich, & Glaser, 1981; Chi, Glaser, & Rees, 1982; Larkin, McDermott, Simon, & Simon, 1980). They found that experts and novices represented information quite differently. Novices tend to represent problems in terms of surface features (e.g., seeing a problem as being about pulleys or inclined planes) whereas experts tend to represent problems in terms of underlying physical principles (e.g., seeing a problem as being one of Newton's first law).

Consider how experts versus novices might go about solving a physics problem or other problem in their domain of expertise. The expert and the novice both will first read the problem but the expert is likely to spend more time reading the statement of the problem than is the novice, or at least more time relative to the total amounts of time each will spend in problem solving (Larkin et al., 1980; Sternberg, 1981). The expert thus spends relatively more time than does the novice in global planning, or strategic planning for solving the problem as a whole. This up-front planning time will save the expert time later on, because the expert will be less likely than the novice to misrepresent the problem and thus pursue blind alleys that later will require starting over.

The novice, in contrast, is more likely to begin problem solution relatively quickly, but with the result that later on during problem solving he or she is more likely to have to restart his or her work. The dividends of more time spent in global planning are later paid in less time that needs to be devoted to local planning, or planning that is done along the way in problem solving. Local planning is the tactical planning that needs to be done as one proceeds through the steps of problem solving. In the long run, it is likely to drain more time from the problem-solving process when global planning was incomplete or inadequate. Experts, therefore, better balance strategic and tactical thinking than do novices.

Because experts can recognize the deep structure of the problem, they are able to solve problems working forward, whereas novices are much more likely to solve problems working backward. In other words, experts look at the terms of the problem and then proceed forward from the problem statement to a conclusion. Novices are more likely to start with the known or intended solution and then to work backward to try to figure out how they could get to the terms of the problem, given where they are trying to go.

Thus, the expert is more likely than the novice initially to draw some kind of schematic representation of the problem, such as a simple diagram outlining the elements of the problem and their interrelations (Larkin & Simon, 1987). In the verbal domain, such as in writing an essay, the expert may use some kind of outline or map of how the essay will be constructed rather than a graphical figure. The expert may also write down formulas for quantitative types of problems but only the formulas that actually are needed; the novice, in contrast, may write down or at least consider the use of a wide range of formulas, trying to figure out which one is appropriate. In other kinds of problem solving as well, experts are likely to zero in quickly on relevant information through selective encoding and selective comparison, while novices seem to muddle through.

The persistent difference in representation of problems (Chi, Glaser, & Farr, 1989) is crucial for understanding an important aspect of the difference between experts and novices. Although the apparent problem being solved by the expert and the novice is the same, the psychological problem being solved, or at least the representation of it, is different. The problem that the expert physicist sees as being about a principle of physics, the novice physicist might see as being about a mechanical device. The problem the layperson might see as being about a person's mood swings, a psychiatrist might see as being about a manic-depressive personality. The differences in representations show how difficult it is to separate knowledge from information processing: The representations experts construct typically would not be possible without very extensive and well-organized knowledge bases.

Experts also need to use sophisticated processes of insightful thinking (Sternberg & Davidson, 1995). They need to be able to engage in *selective encoding*, distinguishing what information is relevant for their purposes. For example, a radiologist needs to know what to look for in an X-ray. A scientist needs to know what to look for in the massive computer outputs that often result from complex data analyses. A lawyer needs to know which facts are relevant to his or her case and which facts, although they might be interesting, are not legally relevant. They also need to be able to integrate large amounts of information in order to make skilled judgments. This is the process Sternberg (1985) has called *selective combination*. For example, a doctor needs to figure out how to put together the different clues presented by an array of symptoms in order to reach a diagnosis. A detective needs to put together clues in order to decide who committed a crime. Finally, they need to be able to do sophisticated *selective compari-*

son, figuring out what information they already possess is relevant for the solution of the problems presented to them.

Doctors, lawyers, scientists, chess players—all, as we shall see—draw on very large-scale knowledge bases in order to solve problems. Thus, we see again the necessity of knowledge for the work of any expert.

The sophisticated use of these processes typically develops over long periods of time. But individuals can be taught to use these processes to good effect. For example, Davidson and Sternberg (1984) gave fourth-grade students (roughly 9 years old) verbal and mathematical insight problems to solve, both initially as a pretest and later as a posttest. An example of such a problem might be "Suppose you have black socks and blue socks placed in a dark room and mixed in a drawer in a ratio of 4 to 5. At most how many socks do you need to withdraw from the drawer in order to be sure that you have two socks of the same color?" In this problem, the ratio information is irrelevant and even misleading. Regardless of the ratio, you need to withdraw three socks, because if the first two socks are not of the same color, the third one has to be of the same color (black or blue) as one of the socks previously withdrawn. Some children were taught for 5 weeks how to use the processes of selective encoding, selective combination, and selective comparison in order to increase the children's expertise in the solution of insight problems. Other children did not receive such instruction. The instructed children gained more from pretest to posttest than did the uninstructed children. In a similar study using only verbal problems, where adults had to learn to use these three processes to figure out meanings of words presented in contexts, individuals instructed in how to use these processes increased more from a pretest to a posttest than did individuals not so instructed (Sternberg, 1987). In effect, instruction can help speed up processes normally acquired during the development of various kinds of expertise.

THE ACQUISITION OF EXPERTISE

Expertise takes a long time to acquire. Simon and Chase (1973) proposed that it typically takes a minimum of 10 years to acquire, and the "10-year rule" has become almost a dictum in the study of expertise. It seems to apply across a number of domains (Charness, Krampe, & Mayr, 1996; Ericsson, 1996a; Ericsson, Krampe, & Tesch-Römer, 1993; Simonton, 1996). What happens over those 10 years? How is expertise acquired? Again, several theories have been proposed of how people may become experts in the acquisition of skills, whether in music, athletics, art, or whatever (Anderson, 1987, 1993; Newell, 1990).

The development of expertise in many domains seems to go through several stages (Bloom, 1985). Interviews with exceptional performers in many domains as well as the parents and teachers of these elite performers suggest that these experts pass through a number of stages.

In Stage I, the elite performers were initially exposed as children to the domain in which they later became experts under fairly relaxed and playful conditions. At this point, the domain is engaged for pleasure. The future expert musician might be involved in piano playing or the artist in painting. Or the future ice skater may skate just for fun. Sooner or later, the parents or teacher recognize that the child shows promise. This recognition may lead to Stage II, in which parents help the child establish a regular practice schedule and arrange for a teacher or coach to work on a fairly intensive basis with the child. The child typically starts practicing daily and the amount of practice increases over time. Further signs of promise may lead to Stage III, in which a major commitment is made. A nationally or even internationally recognized teacher is sought out and the initial teacher abandoned. The parents may move in order to have access to this acclaimed teacher or may make arrangements so that the child otherwise can have access. This stage represents a major commitment of time and resources to the development of expertise in the child and is, in a sense, the point at which there is no easy turning back: A decision to develop an expert has been made. The investment on the part of the parents can be extremely substantial. They must invest money in the cost of lessons and possibly equipment or other material resources, time in driving their child to lessons or practice, and usually must give up some of their own personal activities in favor of the development of expertise in their child. Because of the investment required of them, typically no more than one child in the family will receive the kinds of efforts required to develop high levels of expertise. Finally, in Stage IV, the now expert performer has learned most of what even the internationally acclaimed teacher has to teach him or her. The individual, now often an adolescent or adult, moves well beyond being merely a student and creatively defines the kind of expertise that he or she will offer to the world. The individual develops a kind of "signature" that represents his or her particular way of expressing expertise.

Granting that these stages exist, an obvious question is: What happens to individual skills, as expertise progresses?

According to John Anderson's (1987) theory, which is embedded within his ACT theory of cognition, skill acquisition proceeds through three main stages that represent successive levels in the development of expertise.

In the *first* stage, the kind of situation that evokes the skill and the method for solving problems in that situation are encoded as declarative knowledge. Usually, this declarative knowledge derives from explicit instruction, which may include both an abstract presentation of the type of problem situation and how to solve it as well as examples of problem solving in action. In this stage of development, individuals are able to solve problems. But problem solving is relatively slow and deliberate. The more a given problem departs from the exact way in which its solution was taught, the harder the problem is, to the point that even minor levels of transfer may fail to occur.

In the *second* stage knowledge comes to be represented procedurally. Knowledge is represented in the form of productions, or condition-action statements that can be used in the performance of a task. For example, one such production might be that of "If you see a dot over a note, play that note in staccato (short and punctuated) fashion."

In the *third* stage the productions are combined into successively more elaborated production systems, or sequences of condition-action statements that can be used to execute a complex series of task requirements. Now performance of the task becomes more highly automatized and requires less conscious effort on the part of the individual doing the task.

Anderson's model is similar to a three-stage model proposed earlier by Paul Fitts and Michael Posner (1967). In their model, the first stage (the cognitive stage) involves declarative encoding of information. The second stage (the associative stage) involves the formation of connections among various elements of the skill. The third stage (the autonomous stage) involves relatively rapid and automatic execution of the skill.

These characterizations of the development of skill apply to many tasks but they do so in a rather decontextualized way. Some investigators have been interested in proposing models of acquisition that deal with the question of how expertise develops in the course of a person's daily life. Not everyone progresses with equal efficacy through the stages described by Anderson. What distinguishes those who achieve the highest levels of individual excellence from those who become routine experts, or remain amateurs all their lives?

A very persuasive suggestion, made by Anders Ericsson, is that deliberate practice is crucial to how individuals develop their exceptional abilities. Deliberate practice is not just any sort of practice, but rather practice in which the task (a) is at an appropriate level of difficulty for the individual, (b) provides informative feedback to the individual, (c) provides for opportunities for repetition, and (d) allows correction of errors (Ericsson, 1996a).

Ericsson and his associates (Ericsson & Charness, 1994; Ericsson & Hastie, 1994) distinguish deliberate practice from both work and play. In work, individuals generate products and services that are rewarded socially or monetarily. As with performance- or ego-oriented instruction (Biggs, 1985; Nicholls, 1990), individuals at work seek to prove their competence to others, not necessarily to deepen their understanding of the task. Play is ambiguous; on the one hand, some enjoyment seems to be necessary if one is going to invest thousands of hours of one's life learning some domain, as suggested by the study of flow (Csikszentmihalyi, 1990, 1997) and of intrinsic, mastery, or task-oriented motivation (Nicholls, 1990). If one is simply playing with no aim to improve and no focus to one's activity, however, then improvement will be slow or nonexistent (Ericsson, Krampe, & Tesch-Römer, 1993).

Ericsson (1996a) seemed to argue that deliberate practice is not just a necessary condition for the development of expertise, but a sufficient condition as well. In other words, engaging in sufficient deliberate practice will, under normal conditions, produce an expert. This is a strong claim but there is some evidence to back it up. For example, Ericsson, Krampe, and Tesch-Römer (1993) have reported that a study of violinists from a music academy in Germany revealed that the primary difference between students at different levels of expertise was the amount of deliberate practice in which they had engaged. The top violinists averaged almost 7,500 hours of deliberate practice by the age of 18 whereas good violinists had averaged only about 5,300. John Sloboda (1991, 1996) also has argued that deliberate practice is sufficient for the development of musical expertise.

The claim of those who believe in the sufficiency of deliberate practice is not limited to music, but rather is assumed to apply in all domains, including those that require creativity. In one study, Chase and Ericsson (1982) trained a college student, S.F., who started with a fairly ordinary digit-span memory to have an exceptional memory, for digits. By the end of an extensive period of training—about 200 hours—S.F. was able to recall as many as 81 digits at the rate of 1 per second. A typical college student might remember 7 ± 2 digits. How did SF become so adept in memorizing digits? As it turned out, he was a runner and so he used his information about races to facilitate his digit-span memory. He converted sets of digits into race times, thereby increasing the size of his chunks. As one might predict, strings of digits that did not translate into sensible race times gave him more trouble. And when asked to memorize letters, his span of recall for letters was no better than that of the average college student. In other words, he did not show transfer of the skill to another related domain.

The deliberate-practice view is becoming increasingly popular (Ericsson, 1996b, chap. 2, this volume; Ericsson & Charness, 1994; Ericsson, Krampe, & Tesch-Römer, 1993; Ericsson & Smith, 1991; Howe, Davidson, & Sloboda, 1998; Zimmerman, chap. 4, this volume) and has an important implication that is accepted by almost all psychologists studying expertise, regardless of whether they hold to this particular view or not. This implication is related to inventor Thomas Edison's comment that creative success is 99% perspiration and only 1% inspiration. It is unlikely that one actually could assign percentages to becoming excellent, but developing expertise has always had its basis in substantial amounts of focused hard work, or what Ericsson calls deliberate practice. Many people give up because they are unwilling to engage in these high levels of deliberate practice. Others hope that they will become experts on the basis of sheer unfocused talent. Neither those who quit nor those who hope for an easy road to expertise are likely ever to become experts in their fields.

The Deliberate Practice Plus Talent View

Many theorists believe that abilities or talents play an important role in the development of expertise, not just deliberate practice (Bloom, 1985; Shiffrin, 1996; Simonton, 1996; Sternberg, 1996; Winner, 1996a, 1996b). They argue that although deliberate practice is likely to be a necessary condition for the development of expertise, it is not likely to be a sufficient one. Scholars supporting this mixture model believe that deliberate practice is necessary but not sufficient for the development of expertise. What are some of their main arguments against the sufficiency of deliberate practice?

First, they argue that behavior-genetic studies show a role for genetic factors in interaction with environmental ones in the development of various kinds of expertise (Plomin & McClearn, 1993). Many different types of abilities seem to have at least some heritable component as a source of individual differences and the kinds of expertise studied by psychologists seem to be no exception. The counter argument proposed by Ericsson (1996b) and his colleagues is that these studies do not apply at the extremely high levels of deliberate practice that they have studied. Nevertheless, there is no reason to believe that performances at high levels of practice somehow would obey different rules.

Second, advocates of the combined talent/practice position argue that the deliberate-practice view is just not plausible. Is one to believe that anyone could become a Mozart if only he or she put in the time? Or that anyone could reach the level of skill shown by Michael Jordan in basketball or Wayne Gretzky in hockey, if only he or she worked hard enough at it, and practiced in the right way? Or, for that matter, that becoming an Einstein is just a matter of deliberate practice? Although this argument is one of plausibility rather than data, on its face it is not a simple matter to refute. Many people have tried to reach the exceptional levels of accomplishment shown by the top people in a given field and most have given up disappointed.

Third, the advocates of the mixed position argue that the demonstrations of deliberate practice lack adequate control groups or contain inadequate controls. They speculate that other people who do not become experts or even become known may put in the same hours of deliberate practice as the experts. But, because these nonexperts disappear from view, they may never make it into studies of expertise.

Fourth, the advocates of the mixed position argue that deliberate practice is itself a confounded measure, representing talent as well as practice. How could deliberate practice be a function of talent? The idea is that only those with high levels of talent continue to put in the deliberate practice it takes to reach high levels of expertise (Sternberg, 1996; Winner, 1996b). Their talent motivates them to try harder and thus rack up more hours of deliberate practice. Consider music lessons, for example. Many millions of children over the years have music lessons but many of them quit. Why? Perhaps because they discover that they lack the talent to become professional musicians or even skilled musicians. So they never put in many hours of practice over the course of their lifetime. The result is that correlations between deliberate practice and expertise, in part, may be affected by levels of talent.

At this point psychologists have insufficient evidence to make a definitive decision about whether deliberate practice is sufficient or merely necessary for developing expertise. But whatever its role, the findings on deliberate practice should give hope to many individuals who might despair of ever becoming experts. The data suggest that deliberate practice can help a great deal in the development of expertise, and may even practically guarantee it, if it is done with sufficient devotion.

If one accepts the point of view of abilities as developing expertise, one designs studies to show the joint effects of abilities and deliberate practice. Rather than looking at the effect of the one or the other, one looks at both kinds of effects simultaneously. We designed a small-scale study as a demonstration of the kind of study we believe better addresses how both abilities and deliberate practice matter to developing expertise. The study is small, but we hope it paves the way for a new type of design that is inclusive of both abilities and deliberate practice rather than focusing on the one or the other.

A Demonstration Study Jointly Assessing Ability and Deliberate Practice

Our study involves the computer game SimCity 2000™, a computer-simulation game developed by MAXIS that requires subjects to (a) design and then govern cities of their own creation, and (b) repair specific problems occurring in existing cities created by experts and provided with the program.

Twenty-one participants (16 males and 5 females) learned to play a computer-simulation game, SimCity 2000™. Participants ranged in age from 18 to 33 years of age ($M = 22.8$, SD $= 3.4$). All were undergraduate and graduate students at Yale University and were paid $50 to work on designing simulated cities in six 2-hour sessions. In addition, as an incentive for the participants to stay with the rather long-term (12-hour) study, participants were told that two names would be selected for two additional $100 prizes from all participants who completed the study. One prize was to be given to the individual who created the most successful SimCity™ simulation and the second prize would be given to an individual chosen at random from all of the participants.

Psychometric test materials included tests of reasoning ability, spatial ability, visual memory ability, mathematical ability, and verbal ability from the *French Kit of Reference Tests for Cognitive Factors* (French, Ekstrom, & Price, 1963). The level of ability was specified as the first principal component (unrotated solution) of the French Kit.

The manipulated independent variable was time given for deliberate practice per session (30 vs. 60 minutes). Abilities and age served as covariates in the data analysis. Participants were assigned to the two practice groups at random.

Over a series of six sessions, participants completed eight psychometric tests to assess their levels of basic cognitive abilities. In addition, participants performed the SimCity 2000™ task. In Session 1, participants completed two tutorials that introduced all of the basic tools, charts, and graphs needed to build a new SimCity™ and to evaluate its prosperity and its simulated quality of life. In Sessions 2 through 5, participants first were given the opportunity to spend either 60 minutes or 30 minutes deliberately practicing the design and governance of one or more simulated cities. During the third through the fifth practice sessions, participants were allowed to continue their work from the previous session's practice simulations, if they so wished. They were allowed to use various kinds of expert advice that the program provides and that appears on the screen. The four kinds of advice were from citizens of the city, compliance with zoning ordinances, advisors to the mayor, and newspapers.

In learning about the task, participants were told that their cities would be evaluated in terms of a number of different criteria. These criteria included (a) economic viability (current funds, cash flow, land value, gross national product, city size, and employment), and (b) quality of life for the simulated inhabitants (pollution, crime, health, and education). Thus, the best city would be one that was as economically viable as possible at the same time that it would maintain the maximum possible quality of life.

Following the deliberate-practice time, participants were given 20 minutes to design a new city. They were not allowed to use the expert advice feature of the SimCity 2000™ program. Instead, participants were told to use their own judgment based on their experience with the task.

In Session 6, participants were told that three cities were in serious trouble and needed help. The participants were then allowed to manipulate conditions in the cities so as to improve their economic indicators and quality of life. Thus, qualities of new cities from Sessions 2 through 5 and of rescued cities from Session 6 (altogether, seven summary indicators of cities' qualities) were treated as independent measures.

So what results did we find? To investigate the relative roles of abilities and deliberate practice on performance in the SimCity™ task, we carried out a set of repeated-measures analyses of variance. The dependent variable was the first principal component of seven measures of city quality (health, average education, pollution, crime, land value, city size, and total value of goods and services of SimCity™ residents) measured on seven different occasions. The manipulated independent variable was amount of deliberate practice (30 minutes or 60 minutes). Ability level and age of participants were treated as continuous covariates.

Means and standard deviations for the various measures are shown in Table 3.1. The patterns of means show that individuals with higher levels of deliberate practice seem to outperform individuals with lower levels of deliberate practice.

The effect of group (level of practice) was significant, $F(1, 17) = 7.73$, $p < .01$. The effect of ability level was also significant, $F(1, 17) = 6.44$, $p < .05$. The effect of age was further significant, $F(1, 17) = 13.83$, $p < .01$. To test the significance of the interactions, four separate models retaining all the main effects and one interaction at a time were fitted. This procedure was used because of the low power obtainable through our small sample. None of the interactions were significant.

TABLE 3.1
Descriptive Statistics

Variables	Low Practice Group (N = 11) Mean (SD)	High Practice Group (N = 10) Mean (SD)	T-values (p)
Dependent Measures			
New City 1 (Session 2)	0.27 (.53)	−.029 (1.38)	.12 (.93)
New City 2 (Session 3)	−.304 (.69)	.334 (1.21)	−1.51 (.15)
New City 3 (Session 4)	−.12 (1.10)	.13 (.913)	−.55 (.59)
New City 4 (Session 5)	−.43 (.88)	.47 (.94)	−2.27 (.04)
Rescued City 1 (Session 6)	.071 (.75)	−.080 (1.26)	.34 (.15)
Rescued City 2 (Session 6)	−.133 (1.10)	.146 (.91)	−.63 (.54)
Rescued City 3 (Session 6)	−.51 (.68)	.56 (1.02)	−2.86 (.01)
Covariates			
Ability level	−.425 (2.29)	.468 (2.54)	−.85 (.54)
Age	21.10 (1.92)	22.50 (4.60)	−.93 (.36)

The estimated marginal means for level of practice for the seven constructed cities are shown in Fig. 3.1. These statistics show comparative performances for each of the cities.

The results of the repeated measures analysis of variance demonstrated the importance of ability, $F(1, 17) = 6.44, p < .05$, as noted earlier. To explore this effect we investigated the distribution of the level of ability in the total sample and recoded it so that those individuals who scored below two standard deviations of the total sample mean were categorized as lower ability participants ($N = 6$), and those individuals who scored above two standard deviations of the total sample mean were categorized as higher ability participants ($N = 5$).

Then we, once again, carried out a repeated measures analysis of variance using the indicators of quality of seven cities as dependent variables. Due to the low power of the sample, these results should be interpreted with caution. In this analysis, the independent variable was level of ability, and level of practice and age were specified as covariates. The effect of ability level was borderline-significant, $F(1, 7) = 3.72, p < .10$, the level of practice was significant, $F(1, 7) = 5.66, p < .05$, and the effect of age was significant, $F(1, 7) = 6.66, p < .05$. The estimated marginal means for level of ability are shown in Fig. 3.2.

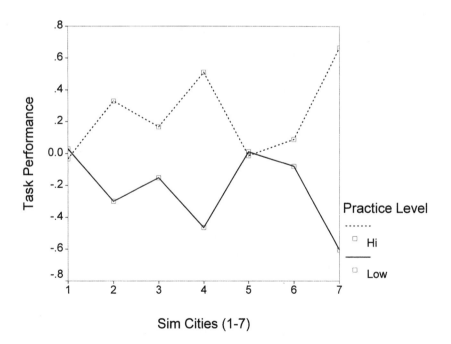

FIG. 3.1. Effect of practice level on SimCity™ performance.

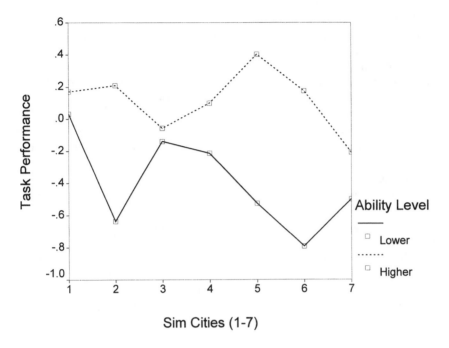

FIG. 3.2.   Effect of ability level on SimCity™ performance.

Taken as a whole, the results of our demonstration study suggest that expertise is not a function exclusively either of abilities or of deliberate practice. It is a function of both simultaneously.

What we mean to suggest with this synthetic point of view is that there is no clear qualitative distinction between abilities and deliberate practice. Higher levels of abilities arise from deliberate practice, but equally, deliberate practice, or at least the desire for it, arises from abilities. On this point of view, abilities are forms of developing expertise that are acquired by deliberate practice. People are born with innate differences, but how these differences manifest themselves depends on deliberate practice and other environmental variables (Sternberg, 1998a, 1998b). The environmental variables may end up being more important in who becomes an expert than are the innate factors. Thus, deliberate practice is a key to the development of expertise, but it builds on a genetic basis for individual differences.

Although we certainly do not believe that the study we have presented here is definitive, it at least uses a design that allows one to simultaneously and systematically examine effects of abilities and deliberate practice on developing expertise. The data suggest that both matter (see also Simonton, 1999). We have no doubt that those favoring more extreme positions will rightfully point out limitations of our demonstration study. The study uses only a small number of participants on a single task at fairly low levels of deliberate practice relative to what would be seen, say, in an expert musician or chess player. We agree with these points: Our study is certainly not definitive. But we would urge those taking extreme positions to design studies that allow one simultaneously to examine effects of both abilities and deliberate practice. The designs that have been used to date to examine this question look at the effects of the one or the other, and not surprisingly, the studies of each side support the positions of the respective sides. We believe this support to be at least partly spurious because the studies typically have not been designed in ways that could examine the effects of both abilities and deliberate practice simultaneously.

CONCLUSION

In this chapter, we have considered how excellence is intimately related to expertise and especially the development of expertise. We have focused particularly on the contrast between views that emphasize static mental abilities and cognitive views that emphasize deliberate practice. Traditional views that emphasize inherent abilities or more contemporary views that emphasize deliberate practice—each to the exclusion of the other—may be oversimplifications with regard to excellence as expertise. The common sense view that both abilities and deliberate practice matter is also the psychologically most viable.

We do not even see the abilities and deliberate-practice positions as mutually exclusive of each other. When abilities are viewed as forms of developing expertise, there no longer is a clear distinction between abilities and deliberate practice. Deliberate practice helps people develop their abilities, and people with higher levels of abilities are more likely to be motivated to engage in deliberate practice. This phenomenon is easy enough to experience in almost any domain. Initially engaging in the domain may be painful and frustrating. Once one reaches a certain level of expertise, however, engagement may become enjoyable and fulfilling. One may become more motivated to develop one's abilities and simultaneously one's expertise.

If there is a lesson to be learned here, it is one that the history of psychology has taught many times. There is little value in false dichotomies. Psychologists will better understand phenomena when they have embraced the dialectical synthetic relation between what often seem to be opposing points of view but what really are points of view that can and should be viewed as compatible (Piaget, 1950; Sternberg, 1999).

ACKNOWLEDGMENTS

The research described in this chapter and preparation of the chapter were supported in part under the Javits Act Program (Grant No. R206R950001) as administered by the Office of Educational Research and Improvement, U.S. Department of Education. Grantees undertaking such projects are encouraged to express freely their professional judgment. This article, therefore, does not necessarily represent the position or policies of the Office of Educational Research and Improvement or the U.S. Department of Education, and no official endorsement should be inferred.

REFERENCES

Adelson, B. (1984). When novices surpass experts: The difficulty of a task may increase with expertise. *Journal of Experimental Psychology, 10*, 483–495.

Anderson, J. R. (1987). Skill acquisition: Compilation of weak-method problem solutions. *Psychological Review, 94*, 192–210.

Anderson, J. R. (1993). *Rules of the mind*. Hillsdale, NJ: Lawrence Erlbaum Associates.

Biggs, J. B. (1985). The role of metalearning in study processes. *British Journal of Educational Psychology, 55*, 185–212.

Bloom, B. S. (Ed.). (1985). *Developing talent in young people*. New York: Ballantine.

Boring, E. G. (1950). *A history of experimental psychology* (2nd ed.). New York: Appleton-Century-Crofts.

Brand, C. (1996). *The g factor: General intelligence and its implications*. Chichester, England: Wiley.

Carroll, J. B. (1993). *Human cognitive abilities*. New York: Cambridge University Press.

Cattell, R. B. (1971). *Abilities: Their structure, growth and action*. Boston: Houghton Mifflin.

Charness, N. (1979). Components of skill in bridge. *Canadian Journal of Psychology, 33*, 1–16.

Charness, N. (1981). Search in chess: Age and skill differences. *Journal of Experimental Psychology: Human Perception and Performance, 7*, 467–476.

Charness, N. (1989). Expertise in chess and bridge. In D. Klahr & K. Kotovsky (Eds.), *Complex information processing: The impact of Herbert A. Simon* (pp. 183–208). Hillsdale, NJ: Lawrence Erlbaum Associates.

Charness, N. (1991). Expertise in chess: The balance between knowledge and search. In K. A. Ericsson & J. Smith (Eds.), *Toward a general theory of expertise* (pp. 39–63). New York: Cambridge University Press.

Charness, N., Krampe, R., & Mayr, U. (1996). The role of practice and coaching in entrepreneurial skill domains: An international comparison of life-span chess skill acquisition. In K. A. Ericsson (Ed.), *The road to excellence: The acquisition of expert performance in the arts and sciences, sports, and games* (pp. 51–80). Mahwah, NJ: Lawrence Erlbaum Associates.

Chase, W. G., & Ericsson, K. A. (1982). Skill and working memory. In G. H. Bower (Ed.), *The psychology of learning and motivation* (Vol. 16, pp. 1–58). New York: Academic Press.

Chase, W. G., & Simon, H. A. (1973). The mind's eye in chess. In W. G. Chase (Ed.), *Visual information processing* (pp. 215–281). New York: Academic Press.

Chi, M. T. H., Feltovich, P. J., & Glaser, R. (1981). Categorization and representation of physics problems by experts and novices. *Cognitive Science, 5*, 121–152.

Chi, M. T. H., Glaser, R., & Farr, M. (Eds.). (1989). *The nature of expertise*. Hillsdale, NJ: Lawrence Erlbaum Associates.

Chi, M. T. H., Glaser, R., & Rees, E. (1982). Expertise in problem solving. In R. J. Sternberg (Ed.), *Advances in the psychology of human intelligence* (Vol. 1, pp. 7–75). Hillsdale, NJ: Lawrence Erlbaum Associates.

Csikszentmihalyi, M. (1990). The domain of creativity. In M. A. Runco & R. S. Albert (Eds.), *Theories of creativity* (pp. 190–212). Newbury Park, CA: Sage.

Csikszentmihalyi, M. (1997). *Finding flow: The psychology of engagement with everyday life*. New York: Basic Books.

Davidson, J. E., & Sternberg, R. J. (1984). The role of insight in intellectual giftedness. *Gifted Child Quarterly, 28*, 58–64.

de Groot, A. (1978). *Thought and choice in chess*. The Hague: Mouton. (Original work published 1946)

Egan, D. E., & Schwartz, B. J. (1979). Chunking in recall of symbolic drawings. *Memory and Cognition, 7*, 149–158.

Engle, R. W., & Bukstel, L. (1978). Memory processes among bridge players of differing expertise. *American Journal of Psychology, 91*, 673–679.

Ericsson, K. A. (1996a). The acquisition of expert performance. In K. A. Ericsson (Ed.), *The road to excellence* (pp. 1–50). Mahwah, NJ: Lawrence Erlbaum Associates.

Ericsson, K. A. (Ed.). (1996b). *The road to excellence*. Mahwah, NJ: Lawrence Erlbaum Associates.

Ericsson, K. A., & Charness, N. (1994). Expert performance: Its structure and acquisition. *American Psychologist, 49*, 725–747.

Ericsson, K. A., & Hastie, R. (1994). Contemporary approaches to the study of thinking and problem solving. In R. J. Sternberg (Ed.), *Handbook of perception and cognition: Thinking and problem solving* (pp. 37–79). San Diego, CA: Academic Press.

Ericsson, K. A., Krampe, R. T., & Tesch-Römer, C. (1993). The role of deliberate practice in the acquisition of expert performance. *Psychological Review, 100*, 363–406.

Ericsson, K. A., & Smith, J. (1991). Prospects and limits in the empirical study of expertise: An introduction. In K. A. Ericsson & J. Smith (Eds.), *Toward a general theory of expertise: Prospects and limits* (pp. 1–38). Cambridge, England: Cambridge University Press.

Ferrari, M. (1996). Observing the observer: Self-regulation in the observational learning of motor skills. *Developmental Review, 16*, 203–240.

Fitts, P. M., & Posner, M. I. (1967). *Human performance*. Belmont, CA: Brooks-Cole.

French, J. W., Ekstrom, R. B., & Price, L. (1963). *Kit of reference tests for cognitive factors*. Princeton, NJ: Educational Testing Service.

Frensch, P. A., & Sternberg, R. J. (1989). Expertise and intelligent thinking: When is it worse to know better? In R. J. Sternberg (Ed.), *Advances in the psychology of human intelligence* (Vol. 5, pp. 157–188). Hillsdale, NJ: Lawrence Erlbaum Associates.

Gott, S. P., Hall, E. P., Pokorny, R. A., Dibble, E., & Glaser, R. (1993). A naturalistic study of transfer: Adaptive expertise in technical domains. In D. K. Detterman & R. J. Sternberg (Eds.), *Transfer on trial: Intelligence, cognition and instruction* (pp. 258–288). Norwood, NJ: Ablex.

Hecht, H., & Proffitt, D. R. (1995). The price of expertise: Effects of experience on the water-level task. *Psychological Science, 6*(2), 90–95.

Horn, J. L. (1994). Theory of fluid and crystallized intelligence. In R. Sternberg (Ed.), *The encyclopedia of intelligence* (Vol. 1, pp. 443–451). New York: Macmillan.

Horn, J. L., & Hofer, S. M. (1992). Major abilities and development in the adult period. In R. J. Sternberg & C. A. Berg (Eds.), *Intellectual development* (pp. 44–99). New York: Cambridge University Press.

Horn, J. L., & Knapp, J. R. (1973). On the subjective character of the empirical base of Guilford's structure-of-intellect model. *Psychological Bulletin, 80*, 33–43.

Howe, M. J., Davidson, J. W., & Sloboda, J. A (1998). Innate talents: Reality or myth? *Behavioral & Brain Sciences, 21*, 399–442.

Jensen, A. R. (1998). *The g factor: The science of mental ability*. Westport, CT: Praeger/Greenwoood.

Joreskog, K. G., & Sorbom, D. (1978). *LISREL IV: Estimation of linear structural equation systems by maximum likelihood methods*. Chicago: National Educational Resources.

Larkin, J., McDermott, J., Simon, D. P., & Simon, H. A. (1980). Expert and novice performance in solving physics problems. *Science, 208*, 1335–1342.

Larkin, J., & Simon, H. A. (1987). Why a diagram is (sometimes) worth 10,000 words. *Cognitive Science, 11*, 65–100.

Lesgold, A., Rubinson, H., Feltovich, P., Glaser, R., Klopfer, D., & Wang, Y. (1985). *Expertise in a complex skill: Diagnosing x-ray pictures* (Tech Rep.). Pittsburgh, PA: University of Pittsburgh, Learning Research and Development Center.

Luchins, A. S. (1942). Mechanization in problem solving. *Psychological Monographs, 54*(6, Serial No. 248).

McNemar, Q. (1964). Lost. Our intelligence. Why? *American Psychologist, 19*, 871–882.

Miller, G. A. (1956). The magical number seven, plus or minus two. *Psychological Review, 63*, 81–97.

Newell, A. (1990). *Unified theories of cognition*. Cambridge, MA: Harvard University Press.

Nicholls, J. G. (1990). What is ability and why are we mindful of it? A developmental perspective. In R. J. Sternberg & J. Kolligian, Jr. (Eds.), *Competence considered* (pp. 11–40). New Haven, CT: Yale University Press.

Patel, V. L., & Groen, G. J. (1991). The general and specific nature of medical expertise: A critical look. In K. A. Ericsson & J. Smith (Eds.), *Toward a general theory of expertise* (pp. 93–125). Hillsdale, NJ: Lawrence Erlbaum Associates.

Piaget, J. (1950). *Introduction à l'épistémologie génétique: Tome 1. La pensée mathématique* [Introduction to genetic epistemology: Volume 1. Mathematical thought]. Paris: Presses Universitaires de France.

Plomin, R., & McClearn, G. E. (Eds.). (1993). *Nature, nurture and psychology*. Washington, DC: APA Books.

Reitman, J. (1976). Skilled perception in GO: Deducing memory structures from interresponse times. *Cognitive Psychology, 8*, 336–356.

Shiffrin, R. M. (1996). Laboratory experimentation on the genesis of expertise. In K. A. Ericsson (Ed.), *The road to excellence* (pp. 337–345). Hillsdale, NJ: Lawrence Erlbaum Associates.

Simon, H. A., & Chase, W. G. (1973). Skill in chess. *American Scientist, 61*, 391–403.

Simon, H. A., & Gilmartin, K. (1973). A simulation of memory for chess positions. *Cognitive Psychology, 8*, 165–190.

Simonton, D. K. (1999). Talent and its development: An emergenic and epigenetic mode. *Psychological Review, 106*, 435–457.

Sloboda, J. A. (1991). Musical expertise. In K. A. Ericsson & J. Smith (Eds.), *Toward a general theory of expertise: Prospects and limits* (pp. 153–171). New York: Cambridge University Press.

Sloboda, J. A. (1996). The acquisition of musical performance expertise: Deconstructing the "talent" account of individual differences in musical expressivity. In K. A. Ericsson (Ed.), *The road to excellence: The acquisition of expert performance in the arts and sciences, sports, and games* (pp. 107–126). Mahwah, NJ: Lawrence Erlbaum Associates.

Spearman, C. (1923). Further.note on the "Theory of Two Factors." *British Journal of Psychology, 13*, 266–270.

Sternberg, R. J. (1977). *Intelligence, information processing, and analogical reasoning: The componential analysis of human abilities*. Hillsdale, NJ: Lawrence Erlbaum Associates.

Sternberg, R. J. (1981). Intelligence and nonentrenchment. *Journal of Educational Psychology*, *73*, 1–16.

Sternberg, R. J. (1985). *Beyond IQ*. New York: Cambridge University Press.

Sternberg, R. J. (1987). Most vocabulary is learned from context. In M. G. McKeown & M. E. Curtis (Eds.), *The nature of vocabulary acquisition* (pp. 89–105). Hillsdale, NJ: Lawrence Erlbaum Associates.

Sternberg, R. J. (1990). *Metaphors of mind*. New York: Cambridge University Press.

Sternberg, R. J. (Ed.). (1994). *Encyclopedia of human intelligence*. New York: MacMillan.

Sternberg, R. J. (1996). Costs of expertise. In K. A. Ericsson (Ed.), *The road to excellence* (pp. 347–354). Mahwah, NJ: Lawrence Erlbaum Associates.

Sternberg, R. J. (1998a). Metacognition, abilites, and developing expertise: What makes an expert student? *Instructional Science, 26*, 127–140.

Sternberg, R. J. (1998b). Abilities are forms of developing expertise. *Educational Researcher, 27*, 11–20.

Sternberg, R. J. (Ed.). (1999). *Handbook of creativity*. New York: Cambridge University Press.

Sternberg, R. J., & Davidson, J. E. (Eds.). (1995). *The nature of insight*. Cambridge, MA: MIT Press.

Sternberg, R. J., & Lubart, T. I. (1995). *Defying the crowd: Cultivating creativity in a culture of conformity*. New York: Free Press.

Whitely, S. E. (1980). Latent trait models in the study of intelligence. *Intelligence, 4*, 97–132.

Winner, E. (1996a). *Gifted children*. New York: Basic.

Winner, E. (1996b). The rage to master: The decisive role of talent in the visual arts. In K. A. Ericsson (Ed.), *The road to excellence* (pp. 271–301). Mahwah, NJ: Lawrence Erlbaum Associates.

Chapter 4

Achieving Academic Excellence: A Self-Regulatory Perspective

Barry J. Zimmerman
City University of New York

The attainment of optimal academic performance requires more than high quality instruction and requisite mental ability on the part of students: It requires personal initiative, diligence, and self-directive skill. Research on self-regulated learning grew out of efforts to understand the nature and source of these forms of students' proactivity, and it has revealed evidence of substantial correlation between their use and academic achievement. Self-regulation refers to self-generated thoughts, feelings, and actions that are planned and cyclically adapted to the attainment of personal goals (Schunk & Zimmerman, 1994). Because use of self-regulatory processes—such as goal setting, use of learning strategies, and self-monitoring—requires both time and effort, a second key issue in understanding students' initiative to excel academically is their sources of motivation. Students' sense of personal agency about the quality of their performance has been hypothesized to play a key self-motivational role (Bandura, 1997). An important self-motivational variable is self-efficacy, which refers to beliefs about one's capabilities to organize and implement actions necessary to attain a designated performance of skill for specific tasks.

This chapter considers research indicating that academic excellence, like other forms of exemplary achievement, depends on expertise in self-regulatory processes and supportive motivational beliefs, especially perceived efficacy (Bandura, 1997; Pajares & Miller, 1994; Zimmerman, 1995). More specifically, I describe the relationship between self-regulation and expert performance, a cyclical theory of academic self-regulation, self-regulation and academic excellence, academic self-regulation and perceived efficacy, the acquisition of self-regulatory expertise, and the emergence of self-regulation through levels.

SELF-REGULATION AND EXPERT PERFORMANCE

There is growing evidence that people's use of self-regulatory processes to systematize their learning and performance play a greater role in developing expertise than their innate talent or ability. Ericsson and his colleagues (Ericsson & Lehmann, 1996) have found that experts across a wide variety of skills, from typing to chess, are distinguished from nonexperts by their *task specific* knowledge and skill rather than by their talent (i.e., generalized ability or capacities). For example, elite athletes do not display superiority in their general perceptual abilities or reaction time (Abernethy, 1987; Starkes & Deakin, 1984). Nor are chess experts distinguished by their IQ (Doll & Mayr, 1987). Experts in recall of digits, such as track and field running times, did not display exceptional memory on more general recall tasks (Ericsson & Staszewski, 1989). Nor is mere exposure to high-quality academic experiences highly predictive of academic success either (Ericsson & Lehmann, 1996). Apparently, contact with relevant instructional activities in a domain is only weakly related to expert performance *unless* it is accompanied by high-quality practice efforts over significant periods of time.

In contrast to the limited effectiveness of measures of basic capacity or instructional experience, Ericsson and colleagues (Ericsson, Krampe, & Tesch-Romer, 1993) have found that measures of personal motivation and the amount and quality of practice much better predict the functioning of experts. These researchers have focused on the role of deliberate practice, which they defined as individualized training activities especially designed by a coach or teacher to improve specific aspects of an individual's performance through repetition and successive refinement. These activities are beneficial because they help learners generate their own feedback, monitor their performance, and, during the early stages of training, form concepts that are necessary for monitoring of performance (Ericsson, 1997).

There is evidence (Ericsson, 1997) that elite performers start their deliberate practice at a younger age than less accomplished performers do and that their expertise is directly related to time spent in such practice, which typically numbers more than 10,000 hours or 10 years for expert achievement in such disciplines as sport, dance, music, and chess. Although deliberate practice usually involves exercises designed by teachers or parents to improve performance, Ericsson noted that in some disciplines, such as chess, practice sessions were generally structured by the students themselves, such as when they personally selected and systematically practiced exemplary moves from written accounts of masters. There are also numerous biographical accounts in the academic skill literature of students who educated themselves by systematic reading and concerted practice, such as Benjamin Franklin (1868) and Thomas Edison (Josephson, 1959). Clearly, self-directed practice episodes, whether planned by others or by oneself, are important to the development of expertise.

This description of deliberate practice reflects learners' use of several classic self-regulatory processes, such as self-monitoring, goal-directed attention, and systematic reliance on feedback (Schunk & Zimmerman, 1994; Zimmerman, 1989). Experts from a wide variety of disciplines have reported use of self-regulation procedures, such as those listed in Table 4.1. I briefly illustrate some interesting personal adaptations of these techniques from the biographies, autobiographies, and instructional texts of successful writers, athletes, and musicians. There is extensive research that each of these self-regulatory techniques can be very effective in attaining excellence in their fields of endeavor (Zimmerman, 1998b). It should also be noted that these techniques represent *categories* of self-regulatory processes whose specific form and effectiveness varies with specific performance task or context. I discuss the underlying mechanisms for such adaptations in the next section of this chapter.

The first self-regulatory technique, *goal setting*, refers to specifying intended actions or outcomes. Before the prolific British novelist Anthony

TABLE 4.1
Definitions of Key Self-Regulatory Techniques

1. *Goal setting* describes specifying intended actions or outcomes of performance, such as pages written.
2. *Task strategies* refer to effective methods of skill execution, such as a mnemonic for recalling information.
3. *Self-instruction* involves overt or covert verbalizations to enhance performance, such as self-relaxation statements to reduce anxiety.
4. *Imagery* refers to imaging a behavioral sequence or setting to enhance performance, such as visualizing a complex performance before attempting to execute it.
5. *Time management* involves estimating and budgeting time for studying, such as organizing one's day to ensure completion of key activities.
6. *Self-monitoring* refers to selective tracking of one's own performance, such as keeping a record of new words learned.
7. *Self-evaluation* involves setting and using realistic standards for one's progress assessment, such as a track athlete's using his or her best running time to compare each day's practice effort.
8. *Environmental structuring* refers to selecting, organizing, and creating effective work settings, such as finding a conducive place to study.
9. *Help seeking* refers to choosing social sources of knowledge and skill, such as models, tutors, or books to learn.

Trollope began a book, he would specify writing goals (Wallace & Pear, 1977). He believed goals focused his daily activities and functioned as implicit standards. When he began each new book, he would organize his personal diary into weeks, and he averaged 40 pages per week, never dropping below 20 pages and topping out at 112 pages for his most productive week. It should be noted that goal setting must be adapted to potentially dynamic personal conditions, and maladaptive forms of goals can retard or even set back learning. For example, quantitative page goals might not be helpful or could even be counterproductive for writers who are struggling to improve the quality of their writing.

Self-regulating *task strategies* refers to the process of analyzing tasks and using specific, advantageous methods for learning. For example, the concert pianist Alicia De Larrocha (Mach, 1991) used a slow playing strategy to focus her attention during practice efforts and described its benefits in the following way: "Slowness not only aids memory, it helps to check note accuracy and phrasing because when you play in slow motion, just as in viewing a movie run slowly, you see every detail and at the same time reinforce the memory" (Mach, 1991, p. 59). Another self-regulatory strategy is *imagery*, which refers to the self-regulatory process of creating or recalling vivid mental images to assist learning. One of history's most successful golf professionals, Jack Nicklaus (1992), regularly uses visual imagery to enhance both practice and competitive play. He described his use of it this way: "Visualize the shot that would best deal with [the situation], and actually 'see' its flight in your mind's eye. Finally, imagine and mentally 'feel' the swing you would need to execute the planned shot" (p. 131). Although a wide variety of types of imagery have been proposed by expert coaches to aid learning (e.g., Dillard, 1998), it is recognized that the individual's goals and outcomes serve as ultimate criteria for interpreting images. For example, using the imagery to put spin on a tennis serve when trying to increase the speed of the serve can impede mastery. Even if a serve is executed as expected, it may not produce the expected outcomes, such as winning a point. For a description of how strategies, such as imagery, are adapted to specific goals and outcomes, see the next section.

The self-regulatory process of *self-instruction* refers to overt or subvocal verbalization to guide performance. For example, elite tennis players attending the Bolletierri Academy in Florida who have trouble controlling their negative outbursts on the court are asked to list all of their negative responses and to find a positive alternative for each one, such as saying "let it go" or "come on" (Loehr, 1991, p. 47) to focus or motivate themselves.

The self-regulatory process of *time management* refers to estimating and budgeting time. For example, the concert pianist Misha Dichter spent as long as 12 hours a day practicing as a youth to develop his competence, but, as an adult, he realized he needed to practice only 4 hours per day when on the road and 6 hours a day when learning new repertoire at home (Mach, 1991). The late pianist Glenn Gould felt that practicing beyond 4 hours a day diminished his effectiveness, and so he avoided it (Mach, 1991). The amount of practice reported by the adult Dichter corresponds quite closely with Gould's as well as with normative data. Ericsson (1997) found that, regardless of their area of skill, experts engage in 4 to 5 hours of practice daily, an amount that they believe optimizes their performance and yet avoids fatigue, stress reactions, and negative consequences.

Another form of self-regulation is *self-monitoring*, which involves observing, tracking, and often recording one's performance and outcomes. For example, the famed British choral instructor Graham Hewitt (1978) advocated that new vocal students keep daily graphs on a variety of vocal techniques, such as breath control, range, agility, vocal resonance, and articulation. He also advocated that singers sit in chairs to help them manually feel whether they provided proper abdominal support for the voice.

The self-regulatory process of *self-evaluation* refers to setting standards and using them for self-judgment. For example, Misha Dichter uses audio recordings of his piano playing to perfect his style (Mach, 1991). He said, "There's something marvelous about being able to hear yourself and study from your own mistakes, from your own performance, and to hear and to study others on records as well" (p. 72). "Things that sounded fine in the practice room sounded quite different in the play-backs. This caused me to rethink many things and has been a very rewarding process" (p. 67).

The self-regulatory process of *environmental structuring* involves selecting or creating effective settings for learning. For example, the British poet and dramatist Ben Jonson believed he wrote best when stimulated by the pungent odor of an orange peel, and warmed by a lot of tea and a purring cat (Barzon, 1964). The French novelist Marcel Proust preferred to write in a cork-lined room he had constructed to screen out distracting sounds (Wallace & Pear, 1977). These two examples indicate considerable diversity in what may be an optimal environment and that the main effects of an environmental feature may be less important than its interactive effects for the individual in question. This is not meant to suggest that subjective preferences about an environmental feature may outweigh its objective impact. Poor students are often handicapped because of their insensitivity to their learning environments and often try to study under highly distracting conditions, such as television or noisy social settings (Zimmerman & Martinez-Pons, 1986, 1988, 1990).

The self-regulatory process of *help seeking* is defined as choosing specific models, teachers, or books to assist oneself to learn. For example, whenever Jack Nicklaus (1992) felt that some bad habits had crept into his golf stroke, he would return to his former golf instructor for assistance in spotting the flaws and correcting them. "In my case, Jack Grout can get me back to fundamentals in minutes, whereas it might take me weeks of trial and error to iron out a basic fault on my own" (p. 136). It is important to note that help seeking differs from social dependence by its selective focus and limited duration, and there is considerable evidence that students who are not self-regulated tend to avoid asking for assistance because of concern about adverse social consequences of such requests (Newman, 1994).

There is extensive anecdotal evidence that use of self-regulatory procedures can increase the perceived efficacy of experts (Zimmerman, 1995). For example, the concert pianist Janina Fialkowska describes how she overcame a lapse in self-efficacy before her debut recital at Carnegie Hall by using self-instruction. She experienced a performance block where she suddenly could not recall the music and felt panic stricken. "Then I told myself that I had been waiting fourteen years for this; it is supposed to be the greatest, happiest moment of my life. I convinced myself that I knew the piece so well that even if the mind is blank, the fingers can do the job. Automatically, it seems, I came in at the right time, I played and everything turned out well. The program was a huge success" (Mach, 1991, p. 66).

What is evident from these anecdotal accounts of learning and performance by experts is that self-regulatory techniques are not merely the methods they used to acquire knowledge during their formative years. Once mastered, these techniques are used throughout life to sustain and to continue their professional development. These techniques were used during both the execution of acclaimed performances in the arts, sports, and writing, as well as to accomplish daily work or practice tasks. There is reason to believe that experts continue to use self-regulation techniques to develop their skills and that these individuals achieve the highest levels of skill. For example, Balzac and Trollope, who kept scrupulous records of their daily literary output, were among the most prolific novelists in history. By contrast, writers who struggled with inflexible self-evaluative standards, such as Truman Capote, were much less prolific. Although there is extensive anecdotal evidence that diverse experts use self-regulation techniques to guide their practice and performance efforts, the typicality of each category of techniques has received little systematic study to date (Zimmerman, 1998a).

A CYCLICAL THEORY OF ACADEMIC SELF-REGULATION

How are these common forms of self-regulation interrelated, and what conditions explain their use? A social cognitive view of self-regulation provides a microanalytic description of how learners discover what works for them on successive efforts when each effort may bring feedback indicating the need for covert, behavioral, and environmental adaptations (Zimmerman, 1989). *Covert* reactions, such as changing levels of knowledge or self-belief, often require changes in one's method of learning. Similarly, shifts in *behavioral* outcomes or *environmental* tasks and contexts also necessitate adjustments in self-regulatory technique. Because change is an inherent characteristic of learning efforts, the effectiveness of each technique must be continuously monitored and adjusted. At the outset of a new learning task, strategies are often general in form but become increasingly particularized as the learner focuses on the various components of the task that need to be acquired and integrated (Kitsantas & Zimmerman, 1998). This contextually adaptive view of learning (Zimmerman, 1983) often leads to differing solutions for different individuals or for the same individual at different times. This variability in strategy use can be best understood as part of a cyclical model of self-regulation.

Social cognitive researchers (Zimmerman, 1998c, 2000) conceptualize people's self-regulatory performance phase processes, such as imagery or task strategies, as dependent on prior forethought and subsequent self-reflection phase processes (see Fig. 4.1). The *forethought* processes and beliefs precede efforts to learn and set the stage for those efforts. The *performance* phase processes occur during learning and influence self-observation and control of those efforts. *Self-reflection* phase processes occur after learning efforts and influence a learner's self-judgments of and self-reactions to that experience. Finally, these self-reflections influence forethought regarding subsequent learning efforts, thus completing the self-regulatory cycle. The various self-regulatory subprocesses or beliefs within these three phases are presented in Table 4.2.

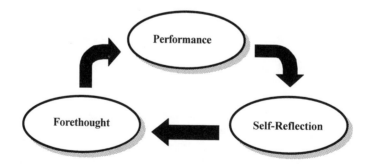

FIG. 4.1. Cyclical phases of self-regulation. From "Developing Self-Fulfilling Cycles of Academic Regulation: An Analysis of Exemplary Instructional Models," by B. J. Zimmerman, 1998, p. 3. In D. H. Schunk & B. J. Zimmerman (Eds.), *Self-Regulated Learning: From Teaching to Self-Reflective Practice*. New York: Guilford Press. Copyright © 1998 by Guilford Press. Reprinted with permission.

TABLE 4.2
Phase Structure and Subprocesses of Self-Regulation

	Cyclical Self-Regulatory Phases	
Forethought	*Performance*	*Self-Reflection*
Task analysis	*Self-control*	*Self-judgment*
Goal setting	Self-instruction	Self-evaluation
Strategic planning	Imagery	Causal attribution
Self-motivation beliefs	Time management	*Self-reaction*
Self-efficacy	Task strategies	Self-satisfaction/affect
Outcome expectations	Help-seeking	Adaptive–defensive
Intrinsic interest	Environmental structuring	
Goal orientation	*Self-observation*	
	Self-monitoring	

The forethought phase processes of goal setting and task strategy planning emerge from personal analyses of a task prior to performance. Highly self-regulated individuals organize their goal systems hierarchically, with process and subprocess goals linked to more distant outcome goals (Carver & Scheier, 1981). This goal system can provide direction to learners over long periods of time. To achieve these goals, learners must choose methods that are appropriate for the task and setting in order to master or perform a skill optimally. Strategic planning is necessary because the effectiveness of strategies depends on their adaptation to fluctuations in covert personal, behavioral, and environmental conditions (Zimmerman, 1989).

Because forethought is anticipatory, it depends on a number of key self-motivational beliefs: self-efficacy, outcome expectations, intrinsic interest, and goal orientation. There is extensive evidence that learners' perceptions of *self-efficacy* influences their motivation to engage and sustain self-regulatory efforts, such as self-monitoring (Bouffard-Bouchard, Parent, & Larivee, 1991), self-evaluation, and goal setting (Zimmerman & Bandura, 1994). *Outcome expectations*, which refer to beliefs about the ultimate ends of performance, motivate people to self-regulate when they are positive, but impede such efforts when they are doubtful or negative (Bandura, 1997). In terms of *goal orientation*, students who value learning progress tend to self-regulate better than those who value performance outcomes (Ames, 1992). Finally, learners with an *intrinsic interest* orientation will continue their learning efforts even in the absence of tangible rewards (Deci, 1975; Lepper & Hodell, 1989). This source of self-motivation is especially important when learners must practice or learn on their own and when social sources of reinforcement are not available or are delayed in time.

To self-control their academic performance, learners use a variety of task strategies as well as more general cognitive, behavioral, and social-environmental processes. As was previously described, self-instruction, imagery, time management, environmental structuring, and help seeking are widely used by experts to control performance phase functioning. However, the effectiveness of these strategic processes depends directly on how closely they are self-monitored, which is a form of self-observation. Students must self-monitor not only their functioning but also the conditions that surround it, and the effects that it produces (Zimmerman & Paulsen, 1995). When the amount of information involved in complex performances exceeds peoples' capacity, it will lead to disorganized or cursory self-monitoring. To avoid this hazard, self-regulated students learn to selectively track their processes. By setting hierarchical process goals during the forethought phase, students shift their selective self-observation quickly to problematic areas of functioning (Kitsantas & Zimmerman, 1998). Self-monitoring can be enhanced by record keeping, which diminishes the need for recall and enables performance outcomes to be studied and adjusted over time and changes in context. In this way, systematic self-monitoring can lead to better control of performance.

Self-evaluation is a key self-reflective phase process (Schunk, 1996). People evaluate themselves according to such criteria as mastery goals, previous performance attainments, or performance of others. Mastery goals involve use of a graduated or hierarchical sequence of criteria ranging from novice to expert. Self-criteria involve comparisons of current performance with earlier levels of one's behavior, and social comparisons involve the performance of others, such as classmates or competitors.

Closely linked to self-evaluation are judgments of causal attribution, such as whether poor performance is due to one's limited ability or to insufficient effort. Attributions for success improve students' self-motivation cyclically, but attributions for errors can easily undermine self-motivation. For example, attributing errors to a fixed ability prompts learners to react negatively and discourages efforts to improve (Weiner, 1979). Fortunately, attributions of errors to learning strategies are highly effective in sustaining motivation during periods of subpar performance (e.g., Zimmerman & Kitsantas, 1997, 1999) because strategy attributions sustain perceptions of efficacy until all possible strategies have been tested. Attributions depend on cognitive appraisal of such factors as perceptions of personal efficacy or mitigating environmental conditions.

These self-evaluative and attributional self-judgments produce several types of self-reactions during self-reflection. One key self-reflection, self-satisfaction, is important because people engage in learning activities that lead to satisfaction and positive affect and they avoid those that produce dissatisfaction and negative affect, such as anxiety (Bandura, 1991). A second self-reaction, adaptive inferences, directs people to new and potentially better forms of performance self-regulation, such as setting a new goal or changing a strategy (Zimmerman & Martinez-Pons, 1992). By contrast, defensive inferences shield people from future dissatisfaction and aversive affect, and unfortunately also undermine successful adaptation. Helplessness, procrastination, task avoidance, cognitive disengagement, and apathy are all forms of defensive inferences (Garcia & Pintrich, 1994).

These self-reactions affect forethought processes in a cyclical fashion. Self-satisfaction or dissatisfaction reactions affect one's self-motivation beliefs, such as self-efficacy, learning goal orientations, and intrinsic interest in the task (Schunk, 1996; Zimmerman & Kitsantas, 1997). Adaptive or defensive inferences influence the subsequent adjustment of goals and strategic planning. These altered self-motivation beliefs, goals, and planning form the basis for further self-regulatory efforts and eventual outcomes. Thus, the key self-regulatory processes used by experts are cyclically interdependent in three distinctive phases.

SELF-REGULATION AND ACADEMIC EXCELLENCE

To investigate the role of these self-regulatory processes in academic excellence, we compared a group of academically successful students with their classmates. Our assessment procedure involved presenting a series of common learning problems or contexts and asking students specifically how they would respond. For example, "teachers often assign their class the task of writing a short paper outside class on a topic such as one's family history. Do you have any particular methods to help you plan and write the paper?" The students' answers to these open-ended questions were then coded into key strategic categories similar to those described in Table 4.1. Some categories, such as task strategies, were subdivided into widely used subtypes, such as seeking information, organizing and transforming, and rehearsing and memorizing. Self-monitoring was separated into record keeping, reviewing records, and self-consequences (arranging or imagining self-consequences for successes and failures). During pilot testing, operational definitions for the categories were developed from students' response protocols using known self-regulation processes. The procedure for scoring the protocols was reliable, and the quality and the quantity of strategies reported were predictive of academic achievement. The differences in the verbal protocols of high and low achievers were sizeable in terms of both the quality and quantity of strategies reported. High achievers reported significantly greater use of 13 and 14 processes that were reported, and used them more than twice as often as low achievers. In our first study (Zimmerman & Martinez-Pons, 1986), students' achievement track in school was predicted with 93% accuracy using these self-regulatory reports, and these reports were correlated with their standardized test performance, $r = .61$. Although causality of students' use of self-regulatory processes could not be determined in this study, these results show that high achievers do use them significantly more frequently.

To determine whether students' self-reported use of self-regulatory processes corresponded to other measures, teachers' rating of their students' self-regulatory strategy use was included in an additional study (Zimmerman & Martinez-Pons, 1988). This scale focused on students' use of learning processes that were either directly or indirectly observable in school (e.g., completing assignments on time or being prepared for class). In this study, the students' academic ability was assessed in two areas: mathematics and English. Most of the items of the teacher rating scale of students' use of self-regulatory processes was found to load on a large first factor (79% of the variance) in an oblique exploratory factor analysis. Several of these items that reflected verbal fluency (e.g., students offering relevant information not mentioned in the textbook or previous class discussions) loaded on a small second factor (12% of the variance). The verbal and math ability measures loaded on a smaller third factor (9%) of the variance. Although very distinctive factors emerged in this analysis, these factors were correlated as expected. For example, the self-regulation factor derived from the teacher ratings correlated .43 with the achievement factor, indicating that students' use of self-regulatory processes was factorially distinctive from but correlated with measures of academic ability. Because verbal fluency can potentially confound self-report assessments of self-regulation, evidence that the two can be separated factorially was important. These three factor scores were correlated with students' self-reports of using self-regulatory processes in a canonical analysis. A substantial correlation was found ($R = .70$), which was due to the teachers' ratings factor of the students' self-regulation according to the large canonical correlation weight. The verbal facility factor and the ability factors had small, negative weights in the canonical correlation. Clearly, students' use of self-regulatory processes is observable to their teacher and is different from their verbal fluency and general academic ability.

Recent research has shown that the students' self-reported use of self-regulated learning processes remains factorially distinctive from aptitude measures even among highly selective populations of middle school students (Ablard & Lipschultz, 1998), but yet have been used successfully to distinguish students requiring remedial courses in college (Ley & Young, 1998).

ACADEMIC SELF-REGULATION AND PERCEIVED EFFICACY

As Ericsson (1996) noted, an essential quality of expert performers is a high degree of motivation to sustain their extensive practice and their performance efforts. Students' perceptions of self-efficacy are hypothesized to be reciprocally related to students' use of self-regulatory processes (Zimmerman, 1989). Students who acquire new self-regulatory skills perceive significant increases in self-efficacy (Schunk, 1994). Conversely, students who perceive themselves as efficacious on a task are more motivated to use known self-regulatory methods (Bouffard-Bouchard, Parent, & Larivee, 1991; Zimmerman, 1995). Thus, self-efficacy beliefs serve as a primary form of academic motivation related to two key aspects of self-regulation: self-monitoring and task-strategy use. Self-efficacy is not the only source of motivation, but it is closely linked to other self-beliefs associated with feelings of personal agency, such as outcome expectations, intrinsic interest, learning goal orientations, and process attributions (Zimmerman, 1998c).

We sought to determine whether a key measure of academic motivation, students' perceptions of efficacy, was related to their development of self-regulatory functioning. Gifted students attending an elite, tuition-free, multiethnic school or regular schools in New York City in grades 5, 8, and 11 were interviewed using our structured interview procedure (Zimmerman & Martinez-Pons, 1990). Students attending the school for the gifted were admitted on the basis of teachers' and counselors' observations of their characteristics and a rigorous entrance test. It was found that gifted youngsters displayed significantly greater use of self-regulated learning processes than regular students at each grade level, but there were developmental increases in use of self-regulatory processes reported by regular as well as by gifted students.

We developed a self-efficacy scale by selecting mathematical problems and verbal definition problems that ranged in difficulty from elementary school to high school levels and by asking students to rate their confidence about answering each item correctly. Corresponding to the increases in use of self-regulatory processes were increases in verbal and mathematical self-efficacy. The correlation between self-regulatory process use and self-efficacy reports was $r = .42$ for verbal functioning and $r = .41$ for mathematical functioning, indicating that self-regulatory competence was related to this key form of motivation. Clearly, developmental increases in the use of self-regulatory processes were accompanied by increases in perceived efficacy.

These findings piqued our interest to study the role of a new aspect of self-efficacy: self-efficacy to self-regulate studying. To investigate this issue, we (Zimmerman, Bandura, & Martinez-Pons, 1992) developed two subscales related to academic studying: (a) self-efficacy for self-regulated learning (i.e., for using studying strategies that were assessed in our structured interview), and (b) self-efficacy for academic achievement (i.e., for a range of academic subjects, such as math, science, and social studies). It was hypothesized that self-efficacy to regulate learning would be linked causally to self-efficacy for academic achievement. Also of special interest was the role of academic goal setting. The goal measure used in this study involved the students' expected grades in their social studies course. We also expected that self-efficacy for academic achievement would predict the grade goals that students set for themselves. It was hypothesized that self-efficacy would be directly linked to the grades the students attained at the end of the academic year as well as be indirectly predictive of the grades through the types of goals they set for themselves. To ascertain the impact of the parents' grade goals, parents were independently asked to respond to the same goal items with regard to their grade expectations for their children. Finally, the students' social studies grades for the prior year were included in the path model because prior achievement in a course area has been historically the best predictor of students' subsequent academic attainment.

The results, which are presented in Fig. 4.2, supported the three main hypotheses. Self-efficacy for self-regulated learning was linked to self-efficacy for academic achievement, which in turn was predictive of the students' grade goals as well as their final grades. Self-efficacy for academic achievement was also indirectly predictive of their final grades through the goals they set. In addition to the impact of the students' self-efficacy beliefs on their goal setting, their parents' grade goals for them affected their goals. This indicated that self and social variables interactively predicted the students' academic goal setting and attainment. The prior course grade predicted the parents' goal setting but not students'. The

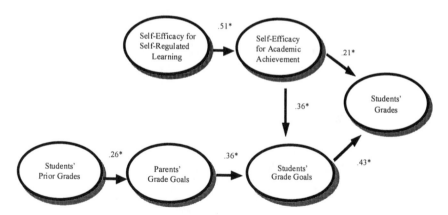

FIG. 4.2. Path coefficients for significant paths between variables in the sociocognitive model of students' self-motivation and class grades (*$p < .05$). From "Self-Motivation for Academic Attainment: The Role of Self-Efficacy Beliefs and Personal Goal-Setting" by B. J. Zimmerman, A. Bandura, & M. Martinez-Pons, 1992, *American Educational Research Journal, 29*, p. 671. Copyright © 1992 by the American Educational Research Association. Adapted with permission.

self-efficacy and goal measures (which were administered early in the fall) greatly increased the prediction of the final grades based on prior course grades by a 31% increase of the variance. This study not only showed the predictive power of self-regulatory beliefs in general, but it also showed that self-beliefs of regulatory efficacy were directly linked to self-beliefs of efficacy regarding academic outcomes.

To establish the generality of these findings, a second study was conducted with students from an elite university enrolled in a writing course (Zimmerman, Bandura, & Martinez-Pons, 1992). The students' verbal aptitude score was included as a background predictor variable (instead of prior grades) because it was used for admission into the college. Despite differences in instruments, age of students, and course content, we found a very similar pattern of results in this second path analytic study to those in the first study (see Fig. 4.3). Once again, self-efficacy for writing was predictive of self-efficacy for academic achievement, which was in turn predictive of the students' writing goals as well as their final grade in the course. Interestingly, verbal aptitude, a primary measure of competence used to predict verbal and written achievement in college, was not directly linked to the final course grade but rather, like the causal impact of prior grades in the earlier study, was mediated through students' use of self-regulatory processes. When comparing the level of prediction afforded by the measure of verbal ability, self-efficacy for academic achievement and goal setting increased the prediction of variance by 35%.

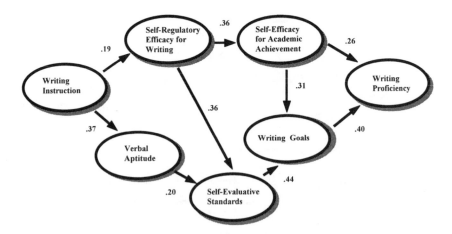

FIG. 4.3. Path coefficients for significant paths between variables in the sociocognitive model of students' self-motivation and class grades (*$p <$ .05). From "Impact of Self-Regulatory Influences on Writing Course Attainment" by B. J. Zimmerman & A. Bandura, 1994, *American Educational Research Journal, 34*, p. 856. Copyright © 1994 by the American Educational Research Association. Adapted with permission.

Thus, the distinction and causal link between self-efficacy for academic self-regulation and self-efficacy for academic achievement in these two studies was cross-replicated and showed generality over subject population, academic task, and assessment instrument. Furthermore, the self-efficacy and self-regulation measures mediated the influence of two of the most predictive measures of academic outcomes: prior grades in the same course and verbal aptitude tests.

ACQUISITION OF SELF-REGULATORY EXPERTISE

This section focuses on a key question that this volume seeks to answer: How does social opportunity interact with individual efforts to develop excellence? As Ericsson (1996) noted, attainment of an expert level of performance requires thousands of hours of deliberate practice, which is usually structured by exemplary teachers and reinforced by supportive parents. Ericsson's research as well as anecdotal descriptions of self-regulatory processes by experts indicate close ties to modeling, coaching, and feedback forms of instruction. But how do socially conveyed skills become sufficiently self-regulated to achieve excellence?

There is a long tradition of theory and research on how social influences and motoric experience combine to influence children's development of competence. John Dewey (1884) was one of the first to stress that developing children draw their mental substance and sense of function (i.e., personal agency beliefs) from their culture. He advocated studying the human mind as it developed in natural cultural settings, such as the school. Cognitive development was not viewed as self-contained but as linked functionally to the environment. However, Dewey rejected efforts to break down purposeful activity into stimuli and responses, arguing that each of these two components defines and causes the other in a reciprocal manner. He disparaged asocial views of cognitive development and saw the impact of socializing influences as instilling direction and purpose in children's unfocused thinking (Dewey, 1902). He also rejected structural reorganization views of children's mental development, arguing instead that the hallmark of adult thinking was its increase in the adaptive range and complexity.

One of the first scholars to focus on the role of imitation in the acquisition of knowledge and skill was J. M. Baldwin (Rosenthal & Zimmerman, 1978). From systematic observations of his own children, Baldwin (1906) concluded that imitative experiences had particular value in the development of children's skill, mental representation, and memory. He conceptualized skill acquisition and refinement as relying heavily on modeling. Baldwin described how a musician first imitates the movements and sounds of his instructor and later plays from printed rules. Eventually the name of a selection elicits "subconscious" (i.e., automatized) sound and muscle movements. In this way, reactions first drawn from imitations of external stimulus may later become governed by internal memory cues that supercede their emulative origins. He took issue with claims that new skills originate in motoric discovery, arguing instead that the child first practices from vicariously induced images and verbal memories before addressing sensorimotor feedback cues. Baldwin suggested that the continuation of motoric efforts are affected by their consequences or absence of consequences.

Vygotsky (1962, 1978) also envisioned children's self-regulation of a skill as growing out of social interactions between adults and more mature peers and learners. These adults provide support within children's zone of proximal development on tasks they cannot perform by themselves. The adults and children collaborate to complete tasks, and the social dialogue between them helps develop children's self-directive speech, which is a key tool for self-regulatory control. According to Vygotsky, there is a shift from social to self-support: At first, a skill is performed with social support by others and only later is performed independently. Thus, children's skilled performance outside the presence of the adult model depends on covert forms of self-instruction. This internalization of verbal regulation was also viewed by Vygotsky as a primary source of personal consciousness.

EMERGENCE OF SELF-REGULATION THROUGH LEVELS

Drawing on these and other traditions, social cognitive researchers (Schunk & Zimmerman, 1997; Zimmerman & Bonner, in press) have proposed that acquisition of a range of task competencies, from motoric skills to academic learning skills, emerges in a series of regulatory levels. At the most elementary level, novices are expected to acquire an exemplary new skill most effectively by watching expert adults or siblings model performance and listening to their verbal explanations and self-expressed beliefs. An *observational level* of skill occurs when learners induce the major features of a skill or strategy from watching a model learn or perform (see Table 4.3). In addition to strategic skill, models convey associated self-regulatory processes, such as performance standards, and motivational orientations, that observers can use personally at subsequent self-regulatory levels. For example, there is evidence (Zimmerman & Ringle, 1981) that the persistence of a model during complex problem solving affects the perseverance of observers. Perceived similarity to a model and vicarious consequences of a model's use of the skill will determine an observer's

TABLE 4.3
Levels of Regulatory Skill

Level	Name	Description
1	Observation	Vicarious induction of a skill from a proficient model.
2	Emulation[a]	Imitative performance of the general pattern or style of a model's skill with social assistance.
3	Self-control	Independent display of the model's skill under structured conditions.
4	Self-regulation	Adaptive use of skill across changing personal and environmental conditions.

[a]This level has been referred to as imitation in prior descriptions.

motivation to develop the skill further (Zimmerman & Rosenthal, 1974). At this initial level, students who watch an expert model perform are hypothesized to have a more detailed concept of the skill in question and its potential benefits than those who must rely on self-discovery.

Efforts to enact a skill motorically produce behavioral feedback that must be integrated with vicariously acquired information. An *emulative level* of self-regulatory skill is attained when a learner's behavioral performance approximates the strategic form of the model. Learners seldom copy the exact actions of the model, but rather they imitate the general pattern or style of functioning, such as the type of question a model asks instead of the model's exact words (Rosenthal, Zimmerman, & Durning, 1970). An observer's accuracy can be improved further when a model adopts a teaching role and provides guidance, feedback, and social reinforcement during practice (Zimmerman & Pike, 1972; Zimmerman & Rosenthal, 1974). The motoric and social consequences of observers' use of this skill will determine their motivation to develop the skill further. At this second level, students who perform a skill using images of and feedback from a skilled model are hypothesized to surpass the motoric performance of students who rely on self-discovery. Ericsson's (1996, 1997) discussions of feedback by master coaches to precocious pupils is reflective of this level of skill acquisition. It should be noted that the source of learning of regulatory skill is primarily social for these first two levels, but at more advanced levels, the locus shifts to self sources.

Acquiring the use of a skill on one's own usually requires more than exposure to a teacher or model, it also depends on extensive deliberate practice on one's own (Ericsson, Krampe, & Tesch-Romer, 1993). Attainment of a third, *self-controlled level* of self-regulatory skill occurs when learners master the use of a skill in structured settings outside the presence of models, such as when a pianist can play scales fluidly in the major and minor keys. At this level, a learner's use of a skill depends on representational standards of a model's performance (e.g., covert images or verbal recollections of a teacher's performance) rather than an overt social referent (Bandura & Jeffrey, 1973). The learner's success in matching that covert standard during practice efforts is expected to determine the amount of self-reinforcement he or she will experience. At this level, learning strategies that focus on fundamental processes rather than outcomes are hypothesized to be most beneficial in producing mastery.

A *self-regulated level* of task skill is achieved when learners can systematically adapt their performance to changing personal and contextual conditions. At this fourth level of skill, learners can vary the use of task strategies and make personal adjustments based on outcomes. Learners can choose a strategy and adapt its features with little or no residual dependence on the model. The motivation to sustain this level of skill depends especially on perceptions of self-efficacy. It is hypothesized that skills at this level can usually be performed with minimal direct process monitoring, and the learners' attention can be shifted toward performance outcomes without detrimental consequences. For instance, a tennis player's attention can be shifted from the execution of the serve to its effective use, such as placing it where it is likely to win a point. It should be noted that the shift from process to outcome monitoring during performance is not expected to preclude learners from interpreting their outcomes indirectly in terms of underlying processes. A tennis player focusing on service outcomes is still expected to attribute point losses to deficient strategy execution and incorrect strategy choice. Tennis players at level four can readily translate their service outcomes into process adjustments because they had already learned the latter's role at level three. Shifting to outcome monitoring can enhance one's ultimate effectiveness only when underlying processes are mastered to the point of automaticity. Carver and Scheier (1981) have cautioned against unconscious views of self-regulation and have suggested that expert learners merely shift their attention from motoric to more inclusive levels of functioning (i.e., where changing contexts and outcomes play a prominent role). The adaptive use of a skill in dynamic situations during level four reflects the hallmark of adult thinking according to Dewey (1884).

Thus, a multilevel social cognitive analysis of the acquisition of self-regulatory competence begins with the most extensive social guidance at the first level, and the need for social support diminishes as learners acquire underlying self-regulatory skill. Notably, this perspective rejects any assumptions that social influences fundamentally conflict with and preclude self-regulation. Instead it envisions social and self influences as reciprocal and interdependent (Bandura, 1986). Social influences are increasingly employed on a self-selective basis from levels 1 to 4 and continue to be used even at level 4, such as when Jack Nicklaus seeks advice from his golf coach during slumps. Because self-regulatory skill is task and context-dependent, new performance applications or contexts can uncover limitations in existing strategies and require additional social learning experiences even at the highest levels of expertise, such as when concert pianists decide to add new composers' works to their concert repertoire.

Unlike developmental stage models, this multilevel social learning formulation does not assume that learners must advance through the four levels in an invariant sequence or that, once the highest level is attained, it will be used universally. Instead, like learning hierarchy models (Gagne, 1968; Zimmerman & Whitehurst, 1979), a multilevel approach assumes that students who master each skill level in sequence will learn more easily and effectively. Although an asocial discovery path to learning complex skills is also available, it is strewn with hazards, dead ends, and confusing results (Bandura, 1986; Schunk & Zimmerman, 1997). By contrast, students who acquire cognitive representations of culturally validated learning strategies from a model and then receive direct social feedback regarding their efforts to imitatively enact those strategies are expected to experience many benefits. They not only learn the basics of the skill better, but they also learn how to set process goals, self-monitor, and adapt their performance when practicing on their own. That is, social learning processes (levels 1 and 2) sets the stage for more self-directed processes (levels 3 and 4).

Furthermore, social models are expected to sustain students' motivation by providing vicarious and direct reinforcement during the initial efforts to learn when students' sense of self-efficacy for the skill has not yet developed. Use of self-regulatory processes to learn is often mentally and physically demanding, and a person may decide to forego their use if he or she feels tired, disinterested, or uncommitted. When such motivation is lacking, even level 4 learners may not choose to perform self-regulatively. For example, a student may not take notes when reading a novel for pleasure but would do so when reading the same novel as part of a formal course or a weekly literary discussion group.

There is evidence that the speed and quality of learners' self-regulatory development can be significantly enhanced if learners proceed according to the proposed four-level hierarchy. A recent study tested the sequentiality of the first and second levels (observational and emulative learning) of acquisition of self-regulation. Recall that this socially guided sequence for initial skill learning was hypothesized to be superior to motoric discovery, although the latter method was expected to work to a lesser degree. In this study, we compared the acquisition of dart-throwing skill by novice learners who learned from modeling with that of learners who learned from motoric discovery (Kitsantas, Zimmerman, & Cleary, 2000). An adult model demonstrated a multistep process strategy involving sighting, throwing, and follow-through steps. Students observed a model perform without errors (a mastery skill), a model gradually overcome errors (a coping model), or no model (a control condition). It was hypothesized that a coping model would produce more accurate observational learning than a mastery model because the former model draws observers' attention to potential errors and their correction. A mastery model was expected to surpass the no model controls because this model demonstrated an effective strategy that control subjects had to discover on their own. During a subsequent enactment learning phase, half of the students in each modeling condition received corrective verbal feedback regarding their performance as they practiced the skill, for example, "You didn't follow through on your throw properly."

It was found that students who had the benefit of coping modeling experiences significantly surpassed the dart-throwing skill of those who attempted to learn from a mastery model who, in turn, surpassed the acquisition of students in the no modeling control group. Furthermore, students who received social feedback learned better than those who practiced on their own, but this feedback was insufficient to make up for the absence of modeling experiences. Students in the coping modeling group also showed higher levels of self-motivation than those in the mastery model or control group according to an array of measures, such as self-efficacy, self-satisfaction, and intrinsic interest. These results confirmed the advantage of engaging in observational learning, especially when it is discriminative (i.e., involving a coping model), before attempting to engage in enactive learning experiences.

A second study (Zimmerman & Kitsantas, 1997) tested the sequentiality of the self-control and self-regulation skill levels by examining the effectiveness of shifting from process goals to outcome goals using the same dart-throwing task described earlier. Recall that process goals were hypothesized to be optimal during the acquisition of self-control but outcome goals were expected to be superior during the acquisition of self-regulation. A key indicator of the transition from level 3 to level 4 is the learner's automatic use of a learning strategy. Once this occurs, learners can shift their attention to performance outcomes without any loss of effectiveness. Although attention is shifted to outcomes, it is expected that learners will continue to interpret outcome deficiencies in terms of the execution of underlying processes.

Using the same dart-throwing task described earlier, all of the subjects were taught the three strategic steps of the skill through observation and emulation (levels 1 and 2). The experiment compared the effects of process goals, outcome goals, and shifting goals from processes (level 3) to outcomes after achieving automaticity (level 4) as well as self-recording during self-directed practice. The results were consistent with a multilevel view of goal setting. Students who shifted goals surpassed classmates who adhered to only process goals or to only outcome goals in posttest dart-throwing skill. In addition to their superior learning outcomes, students who shifted their goals displayed superior self-efficacy perceptions and intrinsic interest in the game. Self-recording enhanced these goal setting effects on dart-throwing skill acquisition. To discern how students would interpret any performance deficiencies during self-directed learning, they were asked to make attributions about a subpar dart-throwing effort when it occurred during practice. Significantly more strategy process attributions were made by students who pursued process goals either temporarily (the shifting group) or consistently (the process group) in comparison to students who adhered to only outcome goals. These results indicate that setting an outcome goal does not preclude strategic process attributions during the self-reflection phase.

A third study (Zimmerman & Kitsantas, 1999) tested the sequentiality of the self-control and self-regulation skill levels by examining the effectiveness of shifting from process goals to outcome goals using a very different task. Unlike the well-defined, highly motoric task of dart throwing, writing is more covert and more subjective. In this study, students were asked to revise a series of sentences from commercially available sentence-combining workbooks. These exercises transformed 6 to 12 simple and often redundant sentences into a single nonredundant sentence. For example, the sentences: "It was a ball. The ball was striped. The ball rolled across the room" could be rewritten as "The striped ball rolled across the room." A scoring system was developed for assessing correspondence between various revisions and the ideal sentence recombination developed by the author of the workbook. The researchers developed a three-step strategy for revising these multisentence problems involving: circling essential information, crossing out redundant information, and connecting the remaining parts in a sentence. All of the subjects were taught the three steps of the revision strategy through observation and emulation (levels 1 and 2). The experiment compared the effects of process goals, outcome goals, and shifting goals as well as self-recording during self-directed practice.

Despite the changes in task, the results parallel those reported in the earlier study of dart-throwing skill: Students who shifted goals from processes to outcomes after reaching level 4 (i.e., having achieved automaticity) surpassed classmates who adhered to only process goals or to only outcome goals in posttest writing revision skill. Self-recording enhanced these goal setting effects on writing skill acquisition. In addition to their superior learning outcomes, students who shifted their goals displayed superior self-efficacy perceptions and intrinsic interest in writing task. Once again, students were asked to make attributions about a subpar revision effort when it occurred during writing practice. Significantly more strategy process attributions were made by students who pursued process goals either temporarily (the shifting group) or consistently (the process group) in comparison to students who adhered to only outcome goals. These results also suggest that an outcome goal does not preclude strategic process interpretations of the outcomes even with an ill-defined writing task.

CONCLUSION

The attainment of academic excellence appears to require more than giftedness or exposure to exemplary instructional experiences. It depends on high levels of motivation and countless hours of practice. What defines an expert's practice as "deliberate" is his or her use of such classic self-regulatory processes as self-monitoring, goal-directed attention, and reliance on systematic feedback. Not only do experts across a wide variety of disciplines report extensive use of self-regulated learning strategies, they also report high levels of motivation and persistence in using them over extended periods of time. Research on academic attainment also has uncovered extensive evidence that self-regulatory processes play a key role. Measures of self-regulation of academic studying are distinctive from measures of academic ability and yet are highly predictive of diverse measures of academic excellence, including membership in gifted groups, advanced tracks in school, performance on standardized tests, and exemplary grades. In terms of students' motivation to learn, efficacy beliefs about use of self-regulatory processes are predictive of students' academic goals and subsequent success. Historically, a number of theorists have suggested that children's self-regulatory control emerges primarily from social learning experiences, and there is now some experimental evidence that interventions that mirror the same pattern are especially effective. Although some learning can occur from autonomous methods, a social cognitive multilevel approach can significantly enhance learners' progress and sustain their motivation until excellence is achieved.

ACKNOWLEDGMENT

I would like to thank Michel Ferrari for his insights and helpful comments regarding this chapter.

REFERENCES

Abernethy, B. (1987). Selective attention in fast ball sports: II. Expert–novice differences. *Australian Journal of Science Medicine and Sports, 19*, 7–16.

Ablard, K. E., & Lipschultz, R. E. (1998). Self-regulated learning in high-achieving students: Relations to advanced reasoning, achievement goals, and gender. *Journal of Educational Psychology, 90*, 94–101.

Ames, C. (1992). Achievement goals and the classroom motivational climate. In D. H. Schunk & J. L. Meece (Eds.), *Student perceptions in the classroom* (pp. 327–348). Hillsdale, NJ: Lawrence Erlbaum Associates.

Baldwin, J. M. (1906). *Mental development in the child and the race* (3rd rev. ed.). New York: Macmillan.

Bandura, A. (1986). *Social foundations of thought and action: A social cognitive theory.* Englewood Cliffs, NJ: Prentice-Hall.

Bandura, A. (1991). Self-regulation of motivation through anticipatory and self-reactive mechanisms. In R. A. Dienstbier (Ed.), *Perspectives on motivation: Nebraska Symposium on Motivation* (Vol. 38, pp. 69–164). Lincoln: University of Nebraska Press.

Bandura, A. (1997). *Self-efficacy: The exercise of control.* New York: W. H. Freeman.

Bandura, A., & Jeffrey, R. W. (1973). Role of symbolic coding and rehearsal processes in observational learning. *Journal of Personality and Social Psychology, 26*, 122–130.

Barzon, J. (1964). Calamaphobia, or hints towards a writer's discipline. In H. Hull (Ed.), *The writers book* (pp. 84–96). New York: Barnes & Noble.

Benjamin Franklin Writings. (1987). New York: Literary Classics of the United States. (Original *Autobiography* published in 1868)

Bouffard-Bouchard, T., Parent, S., & Larivee, S. (1991). Influence of self-efficacy on self-regulation and performance among junior and senior high-school age students. *International Journal of Behavior Development, 14*, 153–164.

Carver, C., & Scheier, M. (1981). *Attention and self-regulation: A control theory approach to human behavior.* New York: Springer-Verlag.

Deci, E. L. (1975). *Intrinsic motivation.* New York: Plenum.

Dewey, J. (1884). The new psychology. *Early works of John Dewey* (Vol. 1, pp. 48–60). Carbondale, IL: Southern Illinois University Press.

Dewey, J. (1902). The child and the curriculum. *Middle works of John Dewey* (Vol. 2, pp. 271–292). Carbondale, IL: Southern Illinois University Press.

Dillard, K. (1998, October). Glide into volleys. *Tennis, 34,* 50.

Doll, J., & Mayr, U. (1987). Intelligenz und Schachleistung—eine Untersuchung an Schachexperten [Intelligence and achievement in chess—a study of chess masters]. *Psychologische Beitrräge, 29,* 270–289.

Ericsson, K. A. (1996). Acquisition of expert performance: An introduction to some of the issues. In K. A. Ericsson (Ed.), *The road to excellence: The acquisition of expert performance in the arts and sciences, sports and games* (pp. 1–50). Mahwah, NJ: Lawrence Erlbaum Associates.

Ericsson, K. A. (1997). Deliberate practice and the acquisition of expert performance: An overview. In H. Jorgensen & A. C. Lehmann (Eds.), *Does practice make perfect?* (pp. 9–51). Stockholm: NIH Publikasjoner.

Ericsson, K. A., Krampe, R. T., & Tesch-Romer, C. (1993). The role of deliberate practice in the acquisition of expert performance. *Psychological Review, 100,* 363–406.

Ericsson, A. K., & Lehmann, A. C. (1996). Expert and exceptional performance: Evidence of maximal adaptation to task constraints. *Annual Review of Psychology, 47,* 273–305.

Ericsson, K. A., & Staszewski, J. (1989). Skilled memory and expertise: Mechanisms of exceptional performance. In D. Klahr & K. Kotosvsky (Eds.), *Complex information processes: The impact of Herbert A. Simon* (pp. 235–267). Hillsdale, NJ: Lawrence Erlbaum Associates.

Gagne, R. M. (1968). Contributions of learning to human development. *Psychological Review, 75,* 177–191.

Garcia, T., & Pintrich, P. R. (1994). Regulating motivation and cognition in the classroom: The role of self-schemas and self-regulatory strategies. In D. H. Schunk & B. J. Zimmerman (Eds.), *Self-regulation of learning and performance: Issues and educational applications* (pp. 127–153). Hillsdale, NJ: Lawrence Erlbaum Associates.

Hewitt, G. (1978). *How to sing.* New York: Taplinger.

Josephson, M. (1959). *Edison: A biography.* New York: McGraw-Hill.

Kitsantas, A., & Zimmerman, B. J. (1998). Self-regulation of motoric learning: A strategic cycle view. *Journal of Applied Sport Psychology, 10,* 220–239.

Kitsantas, A., Zimmerman, B. J., & Cleary, T. (2000). The role of observation and emulation in the development of athletic self-regulation. *Journal of Educational Psychology, 92,* 811–817.

Lepper, M. R., & Hodell, M. (1989). Intrinsic motivation in the classroom. In C. Ames & R. Ames (Eds.), *Research on motivation in education* (Vol. E., pp. 255–296). Hillsdale, NJ: Lawrence Erlbaum Associates.

Ley, K., & Young, D. B. (1998). Self-regulation behaviors in underprepared (developmental) and regular admission college students. *Contemporary Educational Psychology, 23,* 42–64.

Loehr, J. E. (1991). *The mental game.* New York: Plume.

Mach, E. (1991). *Great contemporary pianists speak for themselves.* Toronto: Dover Books.

Newman, R. (1994). Academic help-seeking: A strategy of self-regulated learning. In D. H. Schunk & B. J. Zimmerman (Eds.), *Self-regulation of learning and performance: Issues and educational applications* (pp. 283–301). Hillsdale, NJ: Lawrence Erlbaum Associates.

Nicklaus, J. (1992). *Jack Nicklaus' lesson tee.* New York: Simon & Schuster.

Pajares, F., & Miller, M. D. (1994). Role of self-efficacy and self-concept beliefs in mathematical problem solving: A path analysis. *Journal of Educational Psychology, 86,* 193–203.

Rosenthal, T. L., & Zimmerman, B. J. (1978). *Social learning and cognition.* New York: Academic Press.

Rosenthal, T. L., Zimmerman, B. J., & Durning, K. (1970). Observationally induced changes in children's interrogative classes. *Journal of Personality and Social Psychology, 16,* 631–688.

Schunk, D. H. (1994). Self-regulation of self-efficacy and attributions in academic settings. In D. H. Schunk & B. J. Zimmerman (Eds.), *Self-regulation of learning and performance: Issues and educational applications* (pp. 75–99). Hillsdale, NJ: Lawrence Erlbaum Associates.

Schunk, D. H. (1996). Goal and self-evaluative influences during children's cognitive skill learning. *American Educational Research Journal, 33,* 359–382.

Schunk, D. H., & Zimmerman, B. J. (1994). *Self-regulation of learning and performance: Issues and educational applications.* Hillsdale, NJ: Lawrence Erlbaum Associates.

Schunk, D. H., & Zimmerman, B. J. (1997). Social origins of self-regulatory competence. *Educational Psychologist, 32,* 195–208.

Starkes, J. L., & Deakin, J. M. (1984). Perception in sport: A cognitive approach to skilled performance. In W. F. Staub & J. M. Williams (Eds.), *Cognitive sport psychology* (pp. 115–128). Lansing, NY: Sport Science Association.

Vygotsky, L. S. (1962). *Thought and language.* Cambridge, MA: MIT Press.

Vygotsky, L. S. (1978). *Mind in society: The development of higher psychological processes.* Cambridge, MA: Harvard University Press.

Wallace, I., & Pear, J. (1977). Self-control techniques of famous novelists. *Journal of Applied Behavioral Analysis, 10,* 515–525.

Weiner, B. (1979). A theory of motivation for some classroom experiences. *Journal of Educational Psychology, 71,* 3–25.

Zimmerman, B. J. (1983). Social learning theory: A contextualist account of cognitive development. In C. J. Brainerd (Ed.), *Recent advances in cognitive developmental theory* (pp. 1–49). New York: Springer.

Zimmerman, B. J. (1989). A social cognitive view of self-regulated academic learning. *Journal of Educational Psychology, 81,* 329–339.

Zimmerman, B. J. (1995). Self-efficacy and educational development. In A. Bandura (Ed.), *Self-efficacy in changing societies* (pp. 202–231). New York: Cambridge University Press.

Zimmerman, B. J. (1998a). Academic studying and the development of personal skill: A self-regulatory perspective. *Educational Psychologist, 33,* 73–86.

Zimmerman, B. J. (1998b). Acquisition of self-regulatory skill: From theory and research to academic practice. In R. Bernhardt, C. N. Hedley, G. Cattaro, & V. Svolopoulous (Eds.), *Curriculum leadership: Redefining schools in the 21st century* (pp. 133–152). Emerson, NJ: Hampton Press.

Zimmerman, B. J. (1998c). Developing self-fulfilling cycles of academic regulation: An analysis of exemplary instructional models. In D. H. Schunk & B. J. Zimmerman (Eds.), *Self-regulated learning: From teaching to self-reflective practice* (pp. 1–19). New York: Guilford Press.

Zimmerman, B. J. (2000). Attainment of self-regulation: A social cognitive perspective. In M. Boekaerts, P. Pintrich, & M. Zeidner (Eds.), *Self-regulation: Theory, research, and applications* (pp. 13–39). Orlando, FL: Academic Press.

Zimmerman, B. J., & Bandura, A. (1994). Impact of self-regulatory influences on writing course attainment. *American Educational Research Journal, 31,* 845–862.

Zimmerman, B. J., Bandura, A., & Martinez-Pons, M. (1992). Self-motivation for academic attainment: The role of self-efficacy beliefs and personal goal setting. *American Educational Research Journal, 29,* 663–676.

Zimmerman, B. J., & Bonner, S. (in press). A social cognitive view of strategic learning. In C. E. Weinstein & B. L. McCombs (Eds.), *Strategic learning: Skill will and self-regulation.* Mahwah, NJ: Lawrence Erlbaum Associates.

Zimmerman, B. J., & Kitsantas, A. (1997). Developmental phases in self-regulation: Shifting from process to outcome goals. *Journal of Educational Psychology, 89,* 29–36.

Zimmerman, B. J., & Kitsantas, A. (1999). Acquiring written revision skill: Shifting from process to outcome self-regulatory goals. *Journal of Educational Psychology, 91,* 1–10.

Zimmerman, B. J., & Martinez-Pons, M. (1986). Development of a structured interview for assessing students' use of self-regulated learning strategies. *American Educational Research Journal, 23,* 614–628.

Zimmerman, B. J., & Martinez-Pons, M. (1988). Construct validation of a strategy model of student self-regulated learning. *Journal of Educational Psychology, 80,* 284–290.

Zimmerman, B. J., & Martinez-Pons, M. (1990). Student differences in self-regulated learning: Relating grade, sex, and giftedness to self-efficacy and strategy use. *Journal of Educational Psychology, 82,* 51–59.

Zimmerman, B. J., & Martinez-Pons, M. (1992). Perceptions of efficacy and strategy use in the self-regulation of learning. In D. H. Schunk & J. Meece (Eds.), *Student perceptions in the classroom: Causes and consequences* (pp. 185–207). Hillsdale, NJ: Lawrence Erlbaum Associates.

Zimmerman, B. J., & Paulsen, A. S. (1995). Self-monitoring during collegiate studying: An invaluable tool for academic self-regulation. In P. Pintrich (Ed.), *New directions in college teaching and learning: Understanding self-regulated learning* (No. 63, Fall, pp. 13–27). San Francisco: Jossey-Bass.

Zimmerman, B. J., & Pike, E. O. (1972). Effects of modeling and reinforcement on acquisition and generalization of question-asking behavior. *Child Development, 43,* 892–907.

Zimmerman, B. J., & Ringle, J. (1981). Effects of model persistence and statements of confidence on children's self-efficacy and problem solving. *Journal of Educational Psychology, 73,* 485–493.

Zimmerman, B. J., & Rosenthal, T. L. (1974). Observational learning of rule-governed behavior by children. *Psychological Bulletin, 81,* 29–42.

Zimmerman, B. J., & Whitehurst, G. J. (1979). Structure and function: A comparison of two views of the development of language and cognition. In G. J. Whitehurst & B. J. Zimmerman (Eds.), *Functions of language and cognition* (pp. 1–22). New York: Academic Press.

CULTURE, SOCIETY, AND THE PURSUIT OF EXCELLENCE

Pathways to Excellence: Value Presuppositions and the Development of Academic and Affective Skills in Educational Contexts

Michael F. Mascolo
Merrimack College

Jin Li
Brown University

Rosalie Fink
Lesley College

Kurt W. Fischer
Harvard University

How can a theory of psychological development inform the pursuit of excellence through education? The concepts of *excellence* and *development* are related in ways that are not always clearly acknowledged. As an evaluative concept, *excellence* is defined in terms of the valued skills and outcomes that are judged to be necessary to function well within one's community. Similarly, as a concept implying directional change, *development* has meaning only with reference to some conception of its developmental outcomes or endpoints. Transformations that move a given skill closer to some specified endpoint would constitute progression; changes involving movement away from such endpoints would constitute regression. Thus, in order for a theory of development to inform the pursuit of excellence through education, one must first articulate the social values that define the developmental outcomes that a given community wishes to promote. Having done so, one can use developmental theory to map out ways in which academic skills develop in the directions of those valued endpoints.

In what follows, we explore the ways in which dynamic skill theory (Fischer, 1980; Fischer & Bidell, 1997; Mascolo & Fischer, 1998, 1999) can provide a framework for charting trajectories in the development of academic skills in different psychological domains and sociocultural contexts. Thereafter, we use skill theory to examine pathways in the development of academic and affective skills as they develop toward culturally valued endpoints. In so doing, we first examine pathways in the development of common academic skills that are valued within Western industrialized societies. Thereafter, by comparing the development of motivation-for-learning in the United States and China, we examine ways in which development can take divergent pathways as it moves toward different culturally defined conceptions of excellence.

THE CONCEPT OF DEVELOPMENT
IN DEVELOPMENTAL THEORY

What does it mean to say that something has *developed*? What is a theory of development a theory of? Many theoretical and empirical analyses of psychological development proceed from an implicit or explicit characterization of development as "age-related changes." However, the concept of development differs from this and related concepts (e.g., *change, history, growth*, etc.) in its dual implications of *directionality* and *structural transformation*. The idea that something is developing implies movement in one or another direction. As such, development implies an implicit or explicit comparison to some type of hypothesized *endpoint*. This is not to say that psychological events necessarily move toward specific endpoints in ontogenesis. Instead, it only implies that when we say a structure is more or less developed, we must compare it to some conception of what that structure would look like in a fully developed form(s).

For example, one might propose a variety of qualities that define *arithmetic proficiency*, including the capacities to recite simple number facts, to understand the comparative value of numbers, to understand the logical relations between addition and subtraction, to use certain algorithms or heuristics to calculate complex sums, and so forth. It is only relative to such a conception that one can speak of the *development* of adding skill. It follows, of course, that differences in the ways in which communities define arithmetic proficiency would imply differences in the pathways through which such skills develop. Pathways in development of arithmetic skill are likely to look different in communities that organize addition around different technologies (e.g., abacus, manipulatives, calculators), or in communities in which counting is founded on conceptual frameworks different than those found in the West (e.g., Saxe, 1995).

A second implication of the concept of development is *structural transformation*. Development is not simply a synonym for *growth*. Growth implies an increase in size or number of a given entity. For example, 17th-century preformationists believed that individual spermatozoa contained elements of fully formed humans (Needham, 1959; Ruestow, 1997). If this were so, ontogenesis would simply be a case of a fully formed human becoming larger over time. In contrast, development implies transformation in the very organization of an entity as it forms and changes over time. This notion of development is embodied in Werner's (1940; Werner & Kaplan, 1963/1984) *orthogenetic principle*, which states that when an entity or process develops, it moves from a more global and undifferentiated state to states of increasing differentiation, integration, and hierarchic integration.

For example, addition skills do not emerge fully formed at a single point in ontogenesis. Instead, they develop gradually as their component parts become increasingly differentiated and hierarchically coordinated over time. For example, simple addition skills often develop in a three-step sequence (Resnick & Ford, 1981; Gelman & Gallistel, 1978). In the first step, children simply count to-be-added objects. In the second step ("counting all"), children begin to differentiate between the two addends of a problem. For example, for a problem like "5 + 2", children might use their fingers to count out items corresponding to the first addend, then do the same for the second addend, and then count them all as a group in order to achieve the sum. In the third step ("counting on"), children bring together their skills for counting each of the two addends into a single integrated skill. Specifically, children understand that if they begin with the first addend ("5"), they need only count upward the number of times indicated by the second addend ("2") to arrive at the sum ("7"). These shifts illustrate what it means to speak of *structural* change in development.

Given this definition of development, it follows that not all changes that occur over time qualify as developmental changes. Indeed, the developmental level of any given psychological act fluctuates from time to time and from context to context (Fischer & Granott, 1995; Fischer, Bullock, Rotenberg, & Raya, 1993). Consequently, the concept of development is a *theoretical* concept, and not simply a *descriptive* one (Kaplan, 1984). Relative to a given developmental endpoint, changes that occur over time may be considered *progressions, regressions, digressions,* or even *deviations* (Kanner, in press; Rogoff, 1990). As such, the concept of development reflects a type of *perspective* that one brings to analyses of psychological change (Kaplan, 1984). From this view, psychological losses that accompany aging might be seen as regressions rather than progressions; compensations for such losses might be seen as progressions (see Baltes, 1983).

Our theoretical postulations about what constitutes ideal human development do not occur in a social vacuum. *Social values* play a definitive role in determining those skills and outcomes that we take to be developmental endpoints (Goodnow, 1980; Kanner, in press; Rogoff, 1990). These include not only the social values of the individuals and social groups that we study, but also the values of the communities of which the developmental theorist is a part. Thus, it follows that there is not one universal trajectory or conception of development; instead, there are as many developmental trajectories as there are skills and outcomes that are valued by members of different communities. Thus, in order for a theory of development to inform the pursuit of excellence through education, one must first articulate the value presuppositions that define excellence in a given domain of functioning. Thereafter, one can use developmental theory to map out specific trajectories in the ways in which target skills undergo transformation in the direction of valued endpoints, and to illuminate the nature of the developmental processes that promote such changes.

DYNAMIC SKILL THEORY AS A FRAMEWORK FOR PREDICTING AND PROMOTING DEVELOPMENTAL TRAJECTORIES TOWARD VALUED ENDPOINTS

Dynamic skill theory (Fischer, 1980; Bidell & Fischer, 1996; Mascolo & Fischer, 1998, 1999) provides a framework for charting developmental trajectories in a variety of academic and emotional domains. Having articulated a series of idealized skills that define the valued endpoints for educational development, one can use dynamic skill theory to chart trajectories in the development of acting, thinking, and feeling within any particular educational domain. Skill theory also provides a framework to understand the ways in which biological, personal, and sociocultural processes interact in the epigenesis of any given trajectory of academic or emotional development (Bidell & Fischer, 1998; Mascolo & Bhatia, in press).

Pathways in the Dynamic Development of Psychological Structures

The central unit in dynamic skill theory is the developing *skill*. A skill refers to the capacity to organize one's actions within a given context. A skill is always an action on something. As such, a skill is not simply a property of single individuals. Instead, a skill is a property of an individual-in-a-context. A change in task or context generally results in a change in the organization of a given skill, and social systems play an important role in the creation of skills within any given domain of activity. Skill theory provides a set of conceptual and methodological tools for making both major and fine-grained assessments of transformations in dynamic structures of action and thought. However, unlike stage theories of development (e.g., Piaget, Erikson, or Kohlberg), developing structures do not reflect generic levels of intellectual or social competence. Instead, skills develop within particular tasks, conceptual and emotional domains, and contexts. With development, individuals are capable of applying and generalizing their skills to new situations and domains. However, it takes effort to relate existing skills to novel contexts and domains; it does not generally occur automatically.

Dynamic skill theory postulates a series of 13 different *levels* of an individual's capacity to organize behavior into skills from birth through adulthood. A schematic outline of skill theory appears in Table 5.1. The theory postulates four tiers of development: *reflexes* (beginning from 1 to 4 months), *sensorimotor actions* (beginning around 4 months), *representations* (beginning around 18–24 months), and *abstractions* (beginning about 10–11 years onward). Within each tier, skills pass through four levels (*single sets*, *mappings*, *systems*, and *systems of systems*). Through a careful analysis of the ways in which specific sets of skill elements are coordinated within any given task and social context, skill theory allows fine-grained specification of an indefinite number of intermediate *steps* between any 2 of the 13 levels specified. Each tier, level, and step in development emerges gradually as a result of the hierarchical coordination of lower level skills into higher order structures within a given context.

To illustrate, consider the development of simple mathematical skills within the representational tier. Beginning around 18 to 24 months, children gain the capacity to coordinate multiple systems of sensorimotor action into *single representations*. Using single representations, children can use one object or word to represent a simple meaning, or can place objects in a simple concrete category. For example, a 2½-year-old might be able to describe a set of marbles or blocks in terms of global categorizes of size, such as "big" or "little." By 3½ to 4 years, children develop the capacity to coordinate two single representations into a *representational mapping*. In so doing, a child can hold in mind relationships between at least two single representations. Using representational mappings, for example, a child can make simple non-numerical comparative judgments about quantity. For example, as described by Griffin and Case (Case & Griffin, 1990; Griffin, 1995; Griffin, Case, & Siegler, 1994), by the age of 4 years, many children can indicate which of two small sets of visible objects is bigger or smaller.

Despite this skill, 4-year-olds respond poorly when asked to make comparative judgments using numerals, such as: "Which is more, 4 or 5?" According to Griffin and Case (1997), to respond appropriately to such ques-

TABLE 5.1
Levels of Skill Development

Level		Reflex	Sensorimotor	Representational	Abstract	Age[a]
			Tier			
Rf1: Single Reflexes		$[\text{A}]$ or $[\text{B}]$				3–4 wks
Rf2: Reflex Mappings		$[\text{A} - \text{B}]$				7–8
Rf3: Reflex Systems		$[\text{A}_\text{F}^\text{E} \leftrightarrow \text{B}_\text{F}^\text{E}]$				10–11
Rf4/S1: Systems of Reflex Systems, Which Are Single Sensorimotor Actions		$\begin{bmatrix} \text{A}_\text{F}^\text{E} \leftrightarrow \text{B}_\text{F}^\text{E} \\ \text{C}_\text{H}^\text{G} \leftrightarrow \text{D}_\text{H}^\text{G} \end{bmatrix} \equiv$	$[\mathbf{I}]$			15–17
S2: Sensorimotor Mappings			$[\mathbf{I} - \mathbf{J}]$			7–8 mths
S3: Sensorimotor Systems			$[\mathbf{I}_\mathbf{N}^\mathbf{M} \leftrightarrow \mathbf{J}_\mathbf{N}^\mathbf{M}]$			11–13

		Age
S4/Rp1: Systems of Sensorimotor Systems, Which Are Single Representations	$\begin{bmatrix} I_N^M & \leftrightarrow & J_N^M \\ \Updownarrow & & \Updownarrow \\ K_P^O & \leftrightarrow & L_P^O \end{bmatrix} \equiv [Q]$	18–24
Rp2: Representational Mappings	$[Q - R]$	3.5–4.5 yrs
Rp3: Representational Systems	$[Q_V^U \leftrightarrow R_V^U]$	6–7
Rp4/Ab1: Systems of Representational Systems, Which Are Single Abstractions	$\begin{bmatrix} Q_V^U & \leftrightarrow & R_V^U \\ \Updownarrow & & \Updownarrow \\ S_X^W & \leftrightarrow & T_X^W \end{bmatrix} \equiv [\mathscr{U}]$	10–12
Ab2: Abstract Mappings	$[\mathscr{U} - \mathscr{V}]$	14–16
Ab3: Abstract Systems	$[\mathscr{U}_\mathcal{D}^e \leftrightarrow \mathscr{V}_\mathcal{D}^e]$	19–20
Ab4: Systems of Abstract Systems, Which Are Principles	$\begin{bmatrix} \mathscr{U}_\mathcal{D}^e & \leftrightarrow & \mathscr{V}_\mathcal{D}^e \\ & \Updownarrow & \\ \mathscr{A}_\mathcal{D}^e & \leftrightarrow & \mathscr{B}_\mathcal{D}^e \end{bmatrix}$	24–25

[a]Ages of emergence specify modal times at which a level first appears, extrapolated from research with middle-class North American and European children. They may differ across individuals, cultures, and other social groups.

tions, children must be able to construct a *mental number line*, which emerges as children coordinate their understanding of counting with their capacity to make comparative judgments. Using a mental number line, a child can represent quantity as a continuous dimension having two poles (e.g., small, large) and a series of intermediate points in between. The capacity to construct mental number lines begins to develop at around 6 years with the capacity to manipulate increasingly complex representational mappings (i.e., at what Case and Griffin call *dimensional thinking*), and becomes more fully developed with the onset of *representational systems* at around age 6 or 7. In this way, neo-Piagetian approaches, such as dynamic skill theory, allow prediction and assessment of precise changes in the development of academic skills and understandings.

One can perform developmental analyses of any given skill only within particular conceptual domains, tasks, and contexts. Even subtle changes in task, domain, or social context can lead to important changes in the structure and level of observed skill. Thus, skill theory does not predict strong associations between the onset of skills in different domains or contexts (e.g., mathematical and reading skills). Further, the developmental level of an individual's skill is directly affected by social context. Social context and the actions of others exert a direct effect on the level of a children's psychological structures (Fischer, Rotenberg, Bullock, & Raya, 1993; Fogel, 1993; Rogoff, 1993; Vygotsky, 1978).

The concept of *developmental range* (Fischer, Rotenberg, Bullock, & Raya, 1993) illustrates the ways in which child and context collaborate in the production of any given level of skilled activity. The developmental range refers to the difference between an individual's *optimal* and *functional* levels of performance. A child's optimal level of performance in any given domain refers to the upper limit of what he or she can control or represent in contexts that provide high levels of support or assistance. The child's functional level refers to the level at which children generally function in everyday tasks that do not provide such support. Studies indicate that children's optimal level performance in supportive contexts often far exceeds their functional level in more spontaneous contexts (Fischer, Bullock, Rotenberg, & Raya, 1993; Rogoff, 1990; Vygotsky, 1978). For example, as indicated previously, the early development of addition skills generally passes through three steps: "counting," "counting all," and "counting on." The developmental range would occur in the case of a 6-year-old who ordinarily functions at Step 1 (i.e., "counting" all to-be-added items) without the benefit of contextual support, but who can exhibit the skill of "counting on" (i.e., starting with one addend and counting upward to reach the sum) after the skill is modeled by a teacher. In this example, "counting on" would approach the child's optimal level. However, in the absence of the teacher's support, the child's level would return to his functional level of "counting" (Bidell & Fischer, 1992). Thus, it is not helpful to locate the developmental level of a person's skills at a single point on a ladder; instead, a person's skills occupy a *range* of different possible points within any given developmental pathway.

Just as the developmental level of any particular skill varies as a function of a wide variety of variables, skills in different psychological, emotional, or behavioral domains develop along different developmental trajectories. In this way, as indicated in Fig. 5.1, it is better to think of development as more like a *web* than a *ladder* (Bidell & Fischer, 1992; Fischer & Bidell, 1997). Whereas a ladder represents development in terms of a single unidirectional sequence of steps, a web represents development in terms of alternative and interconnected pathways, each with potentially different starting and endpoints. Development is web-like in many ways. Not only do different individual skills (e.g., arithmetic, reading, social understanding) develop along different trajectories, the same skills exhibited by different people may develop along alternative pathways. This can occur as a function of differences between people in their temperament, culture, personal history, or the presence of disability. Further, to the extent that social values frame the endpoints against which de-

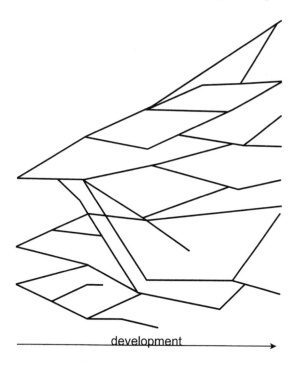

development

FIG. 5.1. The developmental web.

velopmental outcomes are judged, it follows that what is seen as development when judged in relation to one developmental endpoint might not be considered as such when judged from the standpoint of another. In this way, development proceeds dynamically along multiple rather than fixed pathways, and toward alternative rather than single endpoints.

Promoting Idealized Development: The Epigenesis of Dynamic Structures

Thus far we have elaborated a dynamic skills approach on what it means to speak of developmental changes in psychological structures. However, through what processes do psychological structures develop? What are the change processes through which we can promote the development of academic skills in the direction of valued endpoints? Drawing on epigenetic systems theory (Gottlieb, 1991, 1992), dynamic skill theory maintains that patterns of acting, thinking, and feeling are emergent products of co-actions within a hierarchy of embedded change processes. For our purposes, we differentiate four broad sets of hierarchical processes within the organism–environment system (Bidell & Fischer, 1996; Mascolo, Craig-Bray, & Neimeyer, 1997; Mascolo & Fischer, 1998). *Biogenetic* processes include the operation of all "subpersonal" systems, from the expression of the genome through the functioning of the nervous system; *individual-agentive* processes refers to the production of meaningful action, thought, and experience at the level of the person as agent (Harré, 1984; Mascolo, Neimeyer, & Fischer, 1999). *Social-relational* processes consist of co-regulated interactions between two or more persons (Fogel, 1993). *Cultural-symbolic* systems consist of socially shared practices, institutions, and meanings and the ways in which language and sign systems represent and communicate such meanings (Mascolo & Bhatia, in press). In what follows, we illustrate the ways in which early mathematical skills arise from co-actions *between* hierarchically embedded change processes, rather than as a result of any particular isolated change process.

Changes in *biogenetic activity* both influence and are influenced by developing psychological structures and processes (Bidell & Fischer, 1996; Gottlieb, 1992; Weiss, 1970). Fischer and Rose (1994) proposed that changes in each of the 13 levels of skill development specified in skill theory are supported by changes in biogenetic substrate. Specifically, the emergence of each new level of skill in high-support contexts is accompanied by developmental discontinuities in brain growth and activity. For example, a spurt in brain development at 18 to 24 months would prompt neurological changes that would support the construction of *single representations* in children, such as the ability to categorize objects into global categories (e.g., "a lot" or "little"; see also Case, 1992). Another spurt in brain growth around 3 to 4 years of age supports the construction of representational mappings, such as the ability to make simple non-numerical comparative judgments (e.g., "this pile is bigger than that one"). Research from studies on changes in EEG, event-related potentials, and head size suggest discontinuities in brain development occur at age ranges corresponding to the first 12 levels proposed by skill theory. (No data exist to assess the proposed brain-behavior relation for the last proposed level.) Of course, even though neurological development supports the production of novel psychological structures, individual action plays a central role in the local organization of neurological substrate (Edelman, 1987; Gottlieb, 1992; Luria, 1973).

Although biogenetic changes play a major role in promoting development, they are insufficient as determinants in explaining new levels of skill. As indicated earlier, higher order skills are composed of coordinations of lower order skills. Thus, in order to take advantage of the possibilities made possible by biogenetic changes, individuals must actively build the skills that biogenetic changes allow. Children must actively put skill components together in order to form any given higher order skill. For example, consider the construction of skills for making comparative judgments about numbers (e.g., "Which is more, 4 or 5?"). To construct this level of skill, a 6- or 7-year-old must bring together lower level representational skills for *counting* (i.e., involving concrete one-to-one correspondence, cardinality, etc.) and for making *non-numerical comparative judgments* (e.g., "Which group of objects is bigger?"). Such coordinations of lower level skills into higher order structures do not occur spontaneously; children must perform tasks in which they actively bring elements of these two skills into correspondence. As such, at the *individual-agentive* frame of functioning, individuals contribute to their own development through the *active, hierarchical coordination of component systems of action into increasingly higher order structures* (Bidell & Fischer, 1996; Mascolo, Fischer, & Neimeyer, 1999; Mascolo, Pollack, & Fischer, 1997).

Despite the importance of the individual-agentive activity in development, children do not coordinate their skills in isolation from other people. How do children differentiate skill elements that they will later put together to form higher order structures? How do they know how to put together skill elements in culturally adaptive ways? *Social-relational processes* play a direct role in the creation of any particular level of acting, thinking, or feeling. Contexts that provide high support (Fischer, Bullock, Rotenberg, & Raya, 1993) or social *scaffolding* (Rogoff, 1990; Wood, Bruner, & Ross, 1976) have the effect of raising a child's skill to levels that he or she would not ordinarily be able to sustain on his or her own. As such, new levels of skills and meanings arise jointly within such interactions. A child's skills develop as he or she comes to coordinate for himself or herself higher order skill structures that have their basis in social inter-actions with others. For example, using a number line, a teacher might ask a child: "Which is bigger, 4 or 5?" In supporting the child, the teacher may direct the child's attention to specific elements of this task. For example, the teacher might say: "Find 4 on the number line . . . find 5 on the num-ber line . . . now, which is bigger?" In so doing, social interaction *directs* and *organizes* children's attempts to coordinate skill components into higher order structures. It is as if social interaction itself communicates to a child: "Put your counting and comparative judgment skills together like this!" As a result, children develop as they become increasingly able to re-construct skills by coordinating, often in unique ways, elements of action, thought, and feeling that have a basis in joint activity with others (Bidell & Fischer, 1996; Mascolo & Fischer, 1998; Raeff & Mascolo, 1996).

Consistent with a systems approach, personal and social-relational proc-esses operate within *cultural-symbolic* in the production of new structures of action, thought, and feeling (Mascolo & Bhatia, in press). Children's activ-ities take place in sociocultural contexts using cultural artifacts and tools, and are mediated by socially shared meanings represented in symbolic systems. For example, mathematical skills require use of cultural tools and representations (e.g., signs, numbers, numerical notions, workbooks, manipulatives, classrooms, calculators, computers, etc.) as well as cultur-ally shared strategies, metaphors, and algorithms for understanding and executing mathematical skills and concepts. Mathematical skills develop with formal education, which itself functions as a culturally constituted practice that has developed in order to address shifting social and eco-nomic needs. Further, cultures differ in their uses for mathematical skills, and in the specific cultural tools that mediate mathematical calculations (Saxe, 1995).

ALTERNATIVE TRAJECTORIES TOWARD COMMON ENDPOINTS: THE DEVELOPMENT OF ACADEMIC SKILLS

Because of their role in modern social and economic systems, literacy and mathematical skills are highly valued among industrialized societies. In the following, we employ dynamic skill theory and related neo-Piagetian approaches (Mascolo, Kanner, & Griffin, 1998) to chart pathways and processes in the development of basic arithmetic and reading skills within Western culture. In so doing, we illustrate how dynamic models of devel-opment can (a) provide specific representations of the structure and con-tent of the valued skills and outcomes that educators wish to promote, (b) describe alternative pathways toward those endpoints, and (c) illuminate the change processes that move development toward those outcomes.

Structures and Processes in the Development of Early Number Sense

On the basis of a neo-Piagetian analysis of the development of number skills (Case, 1985, 1991; Case & Griffin, 1990; Case, Okamoto, et al., 1996), Griffin, Case, and others (Griffin, in press; Griffin & Case, 1990; Griffin, Case, & Carpenter, 1992; Griffin, Case, & Siegler, 1994) have formulated a curriculum, called *Number Worlds*, for teaching basic number sense to kindergarten children. Case and Griffin's analysis begins with a detailed specification of the organization of basic numbers skills. Griffin et al. (1994) define the 6-year-old conceptual structure for numerical skill in terms of the capacity to construct a *mental number line*. The mental number line is defined in terms of six interrelated concepts, which include the ability to understand (a) the number sequence from 1 up to 10 and from 10 down to 1, (b) one-to-one correspondence between numbers and objects when counting, (c) the cardinal value of each number, (d) the +1 increment rule and the –1 decrement rule (the number line moves from left to right in +1 increments, and from right to left in –1 decrements), and (e) that numbers have a relative value along any variable and can be used to make dimensional assessments. This central conceptual structure provides a specific representation of the local endpoint toward which early number skills develop.

Case and Griffin suggest the capacity to construct a mental number line requires the onset of *dimensional thinking*, which begins to emerge around 6 years of age. Using dimensional representations, children can represent number in terms of a single continuous dimension—a number line representing specific numerical values, from small to large and with a series of points in between. Using this structure, children can not only represent the graded nature of quantity (e.g., hours are divisible into minutes, dollars into cents), but they can also move up and down the number line to perform simple addition and subtraction. Research conducted within Case's neo-Piagetian framework, reviewed earlier, describes the specific steps leading to the development of this conceptual structure.

To promote skill development in the direction of the mental number line, Griffin and Case (Griffin et al., 1994) invented a series of 30 interactive games that children play together under the guidance of a teacher. In the *number line game*, for example, a small group of children use a game board equipped with a different number line for each player. Players roll a die to determine who starts the game. The first player then rolls the die, computes the quantity, asks the "banker" for that many counting chips. Counting out the chips, the player places them in sequence along his or her number line. The player then moves the playing piece along the counting chips, while counting once again, until the playing piece rests on the last chip. The next player then takes a turn, and play continues until one player reaches the winner's circle. Children watch and listen to each other in order to point out mistakes. Disagreements are resolved by recounting and discussion.

In a series of studies (Griffin, Case, & Capodilupo, 1995; Griffin, Case, & Siegler, 1994; Griffin, in press), Griffin and her colleagues demonstrated the efficacy of the *Number World* curriculum for promoting the development of number sense in low SES children in Canada, California, and Massachusetts, in inner cities containing large minority populations. The performance of children receiving the *Number Worlds* program was compared to that of a variety of control groups who did not receive such instruction (including groups of children matched for number knowledge and cultural background, groups of more advantaged children, and children receiving alternative mathematical training). Posttests assessing number knowledge, strategy use, and a series of related tasks (i.e., balance beam task, time telling, money handling, distributive justice) indicated that not only did children profit from the program, but posttest performance in treatment groups surpassed that of control groups, often by a very wide margin. Further, the performance of low SES children who received the *Number Worlds* program was commensurate with that of normative and more advantaged samples of kindergartners and first graders. These findings strongly indicate the effectiveness of the theory-based *Number Worlds* program for promoting early number sense.

Construction and implementation of the *Number World* program illustrates the ways in which developmental theory can inform the pursuit of excellence through education. Neo-Piagetian theory not only provides tools for specifying the precise organization of valued skills and outcomes, it also provides ways of charting transformations in skills as they develop toward these endpoints. Further, the *Number World* curriculum works by drawing on each embedded layer of the epigenetic processes through which children construct mathematical skills. Assuming that kindergartners possess the requisite degree of biogenetic functioning, the *Number World* curriculum incorporates processes at the level of individual agents processes by involving children in games where *they must effortfully perform actions designed to integrate specific lower level actions and understandings into higher order skills.* Through their involvement in social-relational processes, children *learn through affectively charged and playful interactions both with each other and with more accomplished experts* (the teacher). Further, *Number Worlds* integrates cultural-symbolic processes through the repeated use of *diverse symbolic tools that direct attention to individual skill components and their relations* (e.g., numbers, number line, board game and pieces, props and colors, "how do you know" questions, diverse symbolic representations skill elements). Such processes function jointly to direct development in the direction of a valued educational outcome (number sense).

Alternative Pathways in the Development of Reading Skills in Young Children

Griffin and Case's analysis of the development of number sense describes a single, richly structured pathway in the development of number sense. It is possible, however, that different children take different routes in the development of academic skills. Research conducted on the development of early reading skills demonstrates this point. Traditionally, theorists and researchers have often assumed a single developmental pathway for reading words in a particular language. Many models of reading (Adams, 1990; Laberge & Samuels, 1974; Mason, 1980) suggest that basic reading requires the coordination of skills in visual-graphic (i.e., identifying visual aspects of letters and words), phonetic (i.e., identifying sounds of letters and words, including rhymes, syllables, and phonemes), and semantic domains (i.e., understanding word meanings). From this view, readers would integrate semantic, visual-graphic, and sound-analytic skills over time in the same basic linear order. From this view, poor readers would pass through the same sequence, albeit at a slower pace, or after a period of being stuck in a given stage.

An alternative view suggests that different children learn to read in different ways. Not only might there be more than one route that even good readers adopt, it is likely that poor readers differ from good readers in the pathways that they take to reading (Stanovich, 1994; Torgesen, Wagner, & Rashotte, 1994; Wolf & Bowers, in press). To explore this possibility, Knight and Fischer (1992; see also Fischer & Knight, 1990; Fischer, Knight, & Van Parys, 1993) tested 120 first, second, and third graders on a variety of basic reading tasks. The performance of children who were considered good (i.e., reading at or above grade level) and poor (i.e., at least one grade below grade level) readers were examined. The tasks included (a) *word definition*, in which children indicated the meaning of an orally presented word (a test of semantic understanding), (b) *letter identification*, in which children named the letters composing visually presented words (a visual-graphic skill), (c) *rhyme recognition* in which children selected, from four orally presented words, the word that rhymed with a visually presented target (i.e., phonemic skill), (d) *reading recognition*, in which children selected from several possible pictures an appropriate match for visually presented words (i.e., visual-graphic/semantic integration), and (e) *reading production*, in which children read target words orally without prompting (i.e., visual-graphic/phonological integration). For each child, performance in each of the tested skills was scored as a pass or fail.

Pathways in the development of reading can be analyzed by drawing on the logic of a Guttman scalogram (Green, 1956; Guttman, 1944). Given a series of tests that assess each step in a proposed developmental sequence, a Guttman scalogram provides a representation of the order in which skills develop in relation to each other. The simplest developmental pathway would be a linear one in which children at a given age pass all tasks in a single order up to a particular point, and fail all tasks thereafter. Statistical procedures (Green, 1956; Guttman, 1944) test the extent to which any given set of behaviors fit a proposed sequence. For example, as children's reading skills develop, they might first pass the word definition tasks, then letter recognition, rhyme recognition, reading recognition, and reading production. Such a progression would suggest a single linear pathway in the development of word reading.

Alternatively, component reading skills may develop along multiple diverging and converging pathways. Drawing on the logic of the Guttman scale (Krus, 1977; Krus & Blackman, 1988), Fischer and his colleagues (Fischer & Knight, 1990; Kuleck, Fischer, & Knight, 1990) have devised a set of techniques for analyzing developmental webs. Rather than analyzing skills in terms of a single, linear developmental ordering, these techniques provide a way to analyze the partial ordered scaling of items (POSI). Using POSI, an investigator can construct a *dendogram*, which provides a visual representation of the sequence in which different skills order relative to each other (i.e., whether a given skill develops prior to or in tandem with any other set of skills). As such, a dendogram provides a way to chart the ways in which any given set of skills or skill components build on each other, branch off from, and develop independent of each other, and/or converge and become integrated with each other over time in development. Drawing on Laberge and Samuels' (1974) model of reading, Knight and Fischer (1992) proposed a simple model of the development of reading skills. In this model, represented in the dendogram depicted in Fig. 5.2, reading skills begin with the capacity to understand the semantic meanings of words. As ontogenesis progresses, letter identification and rhyme recognition develop independent of each other along diverging pathways. Finally, visual-graphemic and phonological skills come together to support the ordered development of reading recognition, rhyme production, and reading production skills, respectively.

Results from Knight and Fischer's (1992) study produced evidence for three different pathways in the development of reading. The first pathway, which might be called the *normative sequence*, is the one hypothesized in Fig. 5.2. This hypothesized sequence described the developmental pathway for the vast majority of children in all grades. After some independence of visual-graphic and phonemic skill, these skills come together and are followed by a linear ordering of reading recognition, rhyme production, and reading production. This sequence suggests that early reading skills involve the integration of visual-graphic and phonological skills. Children exhibiting the normative sequence read at or above grade level.

In addition to this pathway, however, results suggested other pathways that were less prevalent in good readers and more common to poor read-

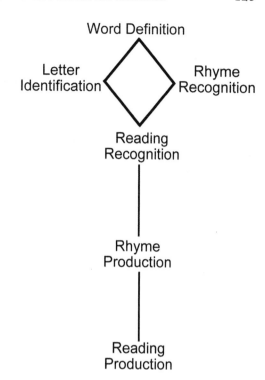

FIG. 5.2.   Normative pathway for the development of word reading.

ers. These pathways are depicted in Fig. 5.3. The *reading and rhyme independent* pathway occurred in readers who have difficulty with phonological skills. In this pathway, reading skills develop independent of rhyme recognition and production, which themselves develop along a separate and delayed pathway. The third pathway was characterized by an *independence of reading, letter identification, and rhyming skills.* This pathway characterized the poorest readers in the study, and was absent among good readers. The very poor readers exhibited problems in both phonological and visual-graphemic processing. These children exhibited difficulty in integrating phonological and visual-graphic skills, which developed independent of each other.

Thus, relative to the standards that define basic reading skills, we see not only alternative trajectories toward what educators would consider good reading skills, but also divergent trajectories from these valued endpoints. Consistent with an orthogenetic conception of development (Werner & Kaplan, 1963/1984), these divergent trajectories involve difficulty in the differentiation of particular skill components (e.g., skills in phonological or visual-graphemic domains) and/or an inability to coordinate these skill domains into increasingly hierarchically integrated structures. By understanding the specific pathways involved, educators can devise interventions to

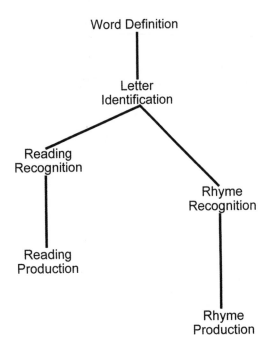

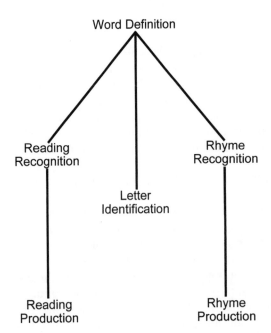

FIG. 5.3. Non-normative pathways in the development of word reading.

prompt the coordination of compensatory skills or to prompt the types of cross-domain integrations that would promote basic word reading.

Continuing the Trajectories: Pathways to Excellence Among Adults With Reading Disabilities

There are many pathways to excellence, even among adults. Fink (1992, 1993, 1995–1996, 1998) examined the ways in which individuals with reading disabilities (RD) have achieved excellence in fields that demand extensive and complex reading. In so doing, Fink (1998) conducted clinical interviews with 60 highly successful adults with reading disabilities. Men and women were sought who would be likely to inspire others currently struggling with RD. Therefore, the sample was not random or representative, but instead was selected by the author on the basis of level of educational and career achievement, field of professional expertise, gender, age, and socioeconomic level. Participants were considered "successful" if they supported themselves financially and demonstrated professional competence recognized by peers in an area of expertise that required sophisticated reading, extensive training, skill, and responsibility. Each adult's history of language-based difficulties was recorded and analyzed based on face-to-face retrospective interviews. Males and females were matched for age, problems, and the severity of their RD. Each participant's high level of success in their respective fields was verified using biographical information collected from their *curriculum vitae*, *Who's Who in America*, publications of the U.S. National Academy of Sciences, as well as journal articles, chapters, and books written by the 60 adults. In addition, six formal and informal literacy tests and life development questionnaires were individually administered to each participant (see Fink, 1998, for details).

As indicated previously, a "normative" pathway for literacy development consists of initial independence of orthographic, phonological, and semantic skills followed later by integration of these components (Laberge & Samuels, 1974). However, reading development in the 60 adult participants with RD was characterized by poor integration of orthographic, phonological, and semantic skills, suggesting alternative developmental pathways. Individuals with RD showed partly linked, partly unlinked, and sometimes independent branches for orthographic, phonological, and semantic skills. This independent branching continued into adulthood for a subset of individuals. Furthermore, their pathways to reading were not neat, unidirectional, or ladder-like in structure. On the contrary, the structure of their developmental pathways for reading was messy and web-like.

Although strands were not strongly integrated, there were some interconnections. Thus, the developmental strands were partly linked. However, making those links was often extremely laborious for adults with RD. The case of Charles Drake, founding Director of the Landmark School in

Prides Crossing, illustrates an alternative literacy pathway that includes separate phonological and semantic strands. Drake reads nearly all materials twice. Each reading is performed for a separate purpose. In Drake's words: "The first time I read something just for the sounds of the words. I . . . work on pronouncing the words. And I do this very, very slowly . . . The second time around I read for the meaning." When Drake reads, phonological processing and semantic processing do not occur simultaneously in a seamless, well-integrated manner; under most conditions they occur somewhat separately, operating largely independently of each other. Drake seems incapable of simultaneous use and integration of sound analysis and meaning skills. These skills proceed along two partly separate, distinct strands. As such, achieving some integration is a laborious enterprise for Drake. First, he uses phonological skills in order to help him later use semantic skills. During the second reading, Drake eventually integrates the two skills to some degree. Thus, his pathway is partially integrated, characterized by partial separation and, at the same time, partial integration between component skills.

As a consequence of his partially separate-stranded pathway, Drake's reading is painstakingly slow, tedious, and effortful. It is neither automatic nor efficient. Yet, it works for him and is relatively reliable insofar as he is able to derive meaning from his reading. Drake is keenly aware of the semantic aspect of reading. He knows that he must think about what the author is saying so that he can construct a meaningful reading of the text (i.e., "I try to think about what the author is saying"). As such, Drake understands reading as an interactive thinking process, a dialogue between himself and an author for the ultimate purpose of constructing meaning.

Another example of a poorly integrated, circuitous developmental pathway is that of George Deem, an artist in New York City and Adjunct Professor of Art at the University of Pennsylvania in Philadelphia. His alternative pathway consists of an additional strand for orthographic processing. Deem shows evidence of extremely weak orthographic skills at the most basic level, the letter identification level. Although Deem reads and comprehends as sophisticated an author as Proust, he still confuses the letters *b* and *d*. He cannot automatically and spontaneously distinguish *b* from *d* in new, unfamiliar words. However, he follows an alternative web-like pathway to enable differentiation of these confusing, look-alike letters. Upon encountering a new, unfamiliar word containing these letters, he scans the page trying to locate a familiar word, such as *but*. "If there is a word I don't know with a 'b' or a 'd' that gets me very mixed up; I have to look at another word in order to find out which letter it is. I have to look at another word to remember that the 'd' goes that way and the 'b' goes this way. . . . Usually the word 'but' was my finder." Deem knows from experience that *but* contains a *b*, so he uses *but* as a guide to cue himself and help identify a *b* in a new word. In this way, when he encounters unfamiliar words with look-alike letters, he takes a detour around the problem, adding an additional circuitous strand for letter identification. This orthographic strand is partly separate and distinct from the sounding out strand of phonological analysis.

The detour that Deem takes is effective in that it enables accurate letter identification. However, it is time consuming and labor intensive, slowing down Deem's reading speed. Indeed, by the time he identifies the letter *b*, he is likely to have forgotten the meaning and context of the sentence he was reading. Consequently, he rereads the sentence to reactivate its meaning. In this way, the orthographic skill of letter identification and the semantic skill of meaning-making are poorly integrated in Deem's alternative developmental pathway.

The cases of Drake and Deem represent and illustrate alternative literacy pathways of successful adults with RD. The alternative pathways show multiple branching of partly independent, web-like structures with poor integration of the three main components of reading: orthographic, phonological, and semantic skills. These component skills are partly linked, or integrated; yet at the same time they remain partly independent, or not integrated. Such paths differ from those adopted by normally developing readers, which show greater integration and automaticity, and are consistent with childhood pathways taken by poor readers (Knight & Fischer, 1992).

Did the slow, poorly integrated alternative developmental pathway of adults with RD preclude their development of skilled reading? Apparently not. Despite following alternative, circuitous routes to reading, these individuals developed into sophisticated readers and writers as indicated by high performance on six different assessments of literacy. The solid performance of these adults with RD on standardized vocabulary and silent reading comprehension tests (Brown, Fishco, & Hanna, 1993; Roswell & Chall, 1992) demonstrates their ability as adults to read, understand, make inferences, and create meaning from text. As such, these individuals demonstrated all the salient characteristics of excellent reading, except speed, and efficiency, which many still lack. Nearly all do a substantial amount of writing in their professions, and all read texts that are technical, specialized and abstract. For many, their books and scholarly articles number in the hundreds.[1] Thus, the pathways exhibited by these persons

---

[1]Among the men and women with dyslexia are Dr. Baruj Benaccerraf, 1980 Nobel laureate in Immunology and Pathology; Lora Brody, TV/radio personality and author of *Cooking With Memories*; Dr. Donald Francis, AIDS researcher/activist and protagonist of the movie "And the Band Played On"; Dr. Florence Haseltine, author of *Woman Doctor* and *Women's Health Research*; Dr. Robert Knapp, Harvard oncologist and author of *Gynecological Oncology*; Professor Ronald W. Davis, genomics researcher and biochemistry textbook author; George Deem, New York City artist; Susan Brown, New York City filmmaker; and Professor Sylvia Law, New York University legal scholar and author of books on poverty, health care, welfare, and the law.

did not prevent them from achieving excellence in their fields. Instead, their pathways demonstrate the multiplicity of pathways to excellence.

DIVERGENT PATHWAYS IN AFFECTIVE DEVELOPMENT: A PASSION FOR LEARNING AMONG THE CHINESE

Up to this point, we have examined the ways in which development can take alternative pathways that eventually *converge* onto particular valued endpoints and outcomes. In this section, we examine the ways in which pathways in the development of a single educational domain—motivation to learn—can *diverge* as development moves toward different culturally valued endpoints. Specifically, we compare the Chinese conception of *hao-xue-xin* (e.g., "heart and mind for wanting to learn") to prevailing Western conceptions of learning motivation. In so doing, we examine the ways in which different conceptions of learning motivation orient development toward different socially valued endpoints.

Diverse Endpoints of Learning Motivation

Skill theory, similar to sociocultural theory approaches to development (Cole & Scribner, 1974; Rogoff, 1990; Wertsch, 1979), holds that one source of variability in developmental endpoints involves cultural backgrounds (Fischer & Bidell, 1997). Motivation to learn is no exception, as the differences between the U.S. and Chinese models illustrate. Although neither culture adopts a monolithic view of learning motivation, research on academic achievement motivation among middle-class Anglo-Americans seems to portray a model of learning motivation consisting of three main components. The first concerns the importance of acquiring skills that support individual success, often defined in terms of economic achievement (McClelland, 1961). A second goal involves individual mastery of achievement and performance standards not linked to economic success (Csikszentmihalyi, 1990; Elliott & Dweck, 1988; Ford, 1992; Nicholls, 1984). Finally, individuals often strive to maintain a sense of individual self-worth, often including a sense of superiority over others (Covington & Omelich, 1979; Ford, 1992).

In pursuing these goals, individuals in the United States often believe that individual *ability* functions as the main determinant of achievement (Covington & Omelich, 1979; Dweck & Bempechat, 1983; Nicholls, 1976; Stevenson & Stigler, 1992; Stipek, 1988; Weiner, 1986). However, individuals have different views regarding the nature of their ability, which in turn influences how they behave in achievement situations. Individuals who believe that their ability is fixed display a "performance orientation" (i.e., toward what others think of oneself), which leads them to avoid difficult tasks that may result in failure. In contrast, persons who believe that their ability can increase by gaining more skill show a "mastery orientation" (i.e., toward learning tasks themselves), which leads them to make a sustained effort even in the face of obstacles and failure, which eventually results in increased learning (Ames & Archer, 1988; Chiu, Hong, & Dweck, 1994; Dweck & Leggett, 1988; Nicholls, 1984). Most individuals in the United States favor an ability over effort orientation for fear of revealing low ability (Covington & Omelich, 1979; Harari & Covington, 1981; Jagacinski & Nicholls, 1987; Nicholls, 1976). As such, people experience happiness and pride upon success and sadness and shame or guilt upon failure (Weiner, 1985). Suarez-Orozco and Suarez-Orozco (1995) suggested that U.S. adolescents (arguably closer to the valued endpoint) display ambivalent attitudes toward school learning, accompanied by considerable frustration, anger, and boredom.

Achievement motivation among the Chinese has been shown to differ from that of the mainstream Americans (Hess, Chang, & McDevitt, 1987; Salili, 1996; Stevenson & Stigler, 1992). In general, Chinese have been described as valuing effort instead of ability, possessing positive attitudes toward school, and taking personal responsibility for their learning. In a recent study attempting to examine underlying reasons for these documented differences, Jin Li (1997) analyzed learning-related terms in Chinese as well as written descriptions of Chinese ideal learners (therefore an endpoint) with college students. She documented what she labeled a Chinese "heart and mind for wanting to learn" (*hao-xue-xin*), a culturally based alternative model of learning motivation.

The first difference with regard to the endpoint is the term itself. Whereas Western scholars speak of "achievement motivation," the Chinese maintain the folk term *hao-xue-xin*, which translates into English literally as "heart and mind for wanting to learn" or, broadly, a passion for learning. This difference is by no means trivial because it reveals clearly where the emphasis lies. Li's cluster analysis of 225 learning-related terms in Chinese shows that the Chinese model stresses *learning* itself instead of achievement. As indicated in Fig. 5.4, most idiomatic expressions (141, or 72%) center around the notion of *seeking knowledge*, compared to a much smaller number of items (54, or 28%) referring to achievement. Within the cluster of "seeking knowledge," the heaviest emphasis (64 terms, or 46%) falls on *hao-xue-xin*, which stresses cultivating one's desire for learning as a lifelong process, humility, and a set of four action-oriented principles regarding learning: *diligence, endurance of hardship, steadfast perseverance,* and *concentration.*

Analyses of written descriptions of ideal learners with *hao-xue-xin* yielded a number of further differences of this learning model. Here *hao-*

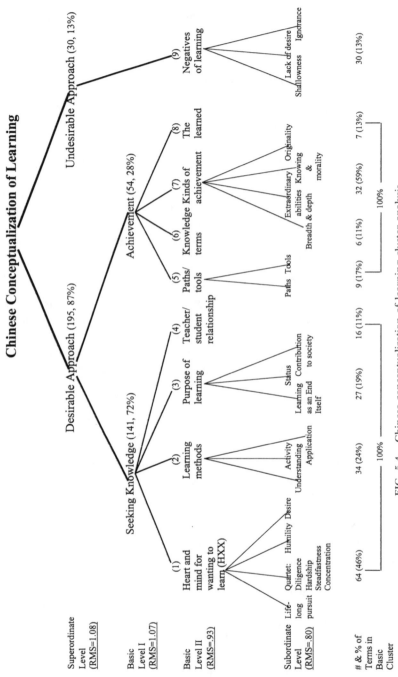

FIG. 5.4. Chinese conceptualization of learning cluster analysis.

xue-xin is described as founded on a culturally specific epistemology and core notions regarding cognition, morality, affect, and behavior. When asked what the purpose of learning might be for their ideal learners, 75% of the subjects referred to the notion that knowledge is a need to perfect oneself. To the question probing if learning has to do with one's moral character, 93% of subjects answered yes. Their further accounts converged on the fact that people with *hao-xue-xin* have a strong moral orientation in their pursuit of learning (see Cheng, 1996). Consistent with the Confucian tradition, perfecting oneself is held as the highest purpose of human life and is taught as reachable by everyone (Lee, 1996). In contrast, the moral dimension is virtually absent in the descriptions of the U.S. model of achievement motivation.

Chinese subjects almost unanimously (95%) provided explanations of how learning can be attained: One must cultivate the utmost, long-lasting, and stable inner desire and love to seek knowledge. To seek knowledge, one must be determined to set one's mind for learning with a singleness of purpose. One must be diligent and prepared to endure the hardships one might encounter in learning. The key to seeking knowledge lies in the learner and what he or she does to acquire knowledge—not in making one's learning dependent on others' teaching. From this view, knowledge neither comes automatically nor is it a matter of luck, favor, or social circumstances. Learning is about how to be a learner and how to learn. Underlying these behavioral principles is the deep belief that "higher" or "lower" intelligence plays little role in *whether* one is capable of learning, *how well*, or *how much* one ends up learning (67% of responses). One can learn to his or her fullest potential and achieve considerable knowledge so long as one is willing to seek it with the degree of effort already outlined.

Subjects also described *hao-xue-xin* related affect. Like previous research on Chinese affect (Bond, 1986; Crittenden, 1996; Fischer & Tangney, 1994; Leung, 1996), two specific emotions were recounted: *shame-guilt* and *modesty*. It is a commonly noted fact that positive emotions such as happiness and pride promote, and negative emotions such as shame and guilt inhibit achievement motivation in the West (Atkinson, 1964; Stipek, 1988; Weiner, 1986). But Chinese subjects (40%) reported a combination of shame-guilt as an emotion associated with poor learning that strongly motivates them to make up for their inadequacies. Also different from the traditional findings were responses (44%) indicating a sense of modesty in both good and poor learning. This emotion was described as an inner force that can counter conceit and complacency, which, in Chinese subjects' belief, may accompany high achievement. Modesty also lifts one's spirit from the "pain and depression" caused by poor learning. These affective tendencies, regardless of success or failure, appear to lead Chinese learners to always want to learn more.

Affect in conventional research has been studied mostly in terms of individuals, including how individuals attribute success and failure and the emotions they associate with their attributions (e.g., pride in success and sadness in failure, Weiner, 1986). However, *hao-xue-xin* related affect is defined in profoundly social terms (Bond, 1986; Leung, 1996; Stipek, 1998). Individuals who fail to learn as a result of a lack of *hao-xue-xin* felt so ashamed-guilty and self-reproaching (52%) that they could not face up to their families. Indeed, nearly one third indicated that their achievement itself must be attributed to their family. Further, participants (73%) reported respect, admiration, and appreciation toward people who possess *hao-xue-xin*, and a strong desire to emulate them.

Divergent Pathways in the Development of Learning Motivation

Literature on the development of Western achievement motivation focuses on children's developing capacity to represent *ability* and *effort*. This work suggests that most kindergarten children hold an undifferentiated view of ability and effort where they believe that hard work means "smartness" and smart people try hard. In middle childhood, children believe that effort itself is the determinant of achievement outcomes. By early adolescence, they have developed a full differentiation that effort alone cannot lead to high achievement without ability, showing that they favor ability over effort (Covington & Omelich, 1979; Dweck & Bempechat, 1983; Harari & Covington, 1981; Nicholls, 1978, 1984; Stipek, 1981).

Chinese *hao-xue-xin* may take a different route. To begin with, ability and effort are not viewed as dichotomous concepts (Stevenson & Stigler, 1992). Chinese children from first to 10th grade have been shown to view effort as a factor that increases one's ability, not as clashing notions (Salili & Hau, 1994). Further, effort, which has been widely recognized as a determinant of Chinese achievement motivation, is only one component of the larger system of *hao-xue-xin* (Li, 1997). We suggest some broad trends in the development of *hao-xue-xin*. At the first level, *initial scaffolding of positive learning*, adults orient preschoolers toward everyday learning activities from an early age. Through their language and action in everyday contexts, parents assign a strong moral value to the process of trying, learning, or doing. A parent might say: "You are a good boy if you try to climb that" or "A good girl will learn to sing." In this way, children's attention to the value of learning is woven into the fabric of everyday activities. At the level of *learning for others' sake*, which coincides with entry into formal schooling, children become increasingly aware of the extreme value that parents and teachers place on performing specific learning tasks. As such, children may begin to perform the tasks of learning (e. g., homework, recitation of poems) with the explicit purpose of pleasing parents and teachers. They are aware that hard work and learning will make parents proud and that the lack of these qualities will engender shame-guilt and embarrassment in parents.

After this period of learning and working hard to please others, children in middle and later childhood may begin to *internalize an orientation to learning as a personal goal*. In so doing, they may begin to realize that engagement in learning would bring about concrete and tangible outcomes (e.g., good grades, getting into a good college, obtaining a desirable job) that bring honor to one's parents, teachers, family, school, community, and self. Learning itself brings about feelings of familial pride, honor, and modesty-respect; failure to learn and to engage in learning brings about guilt-shame and embarrassment. At the final level, *integrated hao-xue-xin*, adolescent and adult Chinese learners would begin to coordinate the various components of *hao-xue-xin* into a coherent skill system. These components are increasingly abstract representations of how learning brings about the perfection in the self, a love of learning for itself, and a belief that learning is a morally positive value that brings honor to community and self.[2]

Change Mechanisms in the Development of Hao-Xue-Xin

What types of cultural-symbolic and social-relational processes promote the development of *hao-xue-xin*? First, there is a cultural intention to foster *hao-xue-xin* in children (Huang & Peng, 1992). Chinese culture deliberately teaches *hao-xue-xin* with tested tools and methods (Vygotsky, 1978; Wertsch, 1979). At least two such tools are worth noting. First, there exists a large vocabulary (over 400) of *hao-xue-xin*-related folk terms and idiomatic expressions that children acquire (Li, in press). Similar to Olson's argument (1994) on the unique cognitive functions English written language affords, these Chinese terms address details of learning situations ranging from the overall importance of learning, to specific study strategies, to warnings of stumbling blocks (e.g., "There is no difficulty in the world that doesn't fear a wanting heart"). Parents and teachers use this language of *hao-xue-xin* to communicate with children about learning on a

---

[2]It is important to note that children's development of achievement motivation or *hao-xue-xin* may also vary as a result of many factors such as the child's personal learning history, experience, social support, and emotional state. No culture is monolithic in its orientation to learning motivation or any other social or psychological process. Variability of any of these factors may cause children's pathways to differ from each other in timing, rates, content, meaning, relationships, and eventually the extent to which the cultural ideal model is attained. Although not all Chinese become great learners, most seem to appreciate the goal of learning and a fundamental ideal of self-perfection (Li, 1997; Stevenson & Lee, 1996).

daily basis. In addition, there is an anthology of stories of real learners throughout Chinese history who serve as models of learning. This ensures that *hao-xue-xin* is not an abstract and nebulous notion but rather is embodied in real people's behaviors, to be emulated by children. Such stories are widely available in both children's books and the curriculum of Chinese formal education (Li, 1997).

Social support for *hao-xue-xin* is extensive and sustained (Li, 1997; Stevenson & Lee, 1996). At the cultural level, family, schools, and the community at large form a coherent tripartite support system through which children hear the same message and observe the same behavior throughout their lives (Li, 1997). Within on-line social interaction, children's learning activities from moment to moment are monitored, guided, and scaffolded (Rogoff, 1990; Vygotsky, 1978). Because *hao-xue-xin* is a deliberately pursued learning goal, children have ample opportunities to emulate living exemplars. Finally, the role of affect and embodied experience must be underscored. Affect is undoubtedly an integral part of Chinese *hao-xue-xin* (Li, 1997). The unique combination of shame-guilt and modesty, which is dynamically coconstructed by children and their social coparticipants including families, teachers, and peers, functions to monitor children's learning and development of *hao-xue-xin* at all levels.

PROMOTING EXCELLENCE: DEVELOPMENTAL THEORY, SOCIAL VALUES, AND EDUCATION

The concept of development has meaning only with reference to some conception of its actual or idealized endpoints. Similarly, the pursuit of excellence through education is defined with reference to the skills and outcomes that are valued by any given culture or social group. Thus, in order for a theory of development to inform the pursuit of excellence through education, one must first articulate the social values that define the developmental outcomes that a given community wishes to promote. Having done so, one can use developmental theory to propose, identify, and explain alternative trajectories in academic or affective skills as they move toward or away from socially valued endpoints. This point is borne out by analyses of multiple pathways in the development of number sense, reading skill, and excellence among learning disabled adults. It follows that if development is defined with reference to proposed endpoints, then ontogenetic changes will look very different when viewed through the lens of different cultural values. The development of a passion for learning among the Chinese illustrates this point. Unlike Americans who tend to organize their conceptions of learning around achievement, effort, and ability, the passion for learning among the Chinese is structured around the principle of a lifelong commitment to the effortful process of learning in and of itself. Thus, what might be considered progress when viewed from the standpoint of American social values may not be seen as such when viewed from a Chinese view. Developmental psychologists can inform educational practice to the extent that they are reflexive about the values that frame their own conceptions of development as well as those of the social groups they study.

REFERENCES

Adams, M. J. (1990). *Beginning to read: Thinking about learning about print*. Cambridge, MA: MIT Press.

Ames, C., & Archer, J. (1988). Achievement goals in the classroom: Students' learning strategies and motivation processes. *Journal of Educational Psychology, 80,* 260–267.

Atkinson, J. (1964). *An introduction to motivation*. Princeton, NJ: Van Nostrand.

Baltes, P. B. (1983). The aging mind: Potential and limits. *The Gerontologist, 33,* 580–594.

Bidell, T., & Fischer, K. W. (1992). Cognitive development in educational contexts: Implications of skill theory. In A. Demetriou, M. Shayer, & A. Efklides (Eds.), *Neo-Piagetian theories of cognitive development: Implications and applications for education* (pp. 9–30). London: Routledge & Kegan Paul.

Bidell, T., & Fischer, K. W. (1996). Between nature and nurture: The role of human agency in the epigenesis of intelligence. In R. Sternberg & E. Grigorenko (Eds.), *Intelligence: Heredity and environment* (pp. 193–242). New York: Cambridge University Press.

Bond, M. (1986). *The psychology of Chinese people*. Hong Kong: Oxford University Press.

Brown, J. I., Fischco, V. V., & Hanna, G. (1993). *Nelson-Denny Reading Test, Form H*. Chicago: Riverside.

Case, R. (1985). *Intellectual development: Birth to adulthood*. New York: Academic Press.

Case, R. (Ed.). (1991). *The mind's staircase*. Hillsdale, NJ: Lawrence Erlbaum Associates.

Case, R. (1992). The role of the frontal lobes in the regulation of human development. *Brain and Cognition, 20,* 51–73.

Case, R., & Griffin, S. (1990). Child cognitive development: The role of central conceptual structures in the development of scientific and social thought. In E. A. Hauert (Ed.), *Developmental psychology: Cognitive, perceptuo-motor, and neurological perspectives* (pp. 193–230). The Netherlands: North-Holland; Elsevier.

Case, R., Okamoto, Y., with Griffin, S., McKeough, A., Bleiker, C., Henderson, B., & Stephenson, K. M. (1996). The role of central conceptual structures in the development of children's thought. *Monographs of the Society for Research in Child Development, 60*(5 & 6, Serial No. 246).

Cheng, K-M. (1996). *The quality of primary education: A case study of Zhejiang Province, China*. Paris: International Institute for Educational Planning.

Chiu, C. Y., Hong, Y. Y., & Dweck, C. S. (1994). Toward an integrative model of personality and intelligence: A general framework and some preliminary steps (pp. 104–134). In R. J. Sternberg & P. Ruzgis (Eds.), *Personality and intelligence*. New York: Cambridge University Press.

Cole, M., & Scribner, S. (1974). *Culture and thought*. New York: Wiley.

Covington, M. V., & Omelich, C. L. (1979). Effort: The double-edged sword in school achievement. *Journal of Educational Psychology, 71,* 169–182.

Crittenden, K. (1996). Causal attribution processes among the Chinese. In M. Bond (Ed.), *The handbook of Chinese psychology* (pp. 263–279). Hong Kong: Oxford University Press.

Csikszentmihalyi, M. (1990). *Flow: The psychology of optimal experience.* New York: Harper & Row.

Dweck, C., & Bempechat, J. (1983). Children's theories of intelligence: Consequences for learning. In S. G. Paris, G. M. Olson, & H. W. Stevenson (Eds.), *Learning and motivation in the classroom* (pp. 239–256). Hillsdale, NJ: Lawrence Erlbaum Associates.

Dweck, C. S., & Leggett, E. L. (1988). A social-cognitive approach to motivation and personality. *Psychological Review, 95,* 256–273.

Edelman, G. M. (1987). *Neural Darwinism.* New York: Basic Books.

Elliott, E. S., & Dweck, C. S. (1988). Goals: An approach to motivation and achievement. *Journal of Personality and Social Psychology, 54,* 5–12.

Fink, R. P. (1992). Successful dyslexics' alternative pathways for reading: A developmental study (Doctoral dissertation, Harvard Graduate School of Education, 1992). *Dissertation Abstracts International,* F4965, Vol. 53 (5-A), 1461.

Fink, R. P. (1993). How successful dyslexics learn to read. *Teaching Thinking and Problem Solving, 15*(5), 1–6.

Fink, R. P. (1995–1996). Successful dyslexics: A constructivist study of passionate interest reading. *Journal of Adolescent and Adult Literacy, 39*(4), 268–280.

Fink, R. P. (1998). Literacy development in successful men and women with dyslexia. *Annals of Dyslexia, 48,* 311–346.

Fischer, K. W. (1980). A theory of cognitive development: The control and construction of hierarchies of skills. *Psychological Review, 87,* 447–531.

Fischer, K. W., & Bidell, T. R. (1997). Dynamic development of psychological structures in action and thought. In R. M. Lerner (Ed.), *Handbook of child psychology: Vol. 1. Theoretical models of human development* (5th ed., pp. 467–561). New York: Wiley.

Fischer, K. W., Bullock, D. H., Rotenberg, E. J., & Raya, P. (1993). The dynamics of competence: How context contributes directly to skill. In R. Wozniak & K. W. Fischer (Eds.), *Development in context: Acting and thinking in specific environments* (pp. 93–117). JPS Series on Knowledge and Development. Hillsdale, NJ: Lawrence Erlbaum Associates.

Fischer, K. W., & Granott, N. (1995). Beyond one-dimensional change: Parallel, concurrent, socially distributed processes in learning and development. *Human Development, 38,* 302–314.

Fischer, K. W., & Knight, C. C. (1990). Cognitive development in real children: Levels and variations. In B. Z. Presseisen (Ed.), *Learning and thinking styles: Classroom interaction* (pp. 43–67). Washington, DC: National Educational Association.

Fischer, K. W., Knight, C. C., & Van Parys, M. (1993). Analyzing diversity in developmental pathways: Methods and concepts. In W. Edelstein & R. Case (Ed.), *Constructivist approaches to development. Contributions to Human Development, 23,* 33–56. Basel, Switzerland: S. Karger.

Fischer, K. W., & Rose, S. P. (1994). Dynamic development of coordination of components in brain and behavior: A framework for theory and research. In G. Dawson & K. W. Fischer (Eds.), *Human behavior and the developing brain* (pp. 3–66). New York: Guilford.

Fischer, K. W., & Tangney, J. P. (1994). Self-conscious emotions and the affect revolution: Framework and overview. In J. P. Tangney & K. W. Fischer (Eds.), *Self-conscious emotions: The psychology of shame, guilt, embarrassment, and pride* (pp. 3–22). New York: Guilford.

Fogel, A. (1993). *Development through relationships: Origins of communication, self and culture.* Chicago: University of Chicago Press.

Ford, E. M. (1992). *Motivating humans: Goals, emotions, and personal agency beliefs.* Newbury Park, CA: Sage.

Gelman, R., & Gallistel, C. R. (1978). *The child's understanding of number.* Cambridge, MA: Harvard University Press.

Goodnow, J. (1980). Everyday concepts of intelligence and its development. In N. Warren (Ed.), *Studies in cross-cultural psychology* (Vol. 2). London: Pergamon.

Gottlieb, G. (1991). Experiential canalization of behavioral development: Theory. *Developmental Psychology, 27*, 4–13.

Gottlieb, G. (1992). *Individual development and evolution: The genesis of novel behavior*. New York: Oxford University Press.

Green, B. G. (1956). A method of scalogram analysis using summary statistics. *Psychometrica, 21*, 79–88.

Griffin, S. (in press). Evaluation of a program to teach Number Sense to children at risk for school failure. *Journal for Research in Mathematics Education*.

Griffin, S., & Case, R. (1997). Re-thinking the primary school math curriculum: An approach based on cognitive science. *Issues in Education*. Greenwich, CT: JAI Press.

Griffin, S. A., Case, R., & Capodilupo, A. (1995). Teaching for understanding: The importance of central conceptual structures in the elementary mathematics curriculum. In A. McKeough, I. Lupert, & A. Marini (Eds.), *Teaching for transfer: Fostering generalization in learning* (pp. 121–151). Hillsdale, NJ: Lawrence Erlbaum Associates.

Griffin, S. A., Case, R., & Carpenter, M. (1992). *Rightstart: A foundational math program for kindergarten*. Worcester, MA: Clark University.

Griffin, S. A., Case, R., & Siegler, R. S. (1994). Rightstart: Providing the central conceptual prerequisites for first formal learning of arithmetic to students at risk for school failure. In K. McGilly (Ed.), *Classroom lessons, integrating cognitive theory and classroom practice*. Cambridge, MA: MIT Press.

Guttman, L. (1944). A basis for scaling qualitative data. *American Sociological Review, 9*, 139–150.

Harari, O., & Covington, M. V. (1981). Reactions to achievement behavior from a teacher and student perspective: A developmental analysis. *American Educational Research Journal, 18*, 15–28.

Harré, R. (1984). *Personal being*. Oxford: Blackwell.

Hess, R. D., Chang, C-M, & McDevitt, T. M. (1987). Cultural variations in family belief about children's performance in mathematics: Comparisons among People's Republic of China, Chinese American, and Caucasian-American families. *Journal of Educational Psychology, 79*, 179–188.

Huang, D. Y., & Peng, H, J. (1992). *San zi jing* [Three character classic]. Taipei, Taiwan: Ruisheng Book & Magazine.

Jagacinski, C. M., & Nicholls, J. G. (1987). Competence and affect in task involvement and ego involvement: The impact of social comparison information. *Journal of Educational Psychology, 79*, 107–114.

Kanner, B. (in press). The cultural framing of the concept of development. In G. Misra (Ed.), *Culture and psychological processes: Issues and perspectives*. New Delhi, India: Sage.

Kaplan, B. (1984). *On development: Psychological or otherwise*. Paper presented at Grand Rounds, McClean's Hospital, Belmont, MA.

Knight, C. C., & Fischer, K. W. (1992). Learning to read words: Individual differences in developmental sequences. *Journal of Applied Developmental Psychology, 13*, 377–404.

Krus, D. J. (1977). Order analysis: An inferential model of dimensional analysis and scaling. *Educational and Psychological Measurement, 37*, 587–601.

Krus, D. J., & Blackman, H. S. (1988). Test reliability and homogeneity from the perspective of the ordinal test theory. *Applied Measurement in Education, 1*, 79–88.

Kuleck, W. J., Fischer, K. W., & Knight, C. C. (1990). *Partially ordered scaling of items: A program and manual*. Cambridge, MA: Harvard University.

Laberge, D., & Samuels, S. J. (1974). Toward a theory of automatic information processing in reading. *Cognitive Psychology, 6*, 293–323.

Lee, W. O. (1996). The cultural context for Chinese learners: Conceptions of learning in the Confucian Tradition. In D. A. Watkins & J. B. Biggs (Eds.), *The Chinese learner* (pp. 45–67). Hong Kong: Comparative Education Research Centre (CERC) & The Australian Council for Educational Research Ltd. (ACER).

Leung, K. (1996). The role of beliefs in Chinese culture. In M. Bond (Ed.), *The handbook of Chinese psychology* (pp. 247–262). Hong Kong: Oxford University Press.

Li, J. (1997). *The Chinese "heart and mind for wanting to learn" (hao-xue-xin): A culturally based learning model.* Unpublished doctoral dissertation, Harvard University, Cambridge, MA.

Li, J. (in press). Conceptualizations of learning in Chinese. *Ethos.*

Luria, A. R. (1973). *The working brain.* (B. Haigh, Trans.). New York: Basic Books.

Maehr, M. L. (1978). Sociocultural origins of achievement motivation. In D. Bar-Tal & L. Saxe (Eds.), *Social psychology and education: Theory and research* (pp. 205–227). New York: Hemisphere.

Mascolo, M. F., & Bhatia, S. (in press). The dynamic construction of culture, self and social relations. In G. Misra (Ed.), *Culture and psychological processes: Issues and perspectives.* New Delhi, India: Sage.

Mascolo, M. F., Craig-Bray, L., & Neimeyer, R. (1997). The construction of meaning and action in development and psychotherapy: An epigenetic systems approach. In G. Neimeyer & R. Neimeyer (Eds.), *Advances in personal construct psychology* (Vol. 4, pp. 3–38). Greenwich, CT: JAI.

Mascolo, M. F., & Fischer, K. W. (1998). The development of self through the coordination of component systems. In M. Ferrari & R. Sternberg (Eds.), *Self-awareness: Its nature and development* (pp. 332–384). New York: Guilford.

Mascolo, M. F., & Fischer, K. W. (1999). The development of representation as the coordination of component systems of action. In I. Sigel (Ed.), *Theoretical perspectives on the concept of representation* (pp. 231–256). Hillsdale, NJ: Lawrence Erlbaum Associates.

Mascolo, M. F., Fischer, K. W., & Neimeyer, R. N. (1999). The dynamic co-development of intentionality, self and social relations. In J. Brandstadter & R. M. Lerner (Eds.), *Action and development: Origins and functions of intentional self-development* (pp. 133–166). Thousand Oaks, CA: Sage.

Mascolo, M. F., Kanner, B. G., & Griffin, S. (1998). Neo-Piagetian systems theory and the education of young children. *Early Child Development and Care, 140,* 31–52.

Mascolo, M. F., Pollack, R., & Fischer, K. W. (1997). Keeping the constructor in constructivism: An epigenetic systems approach. *Journal of Constructivist Psychology, 10,* 25–29.

Mason, J. M. (1980). When do children begin to read: An exploration of four-year-old children's letter and word reading competencies. *Reading Research Quarterly, 15,* 203–227.

McClelland, D. C. (1961). *The achieving society.* New York: Van Nostrand.

Needham, J. (1959). *A history of embryology* (2nd ed.). Cambridge, England: Cambridge University Press.

Nicholls, J. G. (1976). Effort is virtue, but it's better to have ability: Evaluative response to perceptions of effort and ability. *Journal of Research in Personality, 10,* 306–315.

Nicholls, J. G. (1978). The development of the concepts of effort and ability, perception of academic attainment, and the understanding that difficult tasks require more ability. *Child Development, 49,* 800–814.

Nicholls, J. G. (1984). Achievement motivation: Conceptions of ability, subjective experience, task choice, and performance. *Psychological Review, 91,* 328–346.

Olson, D. R. (1994). *The world on paper: The conceptual and cognitive implications of writing and reading.* New York: Cambridge University Press.

Pinker, S. (1994). *The language instinct: How the mind creates language.* New York: Harper Perennial.

Raeff, C., & Mascolo, M. F. (1996, June). *Co-regulated coordination: Representational activities at the intersection of individual, social and cultural processes.* Paper presented at the 26th annual symposium of the Jean Piaget Society, Philadelphia, PA.

Resnick, L. B., & Ford, W. (1981). *The psychology of mathematics for instruction.* Hillsdale, NJ: Lawrence Erlbaum Associates.

Rogoff, B. (1990). *Apprenticeship in thinking.* New York: Oxford University Press.

Rogoff, B. (1993). Children's guided participation and participatory appropriation in sociocultural activity. In R. Wozniak & K. W. Fischer (Eds.), *Development in context: Acting and thinking in specific learning environments* (pp. 121–154). Hillsdale, NJ: Lawrence Erlbaum Associates.

Roswell, F. G., & Chall, J. S. (1992). *Diagnostic assessments of reading with trial teaching strategies.* Chicago: Riverside.

Ruestow, E. G. (1983). Leeuwnhoek's perception of the spermatozoa. *Journal of the History of Biology, 16,* 185–224.

Salili, F. (1996). Accepting personal responsibility for learning. In D. A. Watkins & J. B. Biggs (Eds.), *The Chinese learner: Cultural, psychological, and contextual influence* (pp. 85–105). Hong Kong: Comparative Education Research Centre (CERC) & The Australian Council for Educational Research Ltd. (ACER).

Salili, F., & Hau, K. T. (1994). The effect of teachers' evaluative feedback on Chinese students' perception of ability: A cultural and situational analysis. *Educational Studies, 20,* 223–236.

Saxe, G. B. (1995). From the field to the classroom: Studies in mathematical understanding. In L. P. Steffe & J. Gale (Eds.), *Constructivism in education* (pp. 287–312). Hillsdale, NJ: Lawrence Erlbaum Associates.

Stanovich, K. E. (1994). Phenotypic performance profile of children with reading disabilities: A regression-based test of the phonological-core variable-difference model. *Journal of Educational Psychology, 86,* 24–53.

Stevenson, H. W., & Lee, S. Y. (1996). The academic achievement of Chinese students. In M. Bond (Ed.), *The handbook of Chinese psychology* (pp. 124–142). Hong Kong: Oxford University Press.

Stevenson, H. W., & Stigler, J. W. (1992). *The learning gap.* New York: Simon & Schuster.

Stipek, D. (1981). Children's perceptions of their own and their classmates' ability. *Journal of Educational Psychology, 73,* 404–410.

Stipek, D. J. (1988). *Motivation to learn: From theory to practice.* Englewood Cliffs, NJ: Prentice-Hall.

Stipek, D. J. (1998). Differences between Americans and Chinese in the circumstances evoking pride, shame, and guilt. *Journal of Cross-Culture Psychology, 29,* 616–629.

Suarez-Orozco, C., & Suarez-Orozco, M. (1995). *Trans-formations: Immigration, family life, and achievement motivation among Latino adolescents.* Stanford, CA: Stanford University Press.

Torgesen, J., Wagner, R., & Rashotte, C. (1994). Longitudinal studies of phonological processes of reading. *Journal of Learning Disabilities, 27,* 276–286.

Vygotsky, L. S. (1978). *Mind in society.* Cambridge, MA: Harvard University Press.

Weber, M. (1930). *The Protestant ethic and the spirit of capitalism.* [T. Parson, trans.]. New York: Scribner. (Originally published, 1904).

Weiner, B. (1985). An attributional theory of achievement motivation and emotion. *Psychological Review, 92,* 548–573.

Weiner, B. (1986). *An attributional theory of motivation and emotion.* New York: Springer Verlag.

Weiss, P. A. (1970). The living system: Determinism stratified. In A. Koestler & J. Smythies (Eds.), *Beyond reductionism: New perspectives in life sciences* (pp. 3–55). New York: Macmillan.

Werner, H. (1948). *Comparative psychology of mental development*. New York: International Universities Press.

Werner, H., & Kaplan, B. (1984/1963). *Symbol formation*. Hillsdale, NJ: Lawrence Erlbaum Associates.

Wertsch, J. V. (1979). From social interaction to higher psychological processes: A clarification and application of Vygotsky's theory. *Human Development, 22*, 1–22.

Wolf, M., & Bowers, P. (in press). The double-deficit hypothesis for the developmental dyslexias. *Journal of Educational Psychology*.

Wood, D. J., Bruner, J. S., & Ross, G. (1976). The role of tutoring in peer problem solving. *Journal of Child Psychology and Psychiatry, 17*, 89–100.

Chapter 6

Creating Standards of Excellence for Residency Training in Neurological Surgery: A Historical Approach

Rosa Lynn Pinkus
University of Pittsburgh

Ryan Sauder
University of Pittsburgh

> *The surgeon and his facility will rise together.*
>
> —Stevens (1971, p. 15)

Neurosurgery is a subspecialty that gained full professional status during the years 1890 to 1930. At the start of this time frame, operation on the brain was a rare and courageous feat (for both surgeon and patient). By 1935, Board certification of practitioners who had completed a specified and rigorous residency program was commonplace. Neurosurgery, along with other subspecialties, was held in awe by a public fascinated both with science and the mystery that operating on the brain involved (Porter, 1997). During these years, the societal scaffolding that would both support and enable the specialty to flourish was also put in place. The Flexner Report was published in 1910. It summarized the condition of 160 medical schools in the United States. Holding them to the rigorous scientific and clinical standards for training developed in Germany, only 55 received the approval of the site visitors (Brown, 1979). The standards mandated the inclusion of 2 years of basic science training within the new medical school curriculum, as well as 2 years of practical clinical experience in an accredited hospital—one that was affiliated with a medical school.

The rise of the modern hospital was intrinsic to the success of new surgical subspecialties. "By 1900," wrote Rosenberg (1987), "the hospital assumed a characteristic physical form, its internal spaces defined by their functions and those functions understood in technical and bureaucratic terms" (p. 6). Its designers championed it as a laboratory for the new science-based medicine. By 1920, in fact, critics both within and outside the medical profession articulated the very same concerns about the hospital that are currently viewed as problems: its coldness, impersonality, and focus on cure rather than prevention. Progressives especially disparaged the hospital's focus on the isolated patient and the subsequent neglect by caretakers to understand the patient's family and community (Rosenberg, 1987). "The hospital," writes Rosenberg (1987), "had become central to medical education and was well integrated into the career patterns of regular physicians . . . perhaps most important, it . . . had been clothed with a legitimating aura of science and almost boundless social expectation" (p. 6).

The history of neurosurgery, which came of age during this timespan, provides a specific example of how one profession resolved the question of setting standards of excellence in practice. What techniques would be taught? How would students demonstrate that they had mastered them? How would they learn the techniques and not harm or fatally injure patients in the process? Knowing that mistakes would occur during the learning process—indeed even in practice—how could they be minimized and learned from? Once certification was earned, what mechanisms could be in place to further "control" for excellent practice? Finally, if attention were merely paid to defining safe practice, how would the field evolve and grow?

These questions are not merely of historical interest. They persist today both in neurosurgery and in other specialized professions. "Up to 1960," wrote Hirsch (1997), "children in need of neurosurgical treatment . . . were either treated in neurosurgical departments where anesthetists, nurses, and neurosurgeons had no specialized training in pediatrics or in departments of pediatric surgery in which the specific aspect of neurosurgery was ignored" (p. 165). It was Hirsch's opinion at the time that some new hybrid field should be developed. Chronicling the creation and achievements of a specific department of Pediatric Neurosurgery, the author concluded, progress has been tremendous (Hirsch, 1997). By 1995, this "hybrid field" gained professional status and recognition with the formation of the Society of Pediatric Neurosurgeons, as well as with specific, peer-reviewed publications about technique and surgical success in pediatric neurosurgery. Given this momentum and the societal pressures of managed care markets, in 1997 a small group of U.S.-based neurosurgeons began to advocate and lobby for the segregation of the practice of pediatric neurosurgery from the rest of neurosurgery. They sought to create separate training standards as well as a qualifying board that was independent from the American Board of Neurological Surgery. Large insurance-based group practices were requiring general neurosurgeons to treat children. As a defensive measure, some within the profession felt that specific certification to identify qualified practitioners was needed.

As heated debates pro and con continue about how to create standards of excellence for pediatric neurosurgery, several questions arise. Is infighting among professionals unsettling for the general public and for the pediatricians responsible for referring patients for treatment? Whom should one consult if the skills of a neurosurgeon are needed for one's child or one's patient? Are there neurosurgeons currently operating without having the skills appropriate for the management of disease in infants and children? Neurosurgeons themselves find the ambiguity regarding standardization disquieting. Should patients suffer a complication after surgery, would they be protected in some way if certification by a new board were obtained? More to the point, if one were not certified, would using skills previously deemed "competent" now create a potential liability issue? This current debate surrounding the development of standards of excellence in neurosurgery, then, echoes debates that occurred almost a century ago when the field was first created.

Focusing attention on the work of two prestigious surgeons, Harvey Cushing and Walter Dandy, this chapter uses history to illustrate that the definition of professional excellence is a context-driven, politically negotiated, and value-laden concept. Case reports in both medicine and law, written from 1889 to 1935, as well as journal articles and books, depict how a two-pronged approach to excellence developed during these years and how these approaches established a tension that, when balanced, has led to advancement within the profession. Using this historical approach promotes a critical distance and invites comparison with the present (Pinkus, 1996, p. 21). Ideally, such a discussion will help to illuminate similar trends that affect and continue to shape the pursuit of excellence in the educational processes of other professions.

TWO PERSPECTIVES OF EXCELLENCE: SETTING STANDARDS BY THE BEDSIDE

The scientist requires a thoroughgoing commitment to the tradition with which, if he is fully successful, he will break.

—Kuhn (1977, p. 235)

In 1905, when Harvey Cushing published his first article discussing the need for a new surgical subspecialty, "the idea of professionalization and specialization of many occupations was a major theme in the agenda of the American Progressives" (Greenblatt, 1997, p. 6). Although concerned with the reform of public health, the Progressives were not especially concerned with medical specialization. They did, however, "model their ideas on the paradigm of scientific rationality" (Greenblatt, 1997, p. 6). The inclusion of science and its rigorous methodology was part and parcel of the training that Cushing received while a resident at the Johns Hopkins Medical School. He would include the scientific methods as part of his reform agenda. Cushing understood the political complexity he needed to tackle if his campaign to create a new subspecialty was to succeed. Aware of the infighting of the medical and surgical community and of the competition for patients, he was witness to a chaotic and ineffective group of practitioners. Cushing was a member of the elite reform group identified by the formation of the American Board of Surgery, which was established in 1913. The Board sought and succeeded in creating training programs for surgeons that focused on safety, replication by example, and dedication to careful training in both technique and moral character. Clearly a "product of his times," Cushing's unique personality was also evident in the standards he created. As a formidable mentor who espoused a strict hierarchy both in and out of the operating room, perfection, honesty, and step-by-step progress, Cushing set a conservative tone for the new profession.

Walter Dandy was one of Cushing's first students. A gifted and talented man 16 years younger than his mentor, he appreciated the need to standardize operating on the "brain's unforgiving biological characteristics" (Pinkus, 1996, p. 32; see Fig. 6.1). He was, after all, trained in this tradition. Under Cushing's guidance he easily mastered the methodical replication of tested procedures. When he completed his training, however, he regarded these procedures as a baseline from which to try innovative approaches. Secure in a professional base that had been built by Cushing, Dandy's goal was to push neurosurgery into new and uncharted ground, much as Cushing had done 20 years earlier. His creative genius and technical skill enabled him to tackle operations and define techniques that Cushing neither sanctioned nor ever mastered. Dandy also finished his residency training during World War I. Unable to serve in the frontlines, he remained at home in an environment that was dedicated to the war effort. Progressive rationality foundered in a world torn asunder by war. Innovation and risk taking were tolerated.

The fact that these two surgeons possessed differing views of surgical excellence and that both contributed a lasting legacy to neurosurgery has proven essential to maintaining excellence in the field. Excellence, according to *The American Heritage College Dictionary* (1997), is the state, quality, or condition of being better than others, surpassing others, or excelling (p. 477). In a profession or an institution, persons may use the phrase "standards of excellence" to characterize the level of performance (by professionals, employees, or students) deemed necessary and sufficient to ensure results or services of an acceptably high quality. In a subspecialty surgical practice such as neurosurgery, for example, standards of excellence are defined and used by the Board of Neurosurgery, which was created in 1934 to certify practitioners amidst a context of general reform of medi-

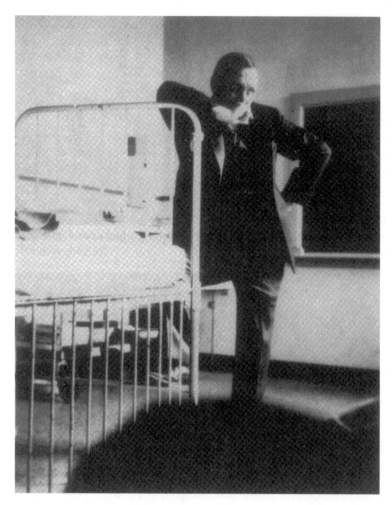

FIG. 6.1. Dandy caught by a candid photographer in a thoughtful moment at Johns Hopkins Hospital. From *Dandy of Johns Hopkins* (p. 103), by W. L. Fox, 1984, Baltimore, MD: Lippincott, Williams & Wilkins. Copyright © 1984 by Lippincott, Williams & Wilkins. Reprinted with permission.

cine and of the development of new surgical subspecialties. These standards seek to insure that a defined set of skills will be used to maximize the efficacy of surgical treatments for particular ailments and to minimize the morbidity and mortality associated with them.

It is notable that, according to the dictionary's definition, standards of excellence can vary in accordance with one's level of skill. A particularly skilled neurosurgeon, for example, may perform successful operations that are inaccessible to the average, yet also competent surgeon. Given hindsight and a recognition of how science progresses, this tension between a standard that is safe and replicable and one that is unique and innovative is identified as being typical in a diverse and evolving field. It provides fodder for arguing whether or not specialized areas within the field should be created to recognize superior skill, or held at bay as dangerous yardsticks to measure the overall competence of practitioners. Referring to this tension, Thomas Kuhn (1977) identifies both "divergent" and "convergent" thinking as being evident in the development of science. "Since these two modes of thought are inevitably in conflict" he surmises, "it will follow that the ability to support a tension that can occasionally become almost unbearable is one of the prime requisites for the very best sort of scientific research" (p. 235). Given that neurosurgery practice is firmly rooted in the scientific method, the existence of a similar tension within it is understandable. Describing the specific circumstances of the infusion of science into neurosurgical practice will help make this observation evident.

FROM MORAL CODE TO STATE REGULATION: TAMING THE DOCTORS

Just before the Great War . . . , the earlier emphasis on moral codes and reflective treatises on medical ethics began to wane . . . The law was beginning to weave its garment of requirements . . . but there was a stillness in medicine and moral philosophy.
—Faden and Beauchamp (1986, p. 86)

Medicine in the early years of the 20th century could not be called a "profession." It was instead characterized by an increase in popularity of various competing medical sects. Practitioners within these rival healing sects included homeopaths, hydropaths, and botanics. Among these, homeopathy was probably the most influential. Following the beliefs of the German physician Samuel Hahnemann, homeopaths believed that a drug that produced a given symptom in a healthy person would cure a similar symptom in the sick and that the potency of a drug increased the more it was diluted (Pernick, 1985). Hydropathy, which also arose out of German romanticism, was also quite popular. Hydropaths banned the use of all drugs and surgery as "artificial" human meddling with nature. They favored the use of water, steam, and ice, in conjunction with exercise, rest, and hygiene, to aid the healing process. Wheat cracker developer Sylvester Graham and flake cereal pioneer John Harvey Kellogg were both influenced by hydropathy (Pernick, 1985). The botanic physicians followed the techniques of American folk healer Samuel Thomson, using purges, blisters, and violent emetics as treatment methods (Pernick, 1985).

It is difficult to approximate the number of practitioners in medical sects during the 19th century. Orthodox medical schools produced more graduates than did sectarian medical schools, but many practitioners in medical sects learned by apprenticeship, and some graduates of orthodox medical programs converted to sectarian practices (Pernick, 1985). Brown stated that, by 1860, regular practitioners outnumbered sectarian practitioners by a ratio of 10 to 1 (Brown, 1979). Although numbers remain somewhat unclear, these sectarian practitioners of medicine were clearly an important minority influence throughout this period (Pernick, 1985).

As the numbers of both orthodox and sectarian physicians continued to increase, organized physicians began to worry because it was clear that increasing the numbers of practitioners would lower rather than raise the prestige and incomes of physicians in the country. Given this situation, medical reformers believed that "[r]aising medical school standards and thereby reducing their enrollment . . . would simultaneously win public confidence in medical practice and reduce the output of doctors" (Brown, 1979, p. 65). It was within this context that the Flexner Reforms were instigated in an attempt to change the standards in medical education. A belief in science and a hefty purse that was filled by the spoils of a post–Civil War industrialized society would foot the bill for the reforms (Brown, 1979).

A first attempt to unite the divided profession admittedly came from within the orthodox groups. This focused on the writing of codes of ethics and an attempt at the internal enforcing of moral codes (Faden & Beauchamp, 1986). Perhaps the most well-known code of ethics to emerge during this period is the one developed by Thomas Percival in the latter part of the 18th century. In his treatise *Medical Ethics*, Percival outlined a code of ethics intended to soothe relations among various staff members of the Manchester Infirmary. Relations among the physicians, surgeons, and apothecaries at the Infirmary were severely strained due to staff changes necessitated by a typhus epidemic in 1789 (Sohl & Bassford, 1986). Although Percival wrote *Medical Ethics* to address a particular situation at the Manchester Infirmary, this code of ethics served as a template for subsequent members of the medical community interested in ethical codes, most notably the American Medical Association's *Code of Ethics* adopted in 1847. There are some significant differences between this code and Percival's code due, in large part, to the different social and professional situations that existed both geographically and chronologically (King, 1982). However, comparison of the two codes clearly demonstrates the marked influence of Percival's code upon the writers of the AMA code. This AMA Code of Ethics was one method by which medical professionals hoped to uphold standards for physicians and to improve medical education in the country (King, 1982).

By the first and second decades of the 20th century, these intraprofessional attempts at unification gave way to the creation of state licensure and other regulatory mechanisms, including the law, to redress grievances from patients (Pinkus, 2000). The influence of widespread regulatory trends affecting medical education and licensure had become quite apparent as early as 1909. State medical examining boards and medical colleges were making notable advances in establishing requirements of preliminary education for medical students. A majority of states required physicians to graduate from a medical college. Many state boards acquired the authority to refuse recognition to low-grade medical colleges, and nearly all states had a unified state medical examining board (Anonymous, 1909).

The Flexner Report, finalized in 1910, created a 4-year educational track for students. Modeled after the prestigious European medical schools that devoted 2 full years to scientific training, the standards essentially prohibited all persons except wealthy or middle-class males from entering the medical profession (Brown, 1979). Specialty training was linked to this reform of medical education as a whole. As stated previously, the American College of Surgeons was created in 1913. Its members decided that only 10% of the new "medical elite" would be offered surgical training and then, only those with superior skill would be selected (Stevens, 1971, p. 149).

Setting these standards protected the general practitioner, who traditionally performed surgical operations, by providing the competent among them with a license and by keeping the incompetent from the professional ranks. It also assured that a mechanism for regulating the new specialists would exist. "Before opening the abdomen and the rise of the surgical specialties," wrote Stevens (1989), "there was relatively little surgery of a major nature which the general practitioner was called upon to undertake. With the development of procedures that made the ill-trained or incompetent surgeon potentially lethal, there arose crucial questions of professional control" (p. 81). Control, it was decided, would rest primarily within the certified training programs that were created at academic teaching hospitals. Criteria included the completion of 4 years of medical school, an internship year, and an additional 5 to 6 years of specialized clinical and scientific work. Those who pursued this training were called House Officers, partly because they actually lived in the hospital during their training. As such, their education included both technical and moral education. Over the years, the descriptive term "residents" was coined to describe these integral troops in medical care.

CREATING SOMETHING OUT OF NOTHING: THE LEGACY OF HARVEY CUSHING

And so here at Hopkins, between the years 1902 and 1908, the modern era of scientific brain surgery was born, conceived and developed by this stubborn, methodical man who refused to give up.

—Denzel (1971, pp. 87–88)

It is against a backdrop of medical competition and incompetence, scientific rigor and wealthy industrialists, that Harvey Cushing's efforts to create a specialty called neurological surgery took place. As mentioned previously, Cushing was the leader of the elitist surgeons during the early decades of the 20th century, holding professorships sequentially at Johns Hopkins, Harvard, and Yale. Surgeons who wanted to create subspecialties were typically trained in Germany where they were taught the latest scientific underpinnings to practice. They disdained practitioners in the United States who represented a therapeutically impoverished and divided medical profession. The infighting and backstabbing among competing sects for dominance resulted in a general societal mistrust of doctors (Pinkus, 2000). Cushing had a deep understanding of the various components of medical practice. He was sensitive to the importance of the ethical aspects of medical care and debated them at length in the hopes of reforming surgical practice. Serving as an expert witness for a legal case of insurance fraud in 1915 must surely have sensitized him to the important interactions between medicine and the law. Finally, as one of an elite group of medical practitioners, he helped shape the new standards that became integral to reforming medical education and practice in the United States. Cushing knew that to teach others the technical and physiological aspects of brain surgery required a massive restructuring of then-current medical practice and education.

Cushing devoted three published articles to defining what he called "The Special Field of Neurological Surgery." In the first, Cushing described how he acquired his expertise and outlined the singular "Hopkins model" of surgical residency that he adopted as the standard for reforming postgraduate medical training.

> Through the generosity of Dr. Halsted [Cushing's well-respected attending surgeon at Johns Hopkins], his junior associates have been given . . . the privilege of directing the work in some of the subdivisions of his large surgical clinic, in order that they may concentrate their efforts toward advancement along particular lines. It has thus fallen to my lot, temporarily and under his guidance, to control the groups of cases which present features chiefly to neurological interest . . . (p. 77)

In addition to such "hands-on" operating experience, Cushing urged that:

> . . . to successfully cope with the many operative problems offered by the various disorders of the nervous system, a man, after a thorough training in pathology and medicine (in its broadest sense) must study, not only in the neurological clinic but also in the laboratory, the pathology of these afflictions in their histological and—what is still more important—their experimental aspects. (Cushing, 1905b, p. 78)

Comparing this approach with the standard method of operating on the nervous system is revealing. Standard practice relied on a technically adept surgeon and a physician trained in neurology. Both doctors were often incompetent in their respective fields, due to inadequate medical education and an absence of state licensure or board certification requirements. Even if both were competent, combining their skills was difficult, commonly leading to cases like the following one reported by Cushing. He noted "Perfect skill and excellent technique" in a laminectomy operation, yet results indicated an "area of anesthesia [corresponding] to a level about three segments higher than the seat of the bony lesion—a level which could not possibly have been exposed by the incision which had been made." This finding was baffling, until it was discovered that "the operator . . . had inserted his finger at the close of the operation into the canal, to be sure that there were no spicules of bone pressing on the cord higher up" (Cushing, 1910, p. 328). The pressure of this finger irreparably damaged the sensitive neural tissue in the spinal canal.

Cushing committed himself to spearheading a campaign to create a new surgical subspecialty, although he knew that such a campaign was politically complex. On the one hand, it required exposing the blatant incompetence of medical practitioners who used their license to operate—and this legitimately, within the bounds of traditional practice. He also needed to criticize the general surgeons who were technically competent, but harmed patients through ignorance of delicate brain structures. Such criticisms needed to be supported by sufficient evidence to justify training a subgroup of specialists to focus on brain surgery. To succeed, Cushing needed to articulate both technical and moral standards for a new profession. He also needed to create an educational environment to teach these new standards. In sum, a new moral was needed for new technical expertise to be fruitfully developed and applied.

Clearly, Cushing's goals in setting a new standard for neurosurgery reflected the general reforms sweeping medicine during the years 1910 to 1945. These Flexnerian reforms played a well-documented role in providing the outline, structure, and financial support needed to "upgrade and standardize" medical education in the United States during these years (Kessel, 1972). The surgical profession's impact on standardizing internship and residency and integrating them into the medical education process was also important (Stevens, 1989; Waitzkin, 1980). Indeed, a subspecialty like neurosurgery could never have developed without this overall standardization in postgraduate medical education.

The American College of Surgeons (ACS), established in 1913 by leading surgeons, promoted the standardization of teaching in hospitals as one of its aims and, over the next 25 years, successfully carved out the form and structure of internship and residency amidst a complex political landscape that involved the American Medical Association (AMA), private foundations, medical schools, and hospital administrations. The system of residency at Johns Hopkins that began in 1898 and existed essentially unchanged until 1941 served as a model for these reforms (Fox, 1984).

Under the Johns Hopkins system, a medical graduate had to train for 8 years to become a neurosurgeon: The first year as a surgical intern; the second as a fellow in experimental surgery; the third and fourth learning surgical pathology, fractures, trauma, and plastic surgery; the two following years were spent in neurosurgery, first as assistant resident, then as a resident; the seventh year graduates served as First Assistant in General Surgery; and finally, one was granted the coveted position of Chief Resident in General Surgery in the eighth year. By 1939, the ACS had accredited 35 medical schools to offer surgical training programs and only 12 of these had residency programs in neurosurgery, each with no more than one to three positions available. In fact, only 24 new positions for neurosurgical residency were available in 1939 (Pevehouse, 1984).

"Upgrading" medical education created a cohort of wealthy and elitist professionals both by distinction of training and by birth, as only wealthy families could delay wage earning for 8 years. A balance was needed, however, between keeping surgery elitist and assuring respect was accorded to the many years of internship and residency training. So it was clearly an accomplishment in creating an acceptable form and structure to teach neurosurgery as a surgical subspecialty. But, still, mentors like Cushing remained fundamentally unprepared for the problems and the responsibilities of having young apprentices living in the hospital (Coughlin, 1917), and of dealing with trainees who left the residency to set up practice before completing the course (Foss, 1931). Cushing's published articles and speeches illustrate how he strove to meet these challenges.

Cushing joined the technical lessons he learned through his operative experiences on Halsted's service with moral tenets central to defining a "good physician" provided by the legendary Sir William Osler and other role models. This two-pronged approach informed the professional maxims he designed specifically to guide new practitioners. For instance, Cushing first described the dangers of operating on patients who had "inaccessible" brain tumors, then he said: "In affording a measure of relief to these distressing cases, one may fulfill the chief of his duties as a physician . . . to prolong life and at the same time alleviate suffering." He added, "the mere lengthening of a patient's months or years without rendering them more livable, is . . . no justification whatsoever of an operative procedure" (Cushing, 1905b, p. 79).

Cushing (1905b), quoting Sir Francis Bacon, stated that "It is easier to evolve truth from error than from certain confusion" (p. 83). For Cushing, this statement was an ethical justification for reporting mistakes. In addition, it was a rationale for constructing "definitive rules" for surgical intervention in specific cases. Cushing cited various harmful mistakes that were seen in patients who had been "needlessly subjected to laminectomy." With the aim of "ordering the confusion" in deciding to operate on patients with spinal cord lesions, all spinal injuries were divided into three categories, and technical criteria and moral justification for operating on each were provided by Cushing. For instance, "In a fracture-dislocation where evidence of a complete transverse lesion is found on clinical exam," he said, "[an] . . . operation can do no harm, but it is an unjustifiable ordeal for both patient and operator" (Cushing, 1905b).

Cushing's early writings were characterized by pairing technical description with moral prescription. These writings expressed his recognition that when a new subspecialty advances there is an associated double responsibility. Learning the science of neurosurgery was not sufficient. Making ethical judgment about the appropriate use of the neurosurgical technique was equally necessary. Based on his experiences, Cushing stated that a neurosurgeon with good training could identify a tumor at an early stage and intervene surgically to prevent irreversible morbidity. Early diagnosis and intervention provided an important justification for the profession of neurosurgery. Cushing (1910) wrote "Allowing a patient to become blind from the pressure of a tumor which does not directly implicate the optic paths is comparable to procrastination in appendicular disease until the onset of general peritonitis." Based on his mistakes, Cushing (1910) knew that "the operation, in the hands of the inexperienced, must usually end with the first protrusion of the naked brain through an open dura, and when abandoned in this way, paralysis, a separated wound, an infected fungus, meningitis and each are, alas, too common" (p. 331). Cushing's judgment and reasoning were acquired, in part, from his mistakes. For him, making mistakes was both acceptable and expectable. He distinguished between gross and unforgivable errors made by incompetent generalists and ones made by the trainee under the supervision of a mentor. He emphasized that the only way of becoming a competent neurosurgeon with technical and judgmental skills was to be trained beyond medical school in the Hopkins residency model. Cushing stated that "[The] transformation of surgery from practices based almost wholly on an anatomical knowledge of the surface and extremities of the body, to ones based on the physiological activity of the viscera, has come rapidly," and he attributed physicians' "reluctance or hesitation to accept surgery as an oft-needed form of therapy . . . for many . . . intracranial conditions . . . to the fear of surgical foolhardiness and its consequences . . ." He advised medical practitioners who referred patients for surgery to examine the successes of mechanical and operative therapeutics. He stated that "the patients' risks were about equal between the physician who knows nothing of surgery and the surgeon who possesses no alternative but the knife" (Cushing, 1910, p. 327; Pinkus, 1996).

Cushing always emphasized the importance of the training he received. During the residency years he established an elite hierarchy in neurosurgical practice. Importance of the hierarchy was that it provided professional control, which in turn was essential for the safety of the patients. It was assumed that trainees would be successful personally and professionally as a consequence of proper performance. The built-in uncertainty (if this is not respected, according to Cushing, it would cause disasters) was the first certainty of neurosurgery. Structure of the brain disease left small amount of time and physical space for operation. Moreover, neurosurgeons needed to be precise due to the biological characteristics of the brain. Death or neurological devastation reports were common obstacles. These disasters were shown graphically in Cushing's early case reports (Pinkus, 1996; see Fig. 6.2A, B, C).

Cushing performed an emergency operation on December 12, 1902. The patient was an 18-year-old woman, who had a penetrating gunshot wound of the head (Cushing, 1903). At the Johns Hopkins Hospital, Cushing first examined her in the "accident" room and saw that she was "almost in the 'Lahmungsstadium' [paralysis stage] of compression, and rapid preparations were made for operation." Moreover, the facts that the patient's husband was the assailant, and that she was pregnant, made the case more difficult.

One year before this case, Cushing had given reports of carefully documented laboratory experiments showing that elevated intracranial pressure could cause respiratory failure but not heart failure (Cushing, 1902). His innovative technique, called "cranial window," demonstrated that with prompt surgical relief, an animal's spontaneous respiration returned: The monkey recovered. This phenomenon was recognized by two surgeons who pioneered operating on the brain: Scottish surgeon Sir William McEwan and British surgeon Sir Victor Horsley. They performed emergency craniotomies to decompress the patient's brain while maintaining respiration artificially until spontaneous breathing occurred (Bailly, 1904; Faden & Beauchamp, 1986; McEwan, 1893). Horsley (1894) identified patients who died due to receiving "a violent blow, frequently in the occipitatemporal region," for example, from a "fist or cricket ball or from an explosion . . ." (p. 309) as early as 1894. Although these people were seen as "deaths by heart failure" he was sure that they were deaths due to respiratory arrest, a fact which he "proved experimentally on the lower animals, with unfailing accuracy." He stated that "we do not observe that any attempt is made to do artificial respiration, although this is just a measure which is universally taught in ambulance classes, and can be practiced by the intelligent layman" (Horsley, 1894, p. 309).

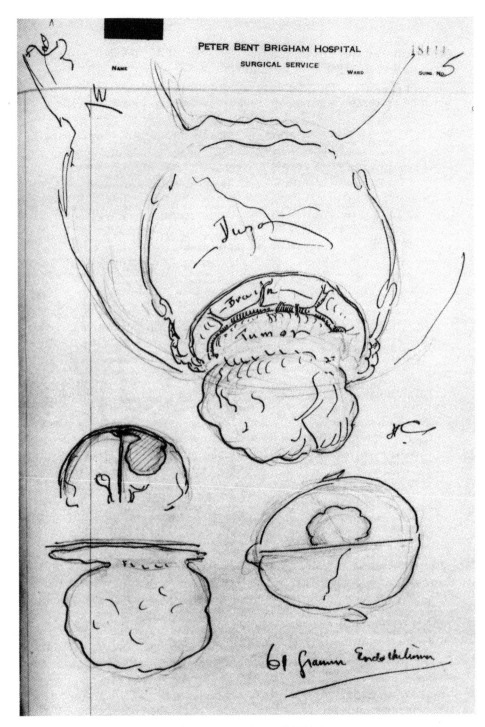

FIG. 6.2A. Case no. 18144.

OPERATIVE NOTE
Jan. 26, 1923
OPERATOR

Right Osteoplastic resection - 1st Stage,
Disclosing tumor. Presumably Endothelioma.

Dr. Cushing

ANAESTHESIA

Ether - Miss Gerrard

Under anaesthesia a large right osteoplastic flap was reflected without
incident, disclosing a tense dura. The flap was so made as to expose the
arm center but was probably too low for the very upper margin of the bone
incision, and slightly thickened dura was observed. Palpation showed
this area to be somewhat more tense than elsewhere and there was a slight
thickening of bone, indenting what was evidently the center of an endothelioma. In order to verify its presence an incision was made in the
dura to the outer margin of what might be tumor about 3 cm. below the central point of indentation. The incision came down directly upon the margin of tumor which was slightly reddish and granular. An extra opening
was made in the bone with the rongeur, so as to give a circle, which it
is hoped may be suffice for tumor removal. This was replaced and closed
in layers by Dr. Horrax.

(Dr. Cushing)

POST-
OPERATIVE NOTE
Jan. 28, 1923.
Dr. McKenzie.

[48 hours postop.]
Sutures removed. Wound inspected by Dr. Horrax. Dressings had
stained through. Coagulation time must be increased in this patient.

OPERATIVE NOTE
Jan. 30, 1923.
OPERATOR

Dr. Cushing.   Second-stage Extirpation of Right Parasagittal Meningioma.

ANAESTHESIA

Novocain

Under local anaesthesia the flap was again reflected there having
been no formation of blood clot. Working fore and aft from the original
small nick made in the dura disclosing the edge of the tumor, a curvi-
linear incision exposing a comparatively small part of the hemisphere
was then made about as in the accompanying sketch. The tumor proved to be
much larger than anticipated, and it was evident that it was going to be
difficult to remove it through the small field. It is possible that I should
have placed more emphasis than I did upon the symptoms which she had in her
foot, but I thought that we were probably going to find a small enucleable
tumor largely limited to the foot area. Encircling the field in which the
nest of the tumor lay was a large vein which finally had to be clipped
though the margin of the cortex was not split. The enucleation would have
been a simple affair had it not been for the fact that the tumor was found
to have a flat expansion which carried its margin to the edge of the
falx. It was necessary to rongeur away considerably more bone even though
the flap was made quite high and although there was a little loss of blood
which caused a lowering of blood pressure. It was possible by the placement
of Kelly clamps along the margin of the flat portion of the growth was tilted
out to control bleeding with the subsequent placement of a few bits of muscle
and some clips.

There was an unusual degree of tension and the tumor practically extruded
itself. At the end of the operation too the fossa from which it had been
removed had filled up completely, and I fear indeed that there may be some
subsequent edema. Over the raw surface of brain a layer of protective
was left in position to encourage an endothelial lining.

The flap was replaced and closed with single layer of sutures in the
galea, though I am not at all sure at this writing that it would not have
been better to have placed some sutures in the scalp for there may possibly
be some danger of herniation. This gutta percha tissue must be removed in
about 10 days.   (Dr. Cushing)

Feb 1/23 Post Operative
HG McKeen Dressing inspected by Dr. Cushing the one suture removed
dressed with rubber tissue & stiff dressing; wound a poor suppuration

FIG. 6.2B. Case no. 18144 continued.

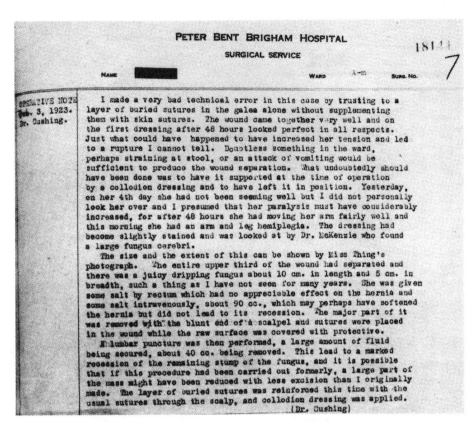

FIG. 6.2C. Case no. 18144 continued. Figures 6.2A, 6.2B, and 6.2C all from
The Surgical Art of Harvey Cushing (pp. 50–52), by P. M. Black (Ed.), 1992, Park
Ridge, IL: American Association of Neurological Surgeons. Copyright © 1992
by American Association of Neurological Surgeons. Reprinted with permission.

According to Cushing's experimental model, Horsley misunderstood
the underlying physiologic process; he thought that medullary paralyses
were produced only by mechanical effect of pressure exerted on the centers so that cardiac action can continue after respiratory failure. However,
according to Cushing, the patient's difficulty was due to "the state of vas-
cular anemia, which paralyzes the centers . . . The regulatory action of the
vasomotor center . . . serves to ward off the condition of threatened anemia by an elevation of blood pressure" (Cushing, 1902, p. 377). He based
his explanation of the situation of the gunshot victim on these assumptions. He showed that the bullet had penetrated the squamous portion of
right temporal bone, and that cerebral substance was protruding from and
squeezed through the wound. This was accompanied by a lethal increase
in intracranial pressure.

The patient was in deep coma. Her respirations were slow, gasping and irregular, with periods of apnea. The pulse was rapid . . . irregular, and the arterial tension was low. Blood pressure observations, which were immediately instituted, demonstrated that a very rapid fall was taking place. The eyes were fixed, staring and prominent with widely and equally dilated pupils. The face was much cyanosed and ecchymoses were already forming in the eyelids and conjunctivae. She vomited soon after her admission, in projectile fashion. (Cushing, 1903, pp. 1038–1044)

Because the woman was in an advanced stage of pregnancy, they rushed her to an adjoining operating room. There, Cushing realized:

. . . the respirations, which had become much more irregular in character, ceased altogether. Artificial respiration, by thoracic compression, was kept up, until the patient could be put upon the table, when a rapid tracheotomy was performed, and the tube inserted in the trachea. After a moment of mouth-to-tube inflation, the color quickly returned to the deeply cyanosed face, and the pulse, which had continued during this interval, greatly improved in character. Meanwhile, an extensive area from the side of the scalp was being shaved; a tourniquet was applied, and a Wagner bone flap, the size of the palm of the hand, was quickly turned down. There was a vain hope that the vasomotor and respiratory failure did not evidence an irrecoverable paralysis of the centers, and that prompt relief from anaemia, due to the extreme degree of intracranial tension, would allow of medullary circulation, sufficient to reawaken the centers to activity.

"With three lives at stake—that of the assailant, his victim and a child—the moments consumed during this partial hemicraniotomy under artificial respiration were exciting enough, and we were rewarded" (p. 1039). After they opened her skull and dura, she took a few gasping inspirations. "The hemisphere bulged under considerable tension from the opening, and a large amount of blood clot was evacuated" (p. 1040). However, this improvement was temporary; the patient could not be saved:

To our great disappointment, the voluntary efforts at respiration did not long continue, and it was once more necessary to resort to artificial means of continuing it. Her blood pressure, continued to fall rapidly and steadily . . . until it had reached its level of complete vasomotor paralysis . . . a condition from which there is probably no recovery. The heart like the isolated mammalian heart of the physiological experiment, continued to beat as long as its circulating blood was kept aerated by the continuance of artificial respiration. As long as there is cardiac pulsation, it is difficult to bring one's self to a realization of the actual presence of death, and artificial breathing was continued for two hours longer before its final abandonment. (Cushing, 1903, p. 1040; Pinkus, 1996, p. 23)

Such reports not only expose the limitations and perils associated with neurosurgical techniques, but also demonstrate the substantial overlap between Cushing's scientific laboratory work and his clinical treatment.

By 1930, such warnings regarding the uncertainties of neurosurgery had been generalized into a common wisdom. "The surgery of brain tumors," Cushing asserted, "may be likened without being trivial to a form of major sport which is played against an invisible but utterly relentless antagonist quick to take advantage of every misplay and faulty move" (Cushing, 1931, p. 130). Honesty in reporting his results was considered integral to learning the technique. "When the time comes to make public one's score, it is done somewhat apologetically," wrote Cushing "but with the expectation that others may profit by it and with the assurance they will come to improve upon it." Still, he qualified the limits of what reading the literature could teach and stressed the importance of the residency program:

> . . . though the general principles may be more or less the same, no two of these operations are precisely alike, and in the process of carrying out what at the best is a complicated and often hazardous procedure, unforeseen circumstances may arise which wholly modify its intended course. When to take great risks; when to force an attempted enucleation of pathologically favorable tumor to its completion with the prospect of an operative fatality, or to abandon the procedure short of completeness with the certainty that after months or years even greater risks may have to be faced at a subsequent session—all this takes surgical judgment which is a matter of long experience and which can scarcely be transmitted by the written word. (Cushing, 1931, p. 130; Pinkus, 1996)

Cushing's emphasis on the need for experiential learning and education in neurosurgery reflected his view regarding the uniqueness of every neurosurgical case. In 1905 Cushing reported a series of six cases of newborn infants. Three days after her birth, one child was diagnosed as having a cephalhematoma (blood under the scalp, usually a birth complication) in the left parietal region. Her swelling increased, and her right pupil was enlarged by the fifth day, her pulse was slow, and she could not eat. Cushing prepared the child for operation because he suspected an intracranial hemorrhage:

> The clot overlying the skull was removed. There was no indication of any connection between it and the intracranial contents. After the evacuation of this clot and exposure of the parietal bone, the latter was turned back almost in its entirety as in the preceding cases. As was expected, a tense, plum-colored dura . . . was brought into view. The dura was opened and a large clot about a centimeter in thickness, which seemed to cover the entire hemisphere, was disclosed. Much of this clot escaped as soon as the opening was

made, and other large pieces of it were lifted off from the surface with a blunt instrument and removed. (1905, p. 579)

After describing the technical procedure, he gave a retrospective review of his decision for continuing the operation:

> Possibly, I should have been satisfied with the relief which this partial operation would have afforded. It doubtless would have been wise to have postponed further interference to another and later occasion, but the child's condition seemed to justify an effort to more thoroughly remove the clotted blood which was within easy access over the anterior and posterior poles of the hemisphere. While irrigating away some of the blood, the child suddenly stopped breathing. Under artificial respiration, the heart beat continued for some minutes, but all efforts to restore spontaneous breathing were unavailing. (Cushing, 1905a, p. 579)

This case shows that pioneering surgeons on the brain succeeded in their profession by understanding the importance of combining technical skill, neurophysiological knowledge, and specific moral virtues. The person had to be bold, honest, and disciplined. Aggressive intervention was required to some extent because of the physiologic aspects of brain disease and knowledge of the brain's temperament. Cushing reported his own experiences and made a generalization that even knowledgeable people are not experienced enough to avoid complications. He proposed that future practitioners should be educated in a hierarchical and strict manner. Further, instruction in every detail of the technique was fundamental. When he was a medical student, Cushing made a mistake in administration of anesthesia and his patient died. In order to prevent this mistake he developed complex blood pressure charts that he appended to both his operating records and published cases (Horrax & Williams, 1955; Pinkus, 1996).

This examination of Cushing's role in reshaping the educational process in residency while promoting the field of neurosurgery demonstrates several tenets that Cushing regarded as paramount in establishing a standard of excellence for the profession: a standardized model of hierarchical learning, respect for uncertainty, and honesty in reporting results (including mistakes). Each of these tenets arises from an implicit, overarching concern for the well-being of surgical patients. Cushing believed that the adoption of a standardized model for medical school and residency training was paramount to ensure that practicing surgeons were competent in their fields. Following medical school, Cushing favored a residency training method designed hierarchically. Cushing's preference for hierarchical learning may have arisen, in part, from his ideas regarding individual responsibility within the professional bounds of neurosurgery. Cushing always assumed responsibility not only for his own mistakes, but also for any mistakes made by residents-in-training beneath him on his service. He believed that teachers in surgery should be held responsible for the actions of their students. Cushing demanded that assistants follow his technique exactly when they operated under his guidance. It was no coincidence that they dressed in a replica of his scrub suit: Cushing was "The Chief." Once he had perfected a surgical technique, Cushing was adamant about the importance of adhering to that precise method (Pinkus, 1996). Because Cushing accepted responsibility for the actions of his students, it was in his best interest to teach them to closely emulate the techniques he himself used. The sense of hierarchy he developed on his service provided an effective way to ensure that his understudies used the surgical methods he felt were most efficacious.

Cushing's respect for uncertainty was closely related to his views on honesty in reporting results of surgical procedures. Because no two patients are exactly alike, no two surgeries are exactly alike. In light of this view, Cushing was hesitant to report surgical successes until he felt confident that he had sufficient data to support the adoption of a particular surgical method. He willingly published his mistakes in hopes that such openness would permit others to learn his technique without duplicating his mistakes. As with the hierarchical teaching method, this emphasis on honesty and openness in establishing standards of excellence for the field presumed that the surgical procedures could be mastered by all neurosurgeons in a manner that minimized morbidity and mortality. Harvey Cushing believed that by establishing set procedures and set technique, all surgeons could reach the standard of excellence to which he held himself. He strongly encouraged such replication by publishing articles that offered the practitioner an operative text (e.g., on removing brain tumors). By 1920, evidence of Cushing's stamp on the new field was abundant.

INNOVATION IN NEUROSURGERY: WALTER DANDY CHALLENGES THE STATUS QUO

> *It is largely due to the frequent comment by Dr. Halstead on the remarkable power of intestinal gases "to perforate bone" that my attention was drawn to its practical possibilities in the brain . . . From these and many other normal and pathological clinical demonstrations . . . it is but a step to the injection of gas into the cerebral ventricles-pneumoventriculography.*
>
> —Scarff (1955, p. 444)

Walter Dandy held a very different view of what constituted the proper standard of excellence for neurosurgery. He also had different ideas regarding how best to achieve that standard. Dandy, who by 1925 was Professor of Neurosurgery at the Johns Hopkins Medical School, was a thorn in Cushing's side beginning from the time he was a resident under Cushing's guidance at Johns Hopkins. Dandy showed his giftedness in surgery and achieved results that only few well-educated surgeons could achieve, while still a student and 16 years younger than his mentor. It is said that Dandy's and Cushing's personalities conflicted (Pinkus, 1996; see Fig. 6.3). However, the rivalry between these two surgeons was not simply a personality conflict; it stemmed in large part from their differing notions of what constituted an adequate standard of excellence for the field of neurosurgery. The historical context and their individual experiences also

FIG. 6.3.   Dandy, left, and Harvey Cushing at Jekyll Island, Georgia, 1921. From *Dandy of Johns Hopkins* (p. 113), by W. L. Fox, 1984, Baltimore, MD: Lippincott, Williams & Wilkins. Copyright © 1984 by Lippincott, Williams & Wilkins. Reprinted with permission. (This well-known picture was taken by Mrs. Harry R. Slack, Jr.)

contributed to their differing views. This can be illustrated by examining several examples; Dandy's promotion of ventriculography, and the perfection of an operation in the posterior *fossa* region of the brain both for the removal of an acoustic tumor and for the cure of *tic doulereaux* are prime cases.

First, some historical background. During World War I, Dandy began his innovative work in the development of ventriculography while Cushing served as an operating surgeon for Base Hospital No. 5 in France. In June of 1918, Cushing was transferred to Medical Headquarters of the American European Front (A.E.F.) as senior consultant in Neurosurgery, and remained there until the war's end in December (Cushing, 1934, pp. ix–x). In January 1919, Cushing was ordered to England to oversee the reconstruction of Base Hospitals. There, he witnessed the

> tragic aftermath of the war for the returning heroes. First, most found someone younger and more vigorous than themselves holding down their former jobs. Many disillusioned veterans were seen literally begging for work. Not the least disillusioned were middle-aged medical officers entitled to wear four blue chevrons on their sleeves, perhaps even a wound stripe or two and some pieces of ribbon on their breast. Home again, but broken in spirit after their four wasted years, they must start in once more at the bottom, replace their out-of-date office equipment and try to recapture some of their lost practice if it ever could be captured. It was a depressing time. . . . (Cushing, 1934, p. 507)

On February 20th, 1919, Cushing embarked on his trip home, which was completed in early April of that year. When he returned, he too was to find that much had changed in the 4 years that he was away (Pinkus, 2000). Cushing's vast operative experience in World War I reinforced the validity of his previous mandate: to standardize procedures so as to train a competent cadre of neurosurgeons. One of his most visible means of doing this was to launch harsh criticism of Walter Dandy, MD.

Dandy, who had remained on the home front, focused on ways to bring new procedures into the field of neurosurgery. Once he experienced personal success at a procedure, he tended to report the success without cautiously warning others of its inherent danger. In 1917, he devised the innovative procedure known as ventriculography that involved injecting air into the ventricles before taking an x-ray of the brain, and proved invaluable in identifying the location and size of an intracranial mass. Scarff (1955) wrote that it "made accessible to direct surgical attack fully 30 or 40 per cent of the intracranial tumors which previously had been unlocalizable by any clinical method of examination . . ." (p. 444). After perfecting his technique Dandy reported his findings at the American Association of Neurological Surgeons meeting, in 1922. However, Cushing challenged him in public and requested a full statistical report of his mortality and morbidity rate. Dandy was frustrated and felt undermined (Fox, 1984). Actually, he was reporting the most important neurosurgical technique of the century.

Dandy published his results that spoke to Cushing's requests, 1 year later. Referring to ventriculography, he stated:

> It is very dangerous. There has been a tremendous mortality from its use. However, if judiciously used and only by one thoroughly skilled in intracranial surgery, the danger is minimal. I had three deaths at the beginning of the series. Since then, I have had none . . . certainly the danger in proper hands is small compared to the danger attending cranial operations based on guesswork. (Dandy, 1923; see Fig. 6.4)

Following Dandy's report, there was a discussion that focused on examining his statistics critically to decide whether cerebral pneumography helps in the localization of brain tumors. In a commentary it was said that "We have to balance its value against its faults" (Dandy, 1923, p. 613). At this time, contradictions in Dandy's published statistics were shown. His honesty was questioned again (in print!) and the famous surgeon was forced to explain the discrepancies.

Dandy's outstanding surgical skills were regarded as criteria against which to evaluate other surgeons. If Dandy could do ventriculography without mortality, it was said that "in hands other than Dandy's, the death rate was 3%" (Dandy, 1923, p. 613). Moreover, it was said that if this was the mortality rate in the hands of an average neurological surgeon, it must have a larger mortality among general surgeons. "We must not allow cerebral pneumography to suggest to the uninitiated a rule of thumb and simple way of locating brain tumors. We must warn of the mortality and the need of experience in making as well as interpreting cerebral pneumogram" (Dandy, 1923, p. 614; Pinkus, 1996).

Dandy fueled further controversy when he reported his preliminary results for a new operation: the complete removal of a tumor of the 8th cranial nerve (acoustic neuroma) at the base of the skull (Dandy, 1922). Attempting a difficult and risky suboccipital exposure, Dandy described complete success based on a single case report. Cushing wrote a scathing letter to the Johns Hopkins journal editor claiming that both Dandy and the editor acted irresponsibly in publishing this case without reference to the larger series complete with operative mortality figures and end results. In a personal letter to Dandy, he stated "after all, it is as important for you as it is for me that you stand in a high plane of professional ethics" (Fox, 1984, pp. 162–163). Dandy was shocked. He defended his report as merely staking claim to the procedure, clearly a major issue for him. Ei-

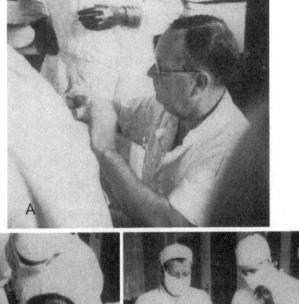

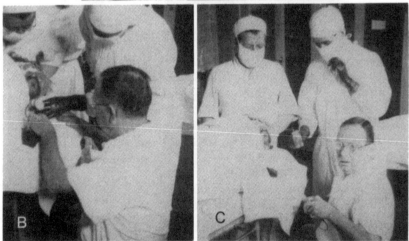

FIG. 6.4. Rare scenes of Dandy later in his career performing a ventriculogram (A, B, C). From *Dandy of Johns Hopkins* (p. 101), by W. L. Fox, 1984, Baltimore, MD: Lippincott, Williams & Wilkins. Copyright © 1984 by Lippincott, Williams & Wilkins. Reprinted with permission.

ther he was unaware that others might use his description and operate on unsuspecting patients, or he simply did not accept responsibility for the actions of others (Pinkus, 2000).

These examples of Dandy's work illustrate a standard of excellence that is quite different from that espoused by Cushing. Much of the discrepancy is attributable to Dandy's view of individual responsibility in neurosurgery. Dandy admitted to being an "iconoclast" and enjoyed the position of being an innovator. He held himself to a high level of excellence and when he taught residents, he followed the same strict hierarchical system of teaching as Cushing, with one major difference. Dandy never allowed an assistant to operate "inside the brain" when he was present. They could participate in the general surgical technique of opening the skull, but once the dura was exposed, Dandy took over, and the resident observed (Fox, 1984, pp. 162–163). By performing each and every technical maneuver personally, he took full responsibility both for the errors committed and for his triumphs.

This observational teaching technique implied that when assistants graduated and operated on their own, they too would assume full responsibility for their surgical errors and triumphs. To amplify this point, Dandy left the operating room when the chief resident took over a case. Moreover, he rarely admitted to mistakes in his published work. Even when he disclosed mortality statistics he minimized them by implying that they were part of a normal learning curve (Pinkus, 1996). Whereas Cushing favored conventional approaches in surgery to ensure that his techniques were accessible to all, Dandy utilized his remarkable surgical skills to perfect treatments that were too difficult to perform for all but the best neurosurgeons. Because Dandy was technically gifted as a surgeon, he was able to develop and perform extremely complex operations while maintaining morbidity and mortality statistics comparable to those of average neurosurgeons performing neurosurgical procedures of average difficulty. Dandy was less concerned with setting the standard of excellence in neurosurgery at a baseline level accessible to all practitioners. He held himself to a standard of excellence that was beyond the reach of all but a few other extremely talented surgeons and espoused the notion that the field should be limited to those who could follow his lead.

EXCELLENCE IN A SOCIAL AND PROFESSIONAL CONTEXT

Any new interpretation of nature, whether a discovery or a theory, emerges first in the mind of one or a few individuals. It is they who first learn to see science and the world differently. . . .

—Kuhn (1962, p. 144)

Contemporaries of Cushing and Dandy described their verbal jousting at professional meetings and disagreements in print as evidence of a feud between mentor and student. This "folklore" has become part of neuro-surgery's history. When one examines the feud within a context of professionalization, however, it becomes evident that the two held differ-ent visions of excellence for the field. The combination of views enabled neurological surgery to progress and develop. Both Cushing and Dandy agreed, for example, that guesswork was no basis for surgery. During his entire professional lifetime, Cushing had tried to discredit the blind ex-ploration of the brain, insisting instead on a thorough understanding of neurology as a prerequisite for neurosurgical training. His fear was about whether incompetent surgeons would try dangerous innovative proce-dures (such as ventriculography) as a fast way of diagnosis, and whether his strict educational criteria would be overlooked. Actually, it was not pos-sible to prevent this technique from being used by surgeons. However, for Cushing, a less harmful way was the traditional way of doing careful neu-rological examination (Pinkus, 1996). His vision of excellence for the field was closely tied to the idea of replication; acceptable surgical procedures, for Cushing, were those that could be successfully replicated by all neuro-surgeons with minimal morbidity and mortality.

Whereas Cushing preferred to take a rather conservative approach to establishing standards of excellence, Dandy had little patience for it. By innovatively injecting air into the ventricles of the brain and then taking an x-ray, Dandy actually took much of the guesswork out of localizing an intracranial mass. Apparently, Dandy was not the only neurosurgeon who favored an approach quite different from that of Cushing. One such prac-titioner, while examining Dandy's statistical inconsistencies, claimed that "the neurological surgeons have been too much to the right politically speaking! They have not had enough of the radical about them. Dr. Dandy is on the extreme left! That is a good thing. It is courageous conduct which will make neurological surgery a living thing" (Dandy, 1923, p. 614; Pinkus, 1996). This evaluation of Dandy's standard of excellence indicates that Dandy's work was viewed by some as promoting vitality and creative expansion in the field of neurosurgery. At the same time, however, it must be noted that the adoption of Dandy's surgical innovations (and thus the expansion enabled by such innovations) occurred via the hands of a very select group of talented neurosurgeons. In describing the creative proce-dure he developed to treat *tic douloureux*, even Dandy, with his arrogant manner, recognized the high level of skill required to operate in the pos-terior fossa. While boasting of his operation's ease, its safety, and its qual-ity results, he also cautioned that "this degree of safety exists only in the hands of an expert. It certainly is not a procedure to be undertaken by anyone except an expert and one who has the proper equipment" (Dandy, 1928, p. 734). Oral accounts of Walter Dandy's appraisal of his contemporary neurosurgeons suggest that by "expert" Dandy was referring to one or two men whom he considered to be competent surgeons (King, 1981; Pinkus, 1984, p. 626).

Although Cushing and Dandy had differing views regarding the methodology of establishing standards of excellence in neurosurgery, these differences were masked in the larger public's view of the overall excellence of the profession. Both men were looked to as experts and their individual differences were dwarfed as academic standards of training gradually began to influence the practice of medicine. Such influence is clearly visible when examining legal cases from this period. The publication of Cushing's "epoch-making" book on pituitary tumors, which contained the results of 47 cases in 1912, symbolized the progress he and his fellow reformers had made in setting new standards for practice. His route of access to tumors set the standard for the next 15 years, reduced mortality from about 30% to 5%, and "offered patients a reasonable chance of prolonged or even permanent improvement from a state of seriously impaired vision" (Horrax & Williams, 1955, pp. 84–85). Recognition in 1915 by legal experts of these standards reconfirmed that they were widely publicized. In that year, the Supreme Court of North Dakota heard *Van Woert v. Modern Woodmen of America* (1915), an insurance appeal by the widow of a man who had died of a "tumor of the brain" (p. 225). Van Woert's widow appealed The Modern Woodmen of America's refusal to pay $3,000 of her husband's insurance benefits. In applying for these benefits, Mr. Van Woert had to answer 35 questions, 2 concerning what we now refer to as a "preexisting condition" (p. 225). Although he had been treated for vision problems, he answered "No" to a query regarding whether or not he had been treated by or consulted a physician in the past 7 years concerning a personal ailment. He also specifically answered that he did not have a tumor and failed to supply the names of physicians and dates of treatment. The widow claimed her late husband had misunderstood the cause of his vision problems and did not intend to deceive the policyholders.

Testimony at trial included detailed evidence from three physicians who diagnosed and treated Mr. Van Woert from 1907 to his death in 1911: Dr. Carr, MD, generalist, Dr. C. E. Riggs, "a specialist in the line of neuro diagnosis," and Harvey Cushing, now of the Department of Neural Surgery at Harvard Medical School (having left Johns Hopkins University). Because the insurer probably would not have issued the policy had it know about the man's condition, the Court held that the withholding of information "even if unintentional" was material and vitiated the policy (Van Woert is documented to have believed his condition originated from a kick in the head by a horse; *Van Woert v. Modern Woodmen of America*, 1915, p. 228). Thus, Mrs. Van Woert never received her $3,000.

This case attests to the influence Cushing had in setting a standard of practice for the field. The court relied on the combined and unanimous testimony of Van Woert's three physicians, specifically, the detailed medical expertise of Harvey Cushing. After citing Cushing's positions at Harvard Medical College and Johns Hopkins University, the court emphasized his expertise. Cushing had written "a book upon disorders of the pituitary body and [was] one of the recognized authorities in the United States upon the subject. He testified that in his opinion Van Woert had been suffering from the disorder, to wit, tumor of the pituitary body, for many years, and that the same was in existence as early as 1907" (*Van Woert v. Modern Woodmen of America*, 1915, p. 226). Cushing's testimony, and that of the others, demonstrated a shared knowledge of the details of the pituitary tumor (Pinkus, 2000).

Approximately 15 years later, in 1933, the Superior Court of Pennsylvania heard an insurance appeal, *Ellis v. Jones & Laughlin Steel Co.*, in which the petitioner sought compensation after her husband died from a head injury. The man was working on a locomotive at the steel plant, when he fell 8 feet and struck his head. Prior to the accident, he was known to have "nickel sized" sarcoma, but after the fall the tumor swelled to the size of a "small hen's egg" (*Ellis v. Jones & Laughlin Steel Co.*, 1933, pp. 264–265). The legal question was whether the fall and the treatment he received from the company doctor, from a local surgeon, and finally from a resident in Walter Dandy's Johns Hopkins clinic "so aggravated and accelerated the growth of the sarcoma from which [decedent] was then suffering as to be the predisposing cause of his death" (*Ellis v. Jones & Laughlin Steel Co.*, 1933, p. 264). The court affirmed the decision of the Commonwealth Court, which awarded insurance compensation to Ellis's widow, but the company appealed the decision (*Ellis v. Jones & Laughlin Steel Co.*, 1933). The case remained on the docket for a variety of reasons and was not heard again until 9 years later, setting a precedent for allowing medical testimony from experts not present at the original trial.

There were three "original players" in the court drama: Dr. Charles H. Gano, the defendant's "company" physician; Dr. H. E. McGuire, chief surgeon for the defendant at the South Side Hospital; and Dr. Deryl Hart, assistant resident surgeon at Johns Hopkins Hospital, where the patient was finally transferred several days after the accident. An excerpt from the original testimony by Dr. McGuire sets the stage:

> There was a swelling there about half the size of an egg, which had a small incision in it. The man gave me a history of having this lump a couple of years, and I thought probably it was a cyst which became larger. On cutting through the scalp I came right into brain tissue, with a terrific hemorrhage. I did not proceed any farther: I passed some deep sutures through the skull,

closing the wound, which stopped the hemorrhage. Then we took X-rays which disclosed he had a tumor of the brain which ate its way through the skull on account of the pressure. I told the family about operating on the man, and that I refused to do it because I thought the man would die. (*Ellis v. Jones & Laughlin Steel Co.*, 169A 264, p. 263; Pinkus, 2000, p. 148)

The size of the growth increased and was twice as large when Ellis left as it was when he entered the hospital. Dr. Hart testified that when Ellis entered Johns Hopkins Hospital he was hardly able to walk and was suffering with intracranial pressure from osteosarcoma of the skull and was vomiting. It was Dr. Hart's opinion that Ellis could not survive more than a few days without the sarcoma being removed. Accordingly, an operation was performed, but the tumor had caused such extensive damage that a successful operation was impossible. In 1932, post hoc testimony by neurosurgeons Dr. L. H. Landon, Dr. Lester Hollender, and Dr. Walter Dandy led the court to conclude:

We find from all the evidence that the blow to the back of decedent's head on December 16, 1924, while in the course of his employment, caused a swelling of the pre-existing sarcoma as the result of a hemorrhage occasioned by the blow. We further find that the incision made into the sarcoma by Dr. Charles H. Gano on the same day aggravated the growth of this sarcoma, and that the operation of Dr. H. E. McGuire in cutting into the sarcoma, the scalp, and the brain tissue, although with reasonable cause, precipitated a terrific hemorrhage and greatly accelerated the growth of the sarcoma, and that the accidental injury and surgical interference were the instant and accelerating cause of the growth of the sarcoma as to be the predisposing and superinducing cause of the death of the decedent some two months and nine days following the accident. (*Ellis v. Jones & Laughlin Steel Co.*, 1933, p. 268; Pinkus, 2000, p. 148)

The testimonies of the neurosurgical experts resulted in an award of compensation in the amount of $4,142.28 (Pinkus, 2000). Although Cushing and Dandy valued different methods of defining standards of excellence in neurosurgery, these cases indicate their intraprofessional differences were not aired in a court of law. Standard procedures for the treatment of pituitary tumors as well as an intracranial sarcoma had been developed.

CONCLUSION: AN ONGOING ETHICAL DEBATE

Professionally, we owe it to ourselves to continue to learn new techniques and to be aware of new developments that could benefit our patients. None of us can be innovators in all aspects of neurosurgery, but we should not wait until we have missed the crest of the wave to support better techniques.

—Rekate (1997, p. 478)

To this day, neurosurgery is characterized by the two opposing yet complementary trends involving replication and innovation that were epitomized by Cushing and Dandy. Consider the fact that neurosurgeons have, within the past several years, developed the first successful "treatment protocol" for brain trauma. Reviewing why agreement in the field has taken so long to standardize, Gladwell (1996) commented that "the complexity and mystery of the brain has led to a culture that rewards intuition, and has thus convinced each neurosurgeon that his own experience is as valid as anyone else's" (p. 34). This tendency is Dandy's legacy. Yet, Cushing's goal of introducing safe and well-understood procedures, based on scientific evidence, is clearly fostered by "organized neurosurgery" and its success in creating a collaborative environment for neurosurgeons to work within (Pinkus, 1996, p. 22; Haines, personal communication, June 8, 1997).

These complementary trends are also visible in recent debates within neurosurgery regarding the possibility of creating specialized Boards or Certifications for subspecialties such as pediatric neurosurgery. Some neurosurgeons have worked hard to innovate procedures in neurosurgery and tailor them to the anatomical needs of pediatric patients. Insofar as these refined procedures benefit pediatric patients and lower mortality and morbidity rates, regard for quality of care indicates that these specialized pediatric procedures should become the new standard for pediatric neurosurgery. However, not all neurosurgeons have sufficient opportunity to perform and perfect the pediatric procedures. If it is time to reassess standards of excellence in neurosurgery in order to account for recent advances in various subspecialties within the field, where should the new standards lie? Neurosurgeons must decide how to ethically integrate innovation in neurosurgical techniques with the establishment of standards of excellence to enable safe replication and stability within their field. "If this process creates great distances between the leaders, innovators, and teachers in general and pediatric neurosurgery," cautions Rekate (1997), "both disciplines will be diminished and our goals of providing the best possible care for our patients will go unrealized" (p. 481).

Such trends are not unique to neurosurgery. In general surgery, the notion of superspecialization demonstrates the tension between the complementary trends pioneered by Cushing and Dandy in neurosurgery. For example, the Shouldice Hospital outside Toronto is a medical center whose 12 surgeons perform only hernia repair operations. Many of the surgeons at Shouldice would not be allowed to practice surgery in an American hospital because they have not completed the 9 or more years of education required for accreditation as a surgeon. However, through replication and cooperation, these surgeons complete hernia operations in half the time required by surgeons in most hospitals and they do it at half the cost. With a remarkably low recurrence rate of 1%, Shouldice Hospital may be the best place in the world to have a hernia repaired (Gawande, 1998). This somewhat extreme example demonstrates the "replication with high quality results" so cherished by Cushing, although these results are achieved by surgeons who have not completed the rigorous training espoused by Cushing. These surgeons and other workers at Shouldice have also found innovative methods by which to cut down on costs and improve results in hernia surgeries. However, such superspecialization also represents a rather fragmented approach to raising standards of excellence in surgery.

We are left asking the question: Is excellence in subspecialty surgical training defined as the ability to replicate safe, tested procedures, or need it also include the ability to tackle innovative and risky operations? Should the primary focus of surgical education be on upgrading the lowest common denominator to a standard of comparative safety; or should it be to create a relatively small, recognizable group of quality? Perhaps, it is a blend of each: an "essential tension" of values that sanctions some practitioners in the field to push ahead to an uncharted ground while others replicate the field as defined by their mentors (Kuhn, 1977). Combined, these values guard against stagnation on the one hand, and, on the other, offer some boundaries for those who would irresponsibly operate on unsuspecting patients.

Neurosurgery as a subspecialty gained full professional status during the years 1890 to 1940. Its history, therefore, provides a specific example of how the question of setting standards of excellence in surgical training was resolved. Focusing attention on the work of two prestigious surgeons, Harvey Cushing and Walter Dandy, during the years 1890 to 1940, we argue that the definition of professional excellence is in part a politically negotiated, context-driven, and value-laden concept. Harvey Cushing elected to pursue the task of pioneering the new surgical subspecialty, neurosurgery. The context within which he worked was one in which a general mistrust of medicine was rampant in society and the first wave of malpractice was evident. New developments in science created opportunities for real progress to be made in the profession but the pioneering of a new surgical subspecialty would have to take these societal realities into account. Cushing thus sought to create a field that was safe, replicable by example, and dedicated to careful training in both technique and moral character. His goal was to create an environment in which neurosurgeons in training could develop and refine their skills safely and with minimal risk to surgical patients.

Walter Dandy was one of Cushing's first students. Under Cushing's guidance Dandy easily mastered the methodical replication of tested procedures. When he completed his training, however, he regarded these procedures as a baseline from which to try innovative approaches. Dandy's goal was to push neurosurgery into new and uncharted ground, much as

Cushing had done 20 years earlier. His creative genius and technical skill enabled him to tackle operations and develop new techniques that were unattainable for most surgeons (including Cushing). He also benefited from Cushing's success in establishing neurosurgery as a specialty field that could help patients. Dandy, furthermore, worked in an era when surgery in general (and brain surgery in particular) held a place of "awe" in the general public (Porter, 1997). When Dandy served as an expert witness to a trial he had no problem criticizing the judgment of his professional colleagues. Not all surgeons, he suggested, were equal. Board requirements aside, excellence was, in his definition, a rare achievement.

This chapter serves to contextualize the debate surrounding the desire to establish an operable baseline by which to measure excellence. It has used the historical development of neurosurgery as a case study. Ideally, such a discussion will help to illuminate similar trends which shape the pursuit of excellence in the educational processes of other professions, and will shed some perspective on the current interest in creating further subspecialties within the field of neurosurgery itself. Thomas Kuhn (1977), reflecting on science in general, proposed that the explanation of progress "must be a description of a value system, an ideology together with an analysis of the institutions through which that system is transmitted and enforced. . . . Knowing what scientists value," he contends, "we may hope to understand what problems they will undertake and what choices they will make in particular circumstances" (p. 235). Residency training has been characterized as "moral training" (Bosk, 1979). We suggest that it is, in fact, moral training for excellence. A tacit ethic is transmitted from experienced practitioners to naive recruits-in-training, which includes a basic and agreed on respect for the unforgiving biological nature of the nervous system. Starting from this tenet there are residencies that favor Cushing's model, and those that follow Dandy's. Given that progress in both scientific understanding and in operative technique is a process that evolves over time, it is understandable why excellence in a profession would be defined as a blend of these two traits.

ACKNOWLEDGMENT

Portions of this chapter were reprinted from "Politics, Paternalism, and the Rise of the Neurosurgeon: The Evolution of Moral Reasoning," by R. L. Pinkus, 1996, *Medical Humanities Review, 10*(2), pp. 20–44. Reprinted with permission of *Medical Humanities Review*.

REFERENCES

American Heritage Dictionary (3rd ed.). (1997). Boston: Houghton Mifflin.
Anonymous. (1909). Medical education and state boards of registration. *Journal of the American Medical Association, 53*(7), 580–585.

Bailly, P. (1904, January 9). Case of brain tumor with autopsy. *New York Neurological Society*, 92–93.

Black, P. M. (Ed.). (1992). *The surgical art of Harvey Cushing*. Park Ridge, IL: American Association of Neurological Surgeons.

Bosk, C. (1979). *Forgive and remember: Managing medical failure*. Chicago: University of Chicago Press.

Brown, R. (1979). *Rockefeller medicine men: Medicine and capitalism in America*. Berkeley: University of California Press.

Coughlin, R. (1920). *The hospital interne*. Paper presented at the Hospital Surgeon's Association, January 9, 1917, Brooklyn, NY.

Cushing, H. (1902). Some experimental and clinical observations concerning states of increased intracranial tension. *The American Journal of Medical Sciences, 124*(3), 375–400.

Cushing, H. (1903). The blood pressure reaction of acute cerebral compression, illustrated as cases of intracranial hemorrhage. *American Journal of Medical Science, 125*(16), 1038–1044.

Cushing, H. (1905a). Concerning surgical interventions for the intracranial hemorrhages of the newborn. *American Journal of Medical Sciences*, 563–581.

Cushing, H. (1905b). The special field of neurological surgery. *Bulletin of the Johns Hopkins Hospital, 16*(168), 77–87.

Cushing, H. (1910). The special field of neurological surgery: Five years later. *Bulletin of the Johns Hopkins Hospital, 21*(236), 325–339.

Cushing, H. (1931). Experiences with the cerebellar astrocytomas. *Surgery, Gynecology and Obstetrics, 52*, 129–130.

Cushing, H. (1934, reprinted 1936). *From a surgeon's journal*. U.S.: Little Brown and Co. in association with The Atlantic Monthly Co.

Dandy, W. E. (1922). An operation for the total extirpation of tumors in the cerebello-pontine angle: A preliminary report. *Bulletin of the Johns Hopkins Hospital, 33*, 344–345.

Dandy, W. (1923). Localization of brain tumors by cerebral pneumography. *American Journal Roentgenology Radium Therapy, 10*(8), 611–661.

Dandy, W. (1928). An operation for the cure of tic douloureux: Partial section of the sensory root at the pons. *Archives of Surgery, 18*, 687–734.

Denzel, J. (1971). *Genius with a scalpel*. New York: Simon & Schuster.

Ellis v. Jones & Laughlin Steel Co., Vol. 169A (Supreme Court of Pennsylvania 1933).

Faden, R. R., & Beauchamp, T. L. (1986). *A history and theory of informed consent*. New York: Oxford University Press.

Foss, H. L. (1931). A plan for the systematic instruction and supervision of interns and resident physicians. *Journal of American College of Surgeons, 6*, 29–31.

Fox, W. L. (1984). *Dandy of Johns Hopkins*. Baltimore: Williams & Wilkins.

Gawande, A. (1998, March 30). No mistake. *The New Yorker*, 74–81.

Gladwell, M. (1996). Conquering coma. *The New Yorker, 68*, no. 20: 34–39.

Greenblatt, S. (1997). Harvey Cushing and the issue of surgical subspecialization: An historical perspective. *Surgical Neurology, 47*(4), 412–413.

Hirsch, J. (1997). The development of pediatric neurosurgery in Paris. *Child's Nervous System, 13*, 465–470.

Horrax, V., & Williams, H. (1955). *Cushing: History of neurological surgery*. Baltimore: Johns Hopkins University Press.

Horsley, V. (1894, July). On the mode of death in cerebral compression, and its prevention. *Quarterly Medical Journal*, 305–309.

Kessel, R. A. (1972). Higher education and the nation's health: A review of the Carnegie Commission Report on medical education. *Journal of Law and Economics, 15*(1), 115–127.

King, A. (1981, February). *Reminiscences of Walter Dandy*. Paper presented to the Mid-Atlantic Neurosurgical Society, Philadelphia.

King, L. (1982). The "Old Code" of medical ethics and some problems it had to face. *Journal of the American Medical Association, 248*(18), 2329–2333.

Kuhn, T. (1962). *The structure of scientific revolutions*. Chicago: University of Chicago Press.

Kuhn, T. (1977). *The essential tension: Selected studies in scientific tradition and change*. Chicago: University of Chicago Press.

McEwan, W. (1893). *Pyogenic infective diseases of the brain and spinal cord*. Glasgow, Scotland: J. Maclehose & Sons.

Pernick, M. (1985). *A calculus of suffering: Pain, professionalism, and anesthesia in nineteenth-century America*. New York: Columbia University Press.

Pevehouse, B. C. (1984). Residency training in neurological surgery, 1934–1984: Evolution over 50 years of trial and tribulation. *Journal of Neurosurgery, 61*, 999–1004.

Pinkus, R. (2000). Learning to keep a cautious tongue: The reporting of mistakes in neurosurgery, 1890–1930. In S. Rubin & L. Zoloft (Eds.), *Margin of error: The ethics of mistakes in the practice of medicine* (pp. 131–153). Hagerstown, MD: University Publishing Group.

Pinkus, R. L. (1984). Innovation in neurosurgery: Walter Dandy in his day. *Neurosurgery, 14*(5), 623–631.

Pinkus, R. L. (1996). Politics, paternalism, and the rise of the neurosurgeon: The evolution of moral reasoning. *Medical Humanities Review, 10*(2), 20–44.

Porter, R. (1997). *The greatest benefit to mankind: A medical history of humanity*. London: HarperCollins.

Rekate, H. (1997). Thoughts on the present and future of pediatric neurosurgery: Skull base surgery, spiral instrumentation, and neuroendoscopy. *Child's Nervous System, 13*, 476–481.

Rosenberg, C. E. (1987). *The care of strangers: The rise of America's hospital system*. New York: Basic Books.

Scarff, J. (1955). Fifty years of neurosurgery, 1905–1955. *International Abstracts of Surgery, 101*(5), 417–513.

Sohl, P., & Bassford, H. (1986). Codes of medical ethics: Traditional foundations and contemporary practice. *Social Science & Medicine, 22*(11), 1175–1179.

Stevens, R. (1971). *American medicine and the public interest*. New Haven: Yale University Press.

Stevens, R. (1989). *In sickness and in wealth: American hospitals in the twentieth century*. New York: Basic Books.

Van Woert v. Modern Woodmen of America, Vol. 151 N.W. (Supreme Court of North Dakota 1915).

Waitzkin, H. (1980, July/August). Medical philanthropies: The band-aid treatment? *The Sciences*, 25–28.

Chapter 7

Achieving Excellence
in Institutions

Herbert A. Simon
Carnegie Mellon University

This volume is concerned with the sorts of social and personal conditions that promote excellence. Many, if not most, of the achievements that individuals and societies value cannot be achieved by people working individually, but only by groups of people who work together in organizations to reach their goals. Our children are educated in schools, our clothing, furniture, food, cars, and computers are manufactured by factories and distributed by stores. Our illnesses are treated in hospitals. Churches, hotels and restaurants, football teams, fire departments, EPA and OSHA—the list of organizations that minister to our needs and wants is almost endless. Thus, our concern with the excellence of members of a society must extend to a concern with the excellence of the organizations through which the society accomplishes its goals, and thereby, through which the society's members accomplish theirs.

But the story must be carried even one step further. In organizations, there are members whose direct contribution to the organization's product is to promote the excellence of the organization itself. They are called executives, managers, administrators, or sometimes entrepreneurs, or leaders. A theory of organizations must explain also the role of leaders in achieving their excellence. In this chapter, I ask what qualities of excellence a person must possess and exercise in order to use social institutions effectively to promote excellence.

I draw on such scientific knowledge on this topic as is available, but much of what I know about it is anecdotal, drawn from my own experience in organizations that, to my great good fortune, turned out to be highly entrepreneurial in their outlook and behavior. In those organizations, I have had the opportunity to be associated with colleagues who possessed high levels of entrepreneurial skill, and I offer as case studies some of their organizational achievements with which I am familiar. In particular, I have something to say about Lee Bach, the founding dean of the Graduate School of Industrial Administration at Carnegie Mellon University, Allen Newell, my close associate in research for over 40 years, Bob Glaser, cofounder and long-time director of the Learning Research and Development Center at the University of Pittsburgh, and Clarence E. Ridley, my first boss and principal mentor in entrepreneurship. The first three were associated with organizations that flourished by exploiting new ideas and technologies that had their origins in World War II. My association with the fourth just preceded the war.

THE TECHNICAL DIMENSIONS OF EXPERTISE

I will assume that we are generally agreed on the characteristics of persons who exhibit excellence in their lives and work. In recent years research on expertise has greatly buttressed with solid empirical evidence our understanding of these characteristics and how they arise (Ericsson, 1996).

First, there are the "technical" dimensions of expertise: the expert knowledge of a domain and the specific skills needed to use that knowledge (Richman, Gobet, Staszewski, & Simon, 1996). We know today that the world-class expert in any domain has stored in memory a large stock of knowledge, in the form of "chunks," that may number 100,000 or upwards. We know that it takes 10 years or more, no matter what the expert's native talents, to acquire these chunks. Each chunk enables the expert to recognize patterns that occur in the situations that professional life presents, and, upon their recognition, to access the knowledge stored in memory that gives meaning to the chunk and suggests actions that are relevant to its presence. As an example, we may think of the expert physician's chunks as including the patterns of symptoms that will be recognized in a patient, which, when seen, evoke a Latin name for the disease and knowledge about prognosis and treatment.

We know that the expert's knowledge, associated with these recognizable patterns and evoked when they are present, contains strategies for dealing with many common situations, and search strategies for solving the problems when appropriate actions are not immediately evoked. Thus, the expert handles problems of practice by recognition (sometimes known as "intuition" or "insight") of common patterns, and by selective search of alternatives when ready solutions are not evoked by recognition.

We may think of these abilities and skills as constituting the substantive dimension of expertise, and hence of excellence.

INSTITUTION BUILDING: THE ENTREPRENEUR

In some cases the qualities just surveyed comprise the whole menu of skills needed by a world-class scientist, who may work essentially alone. Even this is a simplification, for no scientist can accumulate the knowledge needed for innovative work without deep acquaintance with the contents of the "blackboard" of publication and public presentation that records and reports what is already known. Writing on that blackboard, where all may read, and reading from it in order to build on the work of others, are the key social activities in the fraternity of science. But scientists need not be experts on organizations (although we must remember that Newton did manage the British Mint for many years, and presided over the Royal Society; perhaps Einstein is the better example of the "pure" scientist).

However, another, and very important, dimension of excellence does require expertise in working with other people and in and with organizations. We become particularly aware of its requirements when it involves not only managing organizations effectively, but also creating and nurturing them. Today, we call persons exercising the latter skills entrepreneurs: persons, whether scientists or business executives or government administrators, who are skilled and successful in building institutions; who can conceive of a system of useful activities that does not now exist, and who can bring together the human, physical, and financial resources that will create the system and carry it to the point where it is self-sustaining. Entrepreneurial skills are needed, not just at the birth of an organization, but at all points in its history when new opportunities and new challenges must be recognized as they present themselves, or must be sought out when they lurk in the shadows.

There is a rich anecdotal literature about entrepreneurs in business, political institutions, and science, but it is mostly biographical and autobiographical and rich in words and phrases like "inspiration," "flash of insight," "intuition," and "persistence," without much hint of how such events and processes actually occur and how they might be nurtured. Serious systematic research on entrepreneurship is just beginning. However, we can guess ("hypothesize" is the more dignified term) at what some of that research will reveal. It will reveal that the entrepreneur must possess or acquire extensive knowledge about the domain of the proposed activity; must store the 100,000 chunks so that opportunities and problems can be recognized and their implications recalled or discovered promptly. It will reveal that the entrepreneur must have good problem-solving skills in order to use that knowledge. More conjectural are the general abilities and skills that entrepreneurs need for effectiveness in building organizations.

Some of the required skills can be learned in a business school or school of public administration (and sometimes are). One can learn about debits and credits, problems of cash flow, making a business plan, marketing strategies, departmentalization, and many other business practices. (Or one can hire, as entrepreneurs sometimes do, people who know these things.) Other skills are not often taught; a number of important ones, central to the entrepreneur's role, have been captured in recent doctoral research at Carnegie Mellon University, by Sarasvathy Krishnamurthy (1998). I mention a few of them.

The entrepreneur is viewed, correctly I think, as an innovator. But to innovate is not necessarily to invent. The English poet Alexander Pope (*Bartlett's Quotations*, 14th ed., 1968, p. 403a) put it well when he said, "Be not the first by whom the new is tried, / nor yet the last to lay the old aside." Krishnamurthy's study shows that entrepreneurship involves finding the path from idea to successful application, which is often as hard as, or harder than, finding the idea. And following that path often brings about large changes in the idea itself—the product—as well as changes in the markets it is aimed to reach, and the ways in which the new company is to be organized and financed. The entrepreneur is skillful at choosing at the forks in the path, indeed, in detecting the possibilities for such forks to remove difficulties or expand opportunities.

As Krishnamurthy also shows, successful entrepreneurs are not interested in predicting the future; they are interested in shaping it. A systematic market survey may predict the size of the potential market for a particular product in a particular public, but the more relevant question for the entrepreneur is whether there are modifications in the product or in the public that will substantially increase market size. Moreover, the successful entrepreneur is not a dreamer who imagines that the future can be pressed into any desired shape. "Shaping the future" implies close attention to the possible and the feasible, and the feasibility of an idea is highly sensitive to the time when it is proposed.

THE GRADUATE SCHOOL OF INDUSTRIAL ADMINISTRATION

That brings me to the first of my examples of entrepreneurship: Dean George Leland Bach's stewardship for a decade of the new business school (GSIA) at what was then the Carnegie Institute of Technology, now Carnegie Mellon University (Simon, 1995, 1996). Important to the story is the fact that the new school was established by a liberal endowment at an institution that had had no business school, and only a very few faculty who were expert in economics or management studies. This meant that the school could begin without presuppositions about what such a school should be.

Also important is the fact that the school began life in 1949, just at the time when new quantitative tools for management decision, developed during World War II for military use under the label of "operations research," were beginning to be turned to civilian use, and just at the time also when the behavioral sciences were developing new theories of human relations in organizations, and applications of these theories to management. This meant that the school had an alternative (or some mixture of two alternatives) to the traditional business school curriculum, and could blend them in any proportion.

Bach, although himself an economist with little mathematical training, was wise enough and strong enough to see the opportunities of these new developments, and to recruit a faculty who brought expertness in the new areas of knowledge and few preconceptions about what business education ought to be. At the same time, like the excellent entrepreneur that he was, Bach maintained some measure of balance between the new and the old, so that the new school, as it developed, could gain acceptance from prospective students and their prospective employers, as well as from other business schools as a part of their community.

As a result, within a matter of 4 or 5 years GSIA had acquired a reputation of excellence that it has never lost, and a major impact on the reshaping of American (and foreign) business schools over the next generation, to the extent that it gradually (but not completely) lost a good deal of its uniqueness.

In doing this, Bach exhibited some remarkable qualities. There was a wide participation of faculty in the decisions about the policies and practices of the school, but never any doubt that the dean was in charge: that it was he who had to make the final decisions. Democracy was never carried to the point (or even close to the point) of deciding policy by majority vote. Bach also was notably unintimidated by the mathematical expertise of his faculty, which he wholly lacked. Possibly because of a year of legal training before he took up economics, he had impressive cross-examining skills that enabled him to quiz his colleagues until he induced them to translate their ideas and proposals into plain English. He was never "bowled over," to use one of his favorite phrases, by technical virtuosity. Possibly for this reason, he was wholly comfortable to have strong colleagues around him.

IMPLICATIONS FOR ENTREPRENEURIAL SKILL

So we would have to put close to the top of the list of entrepreneurial skills the skills of shaping a feasible venture and creating an institution that can house it. As we have seen from the findings of Krishnamurthy's (1998) study, the task is not one of building a fixed plan, but of developing an idea step by step, with each successive action providing feedback that signals the need for modifying the plan. Launching a venture is a process of exploring a space, gradually adapting the growing institution to the opportunities that appear in the course of the exploration. It is a little like building a house when the shape and contour of the lot and the solidity of the foundation will become known only as the construction proceeds.

In this process, the entrepreneur is never given (as is the businessperson of the economics textbook) a set of clear alternatives, among which to choose. The new institution and its program must be designed, starting with goals that may themselves be somewhat nebulous, and gradually taking on new commitments and new constraints. There is no thought or possibility of "optimizing," for that would require exactly what is missing—given alternatives from which the choice is to be made, rather than design of new alternatives. In building new institutions, and in adapting them to new situations, the best is frequently the enemy of the good. We must seize promising opportunities because we will never know when the "best" opportunity has presented itself.

In assembling resources for the new organization, human resources are perhaps the most important of all. And one essential characteristic of these human resources is a shared vision of the goals of the new activity: not goals spelled out in terms of a specific program, but goals that can guide the process of search and adaptation and that permit each employee who shares them to participate in this process. Krishnamurthy found that, in building a team, entrepreneurs look for a variety of general and special talents, but they place an especially great stress on "loyalty," by which they typically mean loyalty to a set of ideas, goals, and a path, not to a person. Let me enlarge on that theme, as it is a crucial component of excellence in organizations.

LOYALTY: ORGANIZATIONAL IDENTIFICATION

We humans congratulate ourselves on our endowment of reason, of capabilities for thinking and learning. But in moments of objectivity, we recognize the feebleness of these capabilities in comparison with the complexities of the world in which we live and to which we must adapt. We are creatures of bounded rationality, who must use all of our resources to find acceptable solutions, almost always far short of optimal solutions, to the problems we must solve.

One powerful means we have acquired for going beyond the bounds of our own rationality and multiplying our knowledge and powers of reason is to live in societies, and to share the knowledge and experience of our fellows. Most of what we know and believe is not primarily the product of our own senses and our own encounters with nature but of learning from others. In the course of evolution, we have acquired strong tendencies to accept the teaching and advice that comes from trusted social sources, and an important part of that teaching urges us to work toward the goals of the groups to which we belong. Group identification is a powerful human trait, reinforced by natural selection, which has important consequences for humankind, both highly beneficial and exceedingly harmful (Simon, 1990).

The harmful side of group identification is illustrated by ethnic, religious, and national loyalties which cause and sustain the large-scale fratricide that is endemic over the globe today (and was in times past, as well). The beneficial side is illustrated by the effectiveness of the large organizations that we count on to carry out our work at levels of productivity that are orders of magnitude higher than isolated individuals could attain. High levels of *loyalty, identification, morale*—the three terms are nearly synonymous—are essential to organizational excellence (Simon, 1991). Tangible rewards, monetary and other, are also needed to retain the services of members of organizations, but the enforceable effort that employees will exert in order to secure such rewards constitutes only a fraction of the effort that effective organizations can command and that they require for excellence. Motivation to work is much more than a response to supervision, salaries, and promotions. My second example of excellence in leading organizations focuses on the creation of organizational loyalties.

ORGANIZATIONAL CULTURE

The present strength of the School of Computer Science at CMU is the product of the work of many persons, among whom one would certainly include President Richard Cyert, Allen Newell, and Alan Perlis (first Head of the CS Department). I will also admit to a part in shaping the school, but this chapter is not the place to boast about that. Instead, I have something to say about the role of Newell, and especially his innovative approaches to strengthening the identifications of faculty and students with the school by creating an internal culture that is widely seen as unique. Of course, everyone, in a sense, participated in its creation, and Perlis also made important contributions to it, but Newell became its spokesperson and exemplar (Simon, 1998).

At the center of the culture is the Reasonable Person Principle. Each member of the community (faculty, student, and staff) is assumed to be and encouraged to act as a reasonable person: to use shared goals and reason rather than formal regulations as the guides for decision and behavior. And each is to presume that the others are also acting in this way. The principle is widely discussed and frequently invoked to deal with specific situations. It is obvious to anyone who lives in this environment that the principle makes a significant difference in behavior, and in particular greatly enhances the feeling of common "ownership" of the enterprise. It has helped the organization to weather two decades of steadily tightened financial constraints imposed by the national research funding situation, and to continue to thrive in a much more austere environment than that in which it initially flourished.

I cite the Reasonable Person Principle as just one of the pieces of the ethos that Newell helped instill into the organization. In addition, he was responsible for identifying and urging the importation and development of important new technical innovations. For example, he played a central role in bringing about the computer networking of the CMU campus, so that the university was one of the pioneers in network design and use.

As I have described Allen's characteristics and style elsewhere (Simon, 1996), I will not repeat that description here, beyond noting that he, like Bach, had the inner strength that made him comfortable with strong-minded colleagues, insisted without compromise upon excellence, and looked for opportunities to shape the future. He had no love for organizing for organization's or expansion's sake, and avoided standard administrative responsibilities (e.g., department headships). Nevertheless, the organizations with which he was associated did seem constantly to grow and innovate.

ADAPTING TO A COMPLEX ENVIRONMENT

Feasibility of an organizational vision is defined in terms of the environment to which it has to adapt. In the case of a business firm, the environment consists at least of employers and managers, investors, customers, financial institutions, and governments. Each of these has its own goals and visions of the future, and each must be induced to contribute resources to the organization. A similar list can be constructed for government agencies, perhaps even a longer list, including the various publics that are affected by an agency's programs.

A university probably faces a still more complex environment: all that has been previously stated, together with students and their families and alumni, and in addition, the responsibilities that a university today typically assumes for the welfare of the community in which it resides and in relation to public policy issues in the nation and the world. The short average tenure of college presidents is often attributed, and perhaps correctly, to this complexity.

THE LEARNING RESEARCH AND DEVELOPMENT CENTER

We have an example of academic entrepreneurship in the Learning Research and Development Center at the University of Pittsburgh and Robert Glaser, its first director, that illustrates the environmental complexities of academia. In his graduate education in psychology at the University of Indiana, Glaser encountered B. F. Skinner, himself an entrepreneur of first magnitude, who was already experimenting with (very primitive) computers used as (very primitive) teaching machines. In that period, it was quite unusual for experimental psychologists to concern themselves with the practicalities of education, for the potential alliance of basic and applied science was not well recognized. In fact, the idea of such an alliance was nearly universally rejected by basic scientists in psychology, who saw discovery as moving on a higher intellectual plane than application. It was even more unusual for an experimental psychologist doing basic research at the high noon of Behaviorism to seek to demonstrate how theory could guide the design of pedagogical methods. But that is exactly what Skinner did, reaching back to the precedent (but not the theories) of Dewey and Thorndike.

Glaser absorbed that lesson, and not many years later, in the city of Pittsburgh, found the opportunity to implement and expand this idea of enlisting the knowledge obtained from basic research to inform the design of real-world educational institutions and practices. The Learning Research and Development Center was the product of that vision, which was amended in several important ways that proved crucial to its success.

One adaptation was to recognize that ideas had to flow both ways: from theory to practice and from practice to theory. This could be achieved if LRDC had links to schools, conducted some of its research in practical educational settings, observed children in such settings, and listened carefully to experienced teachers as a source of hypotheses and ideas for new basic research. For example, contemporary theory on how students can learn from worked-out examples, owes much to observations of excellent students who, in studying textbooks, spent little time reading the verbal exposition, but much time studying the worked-out examples in the text (Chi, Bassok, Lewis, Reimann, & Glaser, 1989).

Another adaptation derived from attention to the changes that were taking place in the discipline of psychology: the so-called "cognitive revolution" that was just then getting under way. The new interest of theoretical and experimental psychology in cognitive processes—in what was going on inside the learner's head—permitted a development of theory along the dimensions that were particularly relevant to its application to instruction. It encouraged a reconciliation of mainstream psychology with the strong Piagetian tradition in developmental psychology, with Gestalt concepts, and ultimately with the child-oriented and group-oriented concerns of figures like Vygotsky.

LRDC, and Glaser, its leader and one of its researchers, soon became a major contributor to the flow of basic research on human learning and thought processes and their relevance to education, and a major conduit for conveying the products of the cognitive revolution to the schools, and the experiences of the schools to the cognitive researchers.

A history of LRDC, which I will not attempt here, would note these directions simply as prominent examples of the many adaptations of the new institution to its environment as that environment was explored and tested. I have not even mentioned, nor am I knowledgeable about, the strategic decisions that enabled LRDC to obtain the funding it needed to pursue its goals. But even the two examples of adaptation that I have cited illustrate admirably the flexibility an institution of this kind requires in its entrepreneurial planning if it is to be successful, and to continue to be so. And that flexibility stems from the adaptiveness and imaginativeness of Glaser and his associates who carried out the entrepreneurial tasks that caused LRDC to grow and to flourish.

THE MORAL DIMENSION

Flexibility is not enough without a sense of direction and goal: what can be called the moral dimension. *Moral* is a word with an old-fashioned sound. I use it to emphasize that there is no excellence without a deep commitment to goals. *Commitment* means striving to reach these goals even in the face of a discouraging or threatening environment. The stress on flexibility in my account of excellence in entrepreneurship should not be interpreted as derogation of morality. Flexibility is not achieved by abandoning goals, but by redoubling efforts to reconcile goals with reality, seeking new alternatives of action that are feasible, yet effective. Flexibility should not be confused with compliancy or mere expediency. I illustrate with an example of another entrepreneur whom I have known and admired, Clarence Ridley, who was my first boss (Simon, 1996).

Ridley, educated as a civil engineer, became a city public works director some time after World War I, and then a city manager. In the course of this career, he learned how organizations, in this case city governments, could be powerful instruments for achieving social goals. As Executive Director, he built the International City Managers Association, the professional association of municipal administrators, into a powerful force for the improvement of city management, which educated and mentored generations of city managers and other municipal officials to become effective leaders in their communities. Among its most important tasks was to instill an esprit de corps in members of a new profession, each isolated geographically from the others, and facing all of the complexities of operating in the political environment of democratic institutions.

Besides organizing professional meetings that brought its scattered members together, ICMA produced textbooks on management for heads of municipal police, fire, public works, finance, planning, and other departments, and operated a correspondence school based on them. It gathered and published statistics on municipal services, their effectiveness, and costs. It published a monthly magazine on public management. To assist municipalities with their problems, it organized and spun off a nonprofit management consulting firm (whose first director, Donald C. Stone, later filled a similar position in the U.S. Budget Bureau, still later became the first dean of the Graduate School of Public and International Affairs at the University of Pittsburgh, and after his retirement from Pitt, served through his eighth decade as a faculty member of the Heinz School at CMU, a proper protégé of Ridley). Although Ridley died more than 20 years ago, and although his name is hardly a household word except in the profession with which he worked, he left a legacy of greatly improved city government in this country from which we all continue to benefit.

On one occasion some time after I had left ICMA for another position, I had breakfast with Ridley, and we were discussing new developments in his organization. Regarding one new program he was initiating, I asked, "Won't the Spelman Foundation [then a major source of funding for ICMA's program] have some qualms about that?" He turned to me, and said, "I earned a living before I ever heard of the Spelman Foundation, and I guess I could earn one again if they went away." Ridley had the flexibility of an entrepreneur, but he had goals, and he did not abandon them.

THE CIVIC CULTURE

In celebrating excellence in entrepreneurship we celebrate the excellence of organizations, for we have seen that organizations are the vehicles that entrepreneurs use to reach their goals. In the case of organizations like the Graduate School of Industrial Administration, the School of Computer Science, the Learning Research and Development Center, or the International City Managers' Association, achievement requires not only their own excellence, but also excellence in their client organizations, in schools and city governments, respectively. The real goal of an entrepreneur's activity, one might say, is excellence once or even twice removed.

In our time, organizations have a bad press. American business organizations suffered great loss in public credibility from their failure to adapt promptly to the challenge of competition from Japan and other developing nations, and by their frequent eagerness to substitute mergers and other financial manipulations for productivity. Government organizations, and even private nonprofit organizations have been, for several decades, under constant attack as wasteful "bureaucracies." Schools, and especially the nation's public schools, have been special targets of censure, with all sorts of home remedies being prescribed for the real or supposed ills from which they suffer. (Not the least of the problems that LRDC has had to deal with is this noisy clamor and even hostility that surrounds the school systems it serves.)

That the public and private organizations in our society have problems goes without saying, but a problem we could well do without is the widespread public mistrust of them that now prevails. The problems will be solved only as a society recognizes the essential role its organizations play, and supports the qualities of entrepreneurial excellence that are needed to make these organizations excellent.

One widely advocated "solution" to today's organizational problems is to replace organizational mechanisms with market mechanisms, to privatize our government services. As this is not the place to debate the pros and cons of such proposals, I make only a few observations. First, privatization does not eliminate organization, much less take "bureaucracy" out of the system; it simply replaces public organizations by private organizations, which we well know are not without their own bureaucratic problems. If we are not convinced of this from our own experience, we need only look at the past decade's experience in Eastern Europe, where the attempt to move to a market economy, starting with a near absence of an infrastructure of effective organizations, is still very far from reaching satisfactory levels of performance.

Second, much of the current criticism of organizations, and especially public and nonprofit organizations, is a caricature of the true situation, not based in any way on systematic review of the facts. The idea that workers in industry are more industrious than workers in government and nonprofits seems ludicrous to any of us who have been exposed to both environments, and especially to those of us who inhabit the "leisurely" environments of academe or of the public schools. Moreover, excellence in entrepreneurship is an equally essential condition for goal achievement in both private and public organizations, and as difficult to come by in the one as in the other.

Third, the current distrust of organizations rests on a myth of a past that never happened. Long before modern large organizations (except for military organizations) came into existence, competitive markets were the chief organizers of economic activity—both for local trade in the cities and towns, and for long-distance trade along routes on land and sea. What changed with industrialization was not the introduction of markets, which existed already, but the introduction and growth of large organizations, which provided goods and services with an efficiency that could not be rivaled by the handicraft and cottage industries that preceded them. Modern organizations provided entrepreneurs with a previously unavailable tool for achieving innovation. Unless we want to retreat to medieval economic conditions, we must recognize that organizations and the leadership skills that produce excellence in organizations are foundation stones of modern society.

Since World War II, our understanding of the skills that underlie excellence of all kinds, including organizational excellence, has taken great strides forward. And yet, I think we all feel a frustration at the slow rate of incorporation of these advances in our institutions. A reasonable conclusion to draw is that we must add two more items to the agenda for excellence: enhancing the excellence of all of our organizations, and especially enhancing the general public's understanding of the need for excellence in our civic institutions and of the possibilities for attaining it. To do that, we will have to understand how to develop, select, and support effective entrepreneurs, themselves excellent in building and managing organizations.

CONCLUSION

In the preceding, I have tried to indicate why a society like ours requires excellent organizations as well as excellent individuals, and, indeed, requires many individuals who can be excellent leaders and entrepreneurs in the environments of organizations. I have described four examples of excellence in leadership and entrepreneurship that I have personally encountered over the past 60 years, each of which illustrates one or more of the dimensions involved in bringing organizations to a state of excellence. In the case of the Graduate School of Industrial Administration, a strong leader exploited new ideas and management methods in the business environment, involving the application of the quantitative methods of management science and of psychological principles for structuring the relations of people in organizations, to create a school that not only exploited these opportunities but played a major role in initiating a national and international revolution in business education.

In the case of the School of Computer Science, a leader who occupied no formal administrative position took leadership in the shaping of that institution through his support of the Responsible Person Principle and his ability to exemplify in his own behavior the organizational goals and values. In the case of the Learning Research and Development Center, a director was able to grow an organization and to shape it to operate effectively over a long span of years in an unusually complex environment, using it to bring the community of cognitive scientists and educational psychologists in productive contact with the real world of educational practice and politics. In the case of the International City Managers Association, the organization's leader combined a steady vision of his organization's goals with a large arsenal of feasible means for achieving them, thereby enabling it to contribute significantly to the excellence of hundreds of other organizations that are engaged in providing essential public services.

I hope that, in focusing my account on individual leaders in each case, it will not be thought that I am promoting a Great Man theory of organizational excellence. The leaders I described were members of teams (for that is what the leadership of an effective organization must be), and part of their skill and the skill of the other team members consisted in attracting and retaining colleagues who could also make major contributions to the quality of the organizations. All of the leaders I described were strong persons who had no problem in working with strong colleagues, a key component of excellence in leadership.

Finally, I remarked on the additional burden that is placed on today's organizational leaders by negative public attitudes about organizations, and the need for a clearer view both of the essential role that organizations, public and private, have played historically and continue to play in our social system, and of the conditions that make for their excellence.

REFERENCES

Chi, M. T. H., Bassok, M., Lewis, M. W. Reimann, P., & Glaser, R. (1989). How students study and use examples in learning to solve problems. *Cognitive Science, 13*, 145–182.

Ericsson, K. A. (Ed.). (1996). *The road to excellence: The acquisition of expert performance in the arts and sciences, sports and games.* Mahwah, NJ: Lawrence Erlbaum Associates.

Krishnamurthy, S. (1998). *How do firms come to be?: Towards a theory of the pre-firm.* Doctoral dissertation, Graduate School of Industrial Administration, Carnegie Mellon University, Pittsburgh, PA.

Richman, H. B., Gobet, F., Staszewski, J. J., & Simon, H. A. (1996). Perceptual and memory processes in the acquisition of expert performance: The EPAM model. In K. A. Ericsson (Ed.), *The road to excellence: The acquisition of expert performance in the arts and sciences, sports and games* (pp. 167–188). Mahwah, NJ: Lawrence Erlbaum Associates.

Simon, H. A. (1990). A mechanism for social selection and successful altruism. *Science, 250,* 1665–1668.

Simon, H. A. (1991). Organizations and markets. *Journal of Economic Perspectives, 5,* 25–44.

Simon, H. A. (1995, Spring). Appreciation of George Leland Bach. *Selections, 11*(3), 15.

Simon, H. A. (1996). *Models of my life.* Boston, MA: MIT Press.

Simon, H. A. (1998). Allen Newell. *IEEE Annals of the History of Computing, 20*(2), 63–76.

Chapter 8

Personal and Institutional Pursuit of Excellence

Michel Ferrari
University of Toronto

This chapter considers how individual aspirations and institutional norms contribute to the pursuit of excellence in individuals and, on a broader scale, in social institutions. The idea is merely to acknowledge the ancient ideal made famous by Socrates that the unexamined life is not worth living. If we believe this to be true, as I do, then as individuals who participate in society we have an obligation to consider what sort of ideals we wish to strive toward and what sort of society we hope to foster. This chapter does not attempt to define the ideal individual or society, not out of modesty or lack of imagination—although they play a part—but because many possible ideals are equally worthy of being debated and pursued, and because any answer must be tailored to specific circumstances of particular situations in which ideals confront each other: The devil is always in the details. It is the implications of this perspective that I hope to explore in the chapter.

CULTURAL NORMS FOR EXCELLENCE

I begin my discussion of the individual and institutional pursuit of excellence with the basic premise that culture is "superorganic" and supervenes on individual interpretations of life and society (Baldwin, 1916; Bruner, 1996; Cole, 1996; Foucault, 1997). Because this is so, it remains unclear whether our ability to entertain certain notions of excellence reflects the

195

nature of our embodied mind or the socially inherited symbolic systems that our mind relies on to think (Baldwin, 1896, 1930; Bruner, 1996; Csordas, 1994; Gardner, 1993).

Excellence requires drawing distinctions that are culturally specific, that reflect what matters to a culture and to the individuals that embody them. Excellence in English pronunciation requires drawing distinctions that individuals raised within other cultures may not even make and thus can't hear or reliably produce. For example, the Japanese are commonly acknowledged to have difficulty distinguishing between r and l (and Japanese has a phoneme that gives English speakers a lot of trouble). Years ago, when I was taking introductory Japanese, my Canadian instructor told us that he was once in a bar in Japan when someone said to him in Japanese, "Admit it, there's no real difference between r and l is there? You guys are just making that up." All he could answer was that he could hear the difference.

Now, granting that this story or one like it is true, where do such differences, with their associated ideals for excellence, come from? I am not the first to suggest that they come both from the individual's embodied experience of the world and from culture—including the tools for thinking, like words and concepts about ideals (Amsterdam & Bruner, 2000; Csordas, 1994). This implies that our views on excellence are not infinitely plastic, but are framed through two sets of constraints.

The first set of constraints is what has been called the *psychic unity* of mankind that grows out of our shared evolutionary past and that prepares us to engage in our culture, an idea that has a long and muddled history in anthropology and psychology (Bruner, 1996; Cole, 1996; Shore, 1996). Clearly though, our biological evolution has adapted us for certain characteristic ways of knowing, thinking, feeling, and perceiving, and hence into characteristic ways of conceiving of excellence (Bruner, 1996). For example, Lorenz (1965) suggested that it might be evolutionary advantageous to find graceful and acrobatic movements excellent, because these are most likely to aid survival. These intrinsic constraints on our capacity to interpret may limit our ways of conceiving "objective" truths about time, space, and causality. And it is these evolved universals that are generally considered to constitute the "psychic unity of mankind" (Bruner, 1996).

Our conceptions of excellence are also limited by the *symbol systems* accessible to human minds (e.g., by the nature of language) but perhaps also by the formative influence of being exposed to different languages and notational systems accessible in different cultures. Bruner (Amsterdam & Bruner, 2000; Bruner, 1996) suggests that our symbol systems are framed in one of two basic ways: the first is narrative and the second is in terms of logical categories. We consider each of these in terms of how they impact on conceptions of excellence.

Narratives

Stories or narratives never stand alone: They are organized into narrative genres. According to Amsterdam and Bruner (2000) narrative genres are mental models that represent possible ways events in the human world can go. They embody and virtually institutionalize possible worlds, and pattern our culture's views on what is ordinary or legitimate, on the point of human striving, the shapes of human trouble, and of human character. With regard to excellence, narrative addresses the questions of what human beings strive for, what constitutes threats to excellence, and what makes individual characters exceptional. Interestingly, such narrative templates are at once cultural and personal.

According to Amsterdam and Bruner (2000), "Story is the favored form of teaching what Ought-to-be, what is the right order, what is the likely agenda of troubles" (p. 131). It is thus one key way that notions of excellence are introduced in culture. Stories don't just state facts, they advocate for certain standards or types of excellence. They also offer advice on how to overcome obstacles to achieving excellence. Narratives of excellence emerge from violations to scripts and must be coherent with the expected story. (Breaking the 4-minute mile in running was considered extraordinary precisely because prevailing wisdom was that the human body could not attain such a speed.) Some narrative genres (like hero tales or saints) have certain stock features that allow them to be exemplary tales (Amsterdam & Bruner, 2000; Bruner, 1990; Propp, 1984). A wonderful illustration of this is in Leonard Cohen's (1991) *Beautiful Losers*, in which he reinterprets the story of Kateri (Catherine) Tekakwitha, who was canonized by Pope John Paul II in 1980, by contrasting her ideal religious image to what is known of Tekakwitha through historical documents from the 17th century. The narrator originally falls in love with (and wants to physically make love to) her idealized religious image, and is shocked to discover that the historical Tekakwitha was scarred by smallpox and unattractive. This sometimes jarring juxtaposition of images is effective precisely because it violates the canonical form for this sort of tale.[1]

For individuals, stock scripts may be embodied in what Bourdieu (1994, 1997) called the *habitus*, that is, implicit ways people frame their experience and their sense of what is good based on the understanding of the social "rules of the game." Similarly, Searle (1998) pointed out that much of our specific actions and beliefs, like something as simple as ordering coffee in a restaurant, take place against an implicit *background* of know-how that is preintentional. The background or habitus sets the stage for certain expectations, and hence for judgments about excellence (or lack of it). For

---

[1]Thanks to Lora Pallota for pointing out this example.

institutions, narratives are embodied in the institutional structures and practices of, for example, schools, churches, or courts.

Some narratives of excellence are thus part of our cultural heritage, providing a way to communicate about implicit standards and forms of excellence valued by our culture. To paraphrase Henry James, excellence may only come to those who can tell stories that illustrate or promote excellence. But stories are just one way in which individuals organize their enculturated experiences. Another major way of organizing human conceptions of excellence is through logical categorization.

Categories

In terms of categorization, excellence seems inherently bound up to the notion of prototypes. For example, an excellent bird necessarily involves considering what is prototypical for a bird. Likewise, considering an excellent sparrow requires considering the prototype for that specific subtype of bird. Perhaps a riskier claim is that the same can be said for abstract categories like good food, or freedom.

Categories become entrenched in practice, which suggests that we should strive to entrench what we hold to be excellent in practice. Consider implicit praxic knowledge in folk psychology in which understanding typically takes the form of "that's the right way to do it" (Amsterdam & Bruner, 2000); such categories imply a normative view of activity on which people base their ideas of excellence. They are often used to determine excellence because they imply an idea of what ideally should happen, regardless of what actually does happen. That categories become entrenched in practice also suggests that we should challenge practices that we do not think are excellent, but just reflect the way things have always been.

Category prototypes, and the standards and criteria for excellence implied, are mentally constructed, not found in the world; thus they are limited only by the human imagination, although some imaginative products come more easily than others given our common evolutionary history (Amsterdam & Bruner, 2000). This point has been made more prosaically. Writing in the *Contra academicos* about how taste is subjective, St. Augustine (386; cited in Matthews, 1999) remarks on how leaves he can't stomach are eaten by goats, "I do not know how [those olive leaves] seem to the goat," he says, "but they are bitter to me" (p. 90).

Judgments of excellence are also bound up with categories that are of relevance to particular reference groups, specifically, with what matters to oneself and to those on whom one depends. It is striking to consider that Plato's dialogue *Charmenides* concerns a category of excellence, *sophrosyne*, for which we have no English equivalent. My *Collected Dialogues of Plato* (Hamilton & Cairns, 1961) says that "[*sophrosyne*] meant accepting the bounds which excellence lays down for human nature, restraining impulses to unrestricted freedom, to all excess, obeying the inner laws of harmony and proportion" (p. 99), and was the spirit behind the great Delphic aphorisms of "Know Yourself" and "Nothing in Excess." This is an inspiring category, but one for which we are not even sure to grasp the ancient Athenian understanding, and lacking a similar ideal, it becomes difficult to gauge whether we are successfully striving toward it.

Like narratives, categories do not stand alone, but are organized into *category systems* that derive from theories and canonical narratives. Categories may change, but category systems do not change as easily. This is why we recognize Gilgamesh or Odysseus as heroes, when so much else has changed, including our foundational theories about god(s) and way the world works. The category system that allows us to categorize them as excellent and that makes them heroes has not changed.

Aesthetic Experience

Bruner (1996) suggested that narrative and logical categorization are incommensurate. In this he echoes Baldwin (1930), who maintained that these two foundational ways of framing experience develop in tandem. On the one hand, narrative is concerned with human inner agency and the search for what is affectively and personally satisfying or good, whereas logical categories are our way of seeking what is objectively and externally true, independent of our own perspective. Both are influenced by culture but are fundamentally at odds.

But Baldwin refused to let the matter rest there. He proposed that through imaginative reconstruction these two ideals are reconciled in *aesthetic experience*, whether that of the artist personally or of the spectator. It is in art that humanity again remakes the world, considering only his or her own creation of something, and limited only by the possibilities of ideal reconstruction set by his or her materials. This new immediacy unites all values: Knowledge becomes infused with feeling, factual truth is converted into a valued end, and the bonds of reality are released by establishing and contemplating an ideal (Baldwin, 1930).

INDIVIDUAL PURSUIT OF EXCELLENCE

Self and Autobiographical Excellence

Whether one agrees with this potential synthesis of major aims, it seems clear that the self is central to the individual aspect of the pursuit of excellence. We often recount our experiences through stories that we tell to ourselves or to others; stories that adopt the narrative genres of our culture (Bruner, 1990; Bruner & Kalmar, 1998). Such stories are often aimed at showing how we are or came to be good, or why circumstances obliged us to behave in ways others considered bad (Augustine, trans. 1998; Freeman & Brockmeier, 2000).

More specifically, Bruner (1996; Bruner & Kalmar, 1998) suggested that the self system fulfills two *functions*. The first is that of *intersubjective communicability*.

> Any individual's idiosyncratic interpretations of the world are constantly subject to judgment against what are taken to be the canonical beliefs of the culture at large. Such communal judgments, although often governed by "rational" and evidentiary criteria, are just as often dominated by commitments, tastes, interests, and expressions of adherence to the good life, decency, legitimacy, or power. (Bruner 1996, p. 14)

Our accounts of self are highly limited by reticence and taboos, so cultures and subcultures characteristically provide us with guides for such self-presentation in dialogue. This is true in both small matters like making excuses, or matters of grave import, like testifying before a court (Bruner & Kalmar, 1998). A distinguished French anthropologist (Sperber, 1985) has even described a culture's characteristic modes of representing things to oneself as akin to what an epidemiology describes in the realm of susceptibility to illness, in other words, a culture's forms of conceptual representations are "catching" for its members.[2] But Bruner and Kalmar (1998) suggested that Sperber's "epidemiological model" is probably much too passive. It isn't simply that we "catch" the culture, we actively seek to engage it to further our goals and projects.

As individuals develop, they increasingly gain access to a wider range of common beliefs, expectations, and other intentional states that require both mutuality and a shared (perhaps coconstructed) conception of canonicity, that is, what particular acts or beliefs are to be expected of others, and what they can expect from us. This sense of legitimacy creates a cultural community that involves not only "shared" thoughts, but also a shared sense of normativity (Bruner & Kalmar, 1998; Searle, 1998). As Ricoeur (1986) put it, we adopt an ideology, not as a distortion that Marxist philosophers attribute to it, but as a legitimizing/authoritative function that was emphasized by Max Weber and by Becker (1974).

Cultures typically ritualize or institutionalize normative prescriptions on selfhood to keep individuation within limits and to preserve needed intersubjectivity (Bruner, 1990). They are also how individuals reduce the

---

[2]A point also made by Dennett (1991) and Blackmore (1999) in their discussion of "memes."

anxiety associated with life and the threat of imminent deaths (Becker, 1974). When individuation exceeds a certain limit, it is typically characterized as insanity, eccentricity, or some other deviance (Becker, 1974; Bruner, 1990). And thus along with adopting an ideology comes an understanding of what tasks are worth pursuing and will be valued by our peers, and what "failure to succeed" holds in store. But the culture's judgment on any individual construal is also typically multivocal, and admit of a "principle of tolerance" (Amsterdam & Bruner, 2000).

The second function of narratives about the self is an *individuation function*. Individuation creates and maintains privacy, a protected and subjective enclave. Individuation gives a form of quasi-autonomy or inviolacy to humans who necessarily live in communities. It thus permits the development of personal standards of excellence, or personal interpretations of cultural standards that may differ from the majority view.

Individuation is both epistemic and deontic, aspects of self that are practically inseparable, or at least deeply intertwined (Bruner & Kalmar, 1998). The epistemic domain consists of what we each experience, know, and believe on our own: our own unique conscious "phenomenology," background knowledge, and beliefs (Searle, 1998) or habitus (Bourdieu, 1997). The deontic domain includes what we value, care about, fear, love, and expect. A general feature of this deontic side of individuation is that it promotes expectations of consistency and predictability for one's self and for others. Individuation may also facilitate cultural change by preserving individual susceptibility to alternative (noncanonical) ways of representing the world and to their implicit notions of excellence (Bruner & Kalmar, 1998).

Baldwin (1899, 1930) adds that individuation also involves a dialectic synthesis of epistemic and deontic aspects of experience that is characteristic of human development. Here many contemporary readers may refuse to follow, but even if one disagrees with this view, it still strikes me as a wonderfully refreshing ideal to strive toward in a personal search for excellence. Consider the following passage, which I think sums up Baldwin's (1913b) position nicely:

> The course of normal individual development shows marked uniformity in two ways. First, the exigencies of life require and produce adaptations that result in a dualism between selves and things, between mind and body, between subject and object. This dualism goes through a series of transformations which, while refining, nevertheless harden and intensify it, up to the rise of the logical and reflective period. It then takes on the most refined and varied forms in the crucible of reflection. But with this goes, *pari passu*, the development of the imaginative function, which shows at each period a return to a sort of semblant or ideal unity. At each stage the finality of the dualism is denied; and an immediate intuition of things, as ideally complete and whole, is revealed, extending to the entire mental life. This reaches its fullest

form in the aesthetic consciousness, which succeeds to the earlier mystic modes of intuition, and clarifies their results. A thing of beauty, whether in nature or in art, is for the time apprehended as being both ideal as a thing and ideal for the self. [. . .] In the individual, in sum, the development of the theoretical reason or intelligence culminates in laws of Truth for him absolute, that of practical reason or will in norms of absolute Goodness, and that of the emotional life, with which the imagination is charged, in rules of absolute Beauty. (pp. 149–150)

Furthermore, it is through dealing with others that individuals gain a sense of their self-identity, along with its correlative term, the social other; both conceptions draw on the same body of experiences. In each social situation this sense of self and other are largely identical; only partially and progressively do they become different (Baldwin, 1930; Bruner & Kalmar, 1998). This dynamic constitutes a "dialectic of personal growth," which is simultaneously that of social organization. The individual's absorption of the culture's "social heritage" generates a continuous body of accretions (language, institutions, customs, etc.) through social traditions and practices. And certainly, the individual pursuit of excellence is intimately connected to the structure of social institutions and practices. This aspect of the pursuit of excellence is discussed next.

INSTITUTIONAL PURSUIT OF EXCELLENCE

Ignace Meyerson (1948) first proposed the view that the main function of collective cultural activity is to produce external "works" (oeuvres). Once created, in many ways such works take on a life of their own as they become available for interpretation and reinterpretation (Bruner, 1996; Popper, 1990). Such objects include the arts and sciences of a culture, institutional structures such as its laws and markets, even its "history," as what a people chose to remember, and how they remember events collectively (Pinsky, 1999).

Cultural institutions are both "accretions" of individual efforts and require people to interpret and embody them in the service of their specific cultural function. Indeed, the institution is only the lasting form in which organizations of individuals carry on particular social functions. The essential thing is not the outer form by which it accomplishes particular ends, but what sort of collective interest and action it involves (Baldwin, 1911). Institutionalization also locks various culturally provided "prosthetic devices" (artifacts and symbol systems) into place, enabling us to navigate the everyday world largely on automatic pilot (Bruner, 1996; Cole, 1996).

Institutions impose their will explicitly through rewards and sanctions and tacitly through expectations. Individuals commonly owe allegiance to many (formal and informal) institutions (e.g., family, profession, city, nation, social class, or ethnicity), each of which imposes its own pattern of rights and privileges. The earliest forms of constraint were probably religious and military because both assume a developing body of social opinion and practice (Baldwin, 1911; Bruner, 1996; Foucault, 1979).

How any given individual forms his interpretation on issues of public concern will usually involve him in a conflict of interests and identities that, while complementary, compete with each other for privilege and power (Bruner, 1996). They often have different standards and criteria for excellence. Indeed, schools, or the courts, and the standards of social excellence they promote, are not absolute, but an expression of culture. Indeed, the church, schools, and courts are not divorced from the broader culture of which they form a part. Institutional change can be both vast and slow; 100 years is not so long for the courts, church, or schools (or for the canonical narratives that frame their activities) (Amsterdam & Bruner, 2000; Baldwin, 1911, 1930; Bruner, 1996).

I now consider three key social institutions that have somewhat different functions in more detail: the school, the courts, and the church.

The Schools

Schools are designed to prepare individuals for society. Educational systems are highly institutionalized and subject to their own values. As with any institution, they also invent lasting ways to distribute skills, attitudes, and ways of thinking and of perpetuating particular practices in the same old, often unjust, demographic patterns (Bruner, 1996).

But at least ideally, education aims to teach people to use a culture's toolkit to become better architects and builders, according to the standards set by their culture. Students are provided the best knowledge that has been developed by culture and are trained to be critical, to establish ever higher standards of excellence. Ericsson (1996) and Gardner (1999) provided many examples of this dynamic at work in schools and in other educational settings.

The French refer to the results of developing special skills as *déformation professionelle* "professional warping": the shaping or warping that occurs through training to become suited to particular professions. The term suggests that being excellent in one way of doing things (with its particular categories) can warp your ability to be excellent (or even competent) in something else. This fact in turn suggests that we should choose what we want to become excellent in carefully, as it will to some extent determine the sort of overall person we become, the sort of excellence we value, and the sort of society we foster (Ferrari & Mahalingam, 1998). Schools also reflect the broader values of the culture of which they are a part. Alessandra Stanley (1999) wrote that when her daughter began kindergarten in Rome, Italy, she noticed that a huge chart was posted on the door of the class that contained entries like the following:

> Emma [her daughter]: Primo (first course): Pasta con pomodoro (pasta with tomato sauce). Tutto. Ottimo (Ate all. Excellent) [. . .] Dolce (dessert). Pera Cotta (stewed pear): Niente. Maggiore impegno. (None. Needs work). (p. 7)

In fact, when Farinelli, supervisor for Rome's public schools, once tried to introduce perch into the school menu, she was questioned about it in parliament (Stanley, 1999).

The Law

Like schools, the law also emerges from culture and tradition as much as it is in service of preserving or improving the culture of which it is a part. "The supreme court is an inescapable player in America's cultural dialectic, and inescapably responsive to it" (Amsterdam & Bruner, 2000, p. 280). Specifically, law is one way that society maintains continuity in value judgments and thus standards of excellence across time and changing conditions, specifically, those value judgments believed to affect the stability of a community (Amsterdam & Bruner, 2000). In this way, key legal decisions by the U.S. Supreme Court reflect the historical and cultural conditions prevailing when they were made.

Indeed, legal work is an ongoing "work in progress" that both binds its members in a common cultural canon and leaves them somewhat free to imagine and sometimes create possible worlds that go beyond existing canon. An example of this was seen in the case of *Brown v. The Board of Education*. In this case, the Supreme Court ruled against segregated schools, even though such a system was consistent with the specific wording of the U.S. Constitution and even though challenges to segregation had been struck down by the Court in the past. In their ruling, the Supreme Court judges essentially granted that the authors of the Constitution would have wished their own conception of racial equality to be surpassed in the interest of the ideals they strove to achieve (Amsterdam & Bruner, 2000).

The Church

Finally, and especially important in discussions of excellence, are religious and artistic institutions that are not justified by any direct practical utility, but rather reflect the flowering of human feeling and aspiration. Religious institutions in particular embody moral laws that are presumed to be binding on its members (Baldwin, 1911; Jonsen & Toulmin, 1988).

Religious institutions and religious law influence the way that this personal idealization takes permanent form in the life and work across generations in the culture. And even in the case of religious narrative, it is striking to consider the differences introduced into canonical religious tales in light of the cultural climate of the times. The story of Jesus in the four Gospels in many ways reflects the different audiences for which they were written, and are very different in focus from recent, sometimes controversial, films like *The Last Temptation of Christ* or *Jesus of Montreal*, which present Christ in a more human light.

Furthermore, the ideal of self-perfection is not just a social ideal that is embodied in particular religious institutions. Rather, as Baldwin wrote,

> The Diety himself is beyond the church. And insofar as the individual is inspired, the mouthpiece of the divine revelation, so far must he himself stand apart and perhaps lead a movement to reform religion. [. . .]// In religious institutions, therefore, we seem to find the collective and the individualistic motives singularly combined. (1911, pp. 139–140)

Importantly, school curriculum and secular and religious law grow out of the same cultural canons, although schools, courts, and churches are each assigned different social tasks. And the most interesting cases appear when different values and standards are maintained by different institutions who fight over the same cultural terrain.

A classic example is the struggle between church and science over the origins of the human mind/soul. For example, the issue of whether humans evolved by chance from previous life forms or were specifically created by God and how this topic should be taught in schools is a case that has been repeatedly decided through the courts. As succinctly recounted by Gould (1999), several states in the 1920s simply forbade teaching evolution, leading to the infamous Scopes trial of 1925 in which a teacher was convicted in Tennessee for teaching the scientific theory. Only in 1968 did the U.S. Supreme Court declare such laws unconstitutional, based on the first amendment right to free speech. This decision was challenged by the states of Louisiana and Arkansas whose representatives asked that "creation science" be given equal time in the classroom, but the Supreme Court rejected this demand. Most recently, the Kansas Board of Education has voted to remove both evolution and the Big Bang theory from the state's science curriculum. Whereas the Board of Education is powerless to forbid teaching the subject, by saying that it will not be on statewide tests used to evaluate science students, they effectively ensure that teaching of these concepts will be deleted or diminished. This action has provoked an outcry from key scientists like Gould (1999), and by writers and social critics concerned with free speech and teaching of critical thinking in the schools (Rushdie, 1999), social criticism that is biting at its best. Few researchers in education would be as bold as Rushdie or have the literary skill to write, "If Charles Darwin were able to visit Kansas in 1999 he would be obliged to concede that here was living proof that natural selection doesn't always work, that the unfittest sometimes survive and the human race is therefore actually capable of evolving backwards" (p. A13). And to conclude, "In the immortal words of Dorothy Gale, 'Toto, something tells me we are not in Kansas any more.' To which one can only add: Thank goodness, baby, and amen." Perhaps the height of irony is that this decision was recently overturned and led to the reconstitution of the board itself as its most radical members were replaced by more moderate ones in next board elections.

DIALECTIC BETWEEN INDIVIDUAL AND INSTITUTIONAL PURSUIT OF EXCELLENCE

Now although both individuals and institutions pursue excellence in different ways, the most interesting question is how these two different pursuits are dialectically related. Thus, any consideration of cultural perspectives on excellence must coordinate objective institutional arrangements and subjective interpretations, or what Amsterdam and Bruner (2000) call the Yin–Yang dialectic that exists between a society's institutions and its imaginings.

Excellence as Social Progress

The genius or great person is often considered the source of cultural or institutional change (Baldwin, 1896; Gardner, 1997; Sternberg & Davidson, 1995). On this view, it is the genius who sees farther than his or her contemporaries and who sets a new standard to be emulated. Ideally, their discoveries and values become the norm from which all members of society benefit, until a new genius comes to push the envelope even further.

Thus, the history of any knowledge domain (and, for some, of world culture) is the history of progress. Although in some ways this is a compelling idea, it has certain unfortunate consequences. In particular, one is then obliged to mark cultural progress and to consider certain cultures less advanced than others, and certain individuals less sophisticated than others. Jonathan D. Spence (1998; cited in Lamolinara, 1999) speaking on "History and politics," at the *Frontiers of the Mind* symposium argued that once well-accepted views of how science relates to history laid out in a similar conference in St. Louis in 1904 (at which Baldwin presented) have all turned out to be wrong or harmful. They now seem "little more than the self-congratulatory stance of a White male Protestant elite, raised in a highly restricted cultural and social setting." We now no longer think that Science reveals a cumulative rise of wisdom and certain truth, but rather is an unmatched force of destruction that has affected everyone. The very idea of the long path of world progress was clearly false, as entire nations and peoples became poorer and lived in more degrading conditions, while others dominated them in the most horrendous ways.

This is chillingly true of Baldwin's view of progress, as this next passage makes clear:

> An artificial humanitarianism [. . .] has so softened the heart of the civilized peoples, and dulled their reflection, that in this matter of capital importance [improving the population by control of heredity through preferential pairing] a laissez-faire policy has been universal. // [. . .] Weaklings, diseased persons, mental and moral incapables are not only freely produced, but they are allowed in turn to perpetuate themselves by further reproduction. Surely it is high time for society, as it becomes conscious of the principles of its own development and of its resources of control, to address itself directly to the problems of eugenics. A movement in this direction is upon us which is destined to do more for humanity, both in its radical provisions and in its beneficent results, than possibly any other that society has seen. (1911, pp. 164–166)

This endorsement of something that the Nazis used to justify the Holocaust, and that Serbs have used to justify "ethnic cleansing," is a sad testimony to the prevalence of this idea that 100 years ago captured some of the greatest psychologists and doctors (Marrus, 2000) of the age, and has probably done the most to undermine any current belief in progress.

The idea of universal progress has been greatly qualified in recent times by the realization that different cultural roles set very different standards of excellence, and different endpoints for development (Mascolo et al., chap. 5, this volume). Nietzsche (1874) was one of the first to ridicule the Hegelians (and Baldwin is very much a "psychological Hegelian") for what he called "the use and abuse of history." For Nietzsche, it is a modern arrogance to think that all of world history rises to produce 19th (and now 21st?) century Europe at its pinnacle. In such a view, there is no room for the future; where could we go from the top but down? But Nietzsche pointed out that different cultures had very different ideals. Certainly ancient Athens, or turn-of-the-century Vienna were beacons of the arts and sciences, rising to heights that they would both lose after a major war destroyed their political dominance (Schorske, 1971). For Nietzsche, and more recently Foucault (1994/1997), the real task for contemporary think-

ers is to prepare a present-day equivalent to the overarching values of
these great cultural moments that we can strive for and endorse now, not
to remain enthralled to shards of value systems from the past.

In this light, consider the French sociologist and criminal lawyer Ga-
briel Tarde's (1896/1904) astonishing tale of a future utopia. In it Tarde
echoes many of Baldwin's views on the power of brilliant individuals to
shape culture, and on the importance of artifacts in stimulating individual
development. However, Tarde also grants that cultural gains can be lost, if
care is not taken to preserve the artifacts and practices that history has
shown to produce a peaceful and charitable social environment, and a rich
inner life for its members.

EXCELLENCE BASED ON PRACTICAL POWER

Amsterdam and Bruner (2000) strongly cautioned against considering
culture as a unified block, and instead suggest that it is a collection of constituencies. Cultures by their very nature are marked by contests for control over conceptions of reality. Their integrity is maintained by seeing
culture as negotiated compromise between the established and imagined
possibilities. This also seems true for cultural conceptions of excellence. In
this sense, estimations of excellence may be seen as an upper limit of canonical normativity, one that shows the way for further enrichment of the
canon. Each such advancement is an imagined possibility that someone
has made actual and that is maintained by people in the culture as something to be emulated. Note that it is impossible to observe any universal
social progress under such a view.

As Bruner (1996) observed, one may legitimately inquire about how individual minds interact with the means by which culture helps or hinders
their realization. Inevitably, this requires an ongoing assessment of the fit
between what members of any particular cultural community deem essential for a good, useful, or worthwhile way of life, and how individuals adapt
to the constraints these demands impose on their lives (Taylor, 1989).
These considerations emphasize the important role of power and rhetoric
in any cultural-psychological discussion of excellence.

Cultural reference groups seem intimately bound up with considerations of excellence in terms of communal power (i.e., creating communal
solidarity through stereotypes). Thus categories sometimes can foster particular types of excellence, but these same categories can be used for hegemony or power of one group over another in the service of a particular
ideology (Amsterdam & Bruner, 2000; Ricoeur, 1986).

Indeed, entire systems of beliefs and practices can be abandoned and
replaced with others that are not better or worse, but just different (Kuhn,

1970, 1993). Choices between different systems of categorization, or foundational narratives (and their associated notions of excellence) thus often depend on hegemony and dominance, or on the particular cultural conditions under which one lives. And entire disciplines can be transformed or lost when new conditions come into place and old distinctions are not fostered, or are no longer even of interest. For example, in trying to heal a Tamil victim of torture in Sri Lanka, a *kotanki* (local diviner-healer priest) laments that "In India, [. . .] they use a horsetail-whip to beat the demon into waking up and trembling [a sign that the person has returned]. My grandfather used to do that. But nobody here knows how" (Daniel, 1994, p. 245).

Although it is impossible to speak of universal progress or appeal when considering different cultural forms of healing or justice, clearly certain values should be upheld. Through such practices the healer attempts to restore the individual power and sense of self lost through the atrocity of torture of an innocent man. Virtually all will agree that the eradication of torture, the emancipation of slaves, and the desegregation of schools mark progress for American and world culture, even granting their underlying diversity (Amsterdam & Bruner, 2000; Taylor, 1989).

Negotiating/Navigating Noetic Space

Ricoeur (1986) suggested that the conjunction of "two opposite sides or complementary functions [ideology and utopia] typifies what could be called social and cultural imagination" (p. 1). This imagination constitutes what Amsterdam and Bruner (2000) called a culture's *noetic space*. According to Amsterdam and Bruner (2000) a culture's noetic space contains its range of imaginative possibilities. What does this distinction say about how different cultures will value and promote different standards of excellence?

This imaginative or noetic space is stocked with narrative genres that serve as tools of narrative problem solving, and seem to have a lot to do with orienting a culture's views on what constitutes normativity (ideology) and excellence (utopia) and how to foster the dialectic between them. Indeed, establishing new genres is crucial to establishing new visions of excellence.

Noetic space is where a culture harbors its notions of excellence, either as ways of being outstanding at canonical tasks or by acknowledging that someone has surpassed what is established in some way. Excellence implies possible worlds that extend the canon or improve on it in ways not imagined by those who uphold it. In this sense, noetic space is one of pragmatic possibilities and not merely wishful thinking, as Simon (chap. 7, this volume) points out in discussing the imagination of successful entrepreneurs; entrepreneurs imagine what is actually possible, not just what they would like in some ideal world.

Importantly, marginality and centrality in noetic space can change, and thereby change institutions and practices (including their implicit notions of excellence). Indeed, cultures institutionalize "sites" to help us build possible worlds (e.g., theatre, fiction, meditation classes, and utopian or distopian fantasies). These sites can become the test bed for movements that end up shaping tomorrow's canonicity. For example, Amsterdam and Bruner (2000) suggested that shifting from an *ideology of fate* to an *ideology of the possible* characterized the transformation of European thought from the age of Faith to the age of Reason, and the very idea of what was considered excellent shifted in the transformation.

> Seeing the obvious as strange requires metacognition, a clumsy word for making one's own thoughts the object of one's own thinking. [. . .] Disturbers of the canonical peace [e.g., artists, philosophers, agitators, dissidents] may be disapproved of by those in charge of the banal and obvious. But they are always left some room to do their thing. This is to lure us into metacognition, into the imaginative space where mind can envision other possible worlds. Each culture maintains its distinctive imaginative space, teeming with alternatives to the actual. (p. 237)

Once a new possibility is established it is often institutionalized, fixed in habitual practice, or off-loaded into artifacts. "We use intelligence to structure our environment so that we can succeed with *less* intelligence. Our brains make the world smart so that we can be dumb in peace!" (Amsterdam & Bruner, 2000, p. 234). As Dennett (1996) pointed out, scissors make us more intelligent just by their very existence, because with a pair of scissors in hand one almost immediately knows how to cut things using them. (And this is even more true if we consider what an apprentice learns when coached in the use of specific tools of a trade.)

Hence one type of excellence is to make things "idiot proof" so that the rest of us can be at peace dealing with others who use systems that help us all act smarter, even if particular individuals may be dumb or virtuous (Aristotle, 1984 version). But as in Hegel's (1807/1967) discussion of the Master/Slave relationship, tools and artifacts also make us their servants in exchange for being ours (Amsterdam & Bruner, 2000). Thus, created artifacts become part of the cultural norm, until another dissident perturbs the noetic space and sets new standards or criteria for excellence.

But what about cases in which society and the individual are at odds? (For example, the greatest artists or dissidents shock us out of our complacency and force us to envisage things in new ways and to deeply consider what we value.) When powerful individuals come into conflict with existing laws and customs, nothing can be done to determine who is right in such extreme conflicts between the individual and society (Baldwin, 1899).

Powerful individuals can marshal social power against prevailing social norms to promote great ideals or monstrous ones. Which is which cannot be stated outside of our own cultural upbringing and sense of excellence. Gandhi is considered a political genius by many today, and by his supporters in his own time, but the British then saw him as a dangerous dissident and imprisoned him for many years (Gandhi, 1957). Or consider the exhibition "Sensation" that was shown at the Brooklyn Museum of Art in the fall of 1999. So much controversy surrounded Chris Ofilie's painting "The virgin Mary" (in which a Black Madonna is adorned with elephant dung and surrounded by small pictures of vaginas), among other controversial works, that the mayor of New York (Giuliani) withheld payment of $7 million to the museum (one third of their yearly budget) and moved to have them evicted because he was so incensed that public money was being spent to support such an exhibit. The museum curator and the board of trustees refused to back down on principle, saying that the work had artistic merit and the show should be presented as it was in London where it was well received. The case was then sent to court as the museum sued to stop the city from withholding payment.

In such cases, dissidents are often marginalized, despite the value (or supposed value) of their ideas. But interestingly, such cases do not concern the lone genius. Rather we see influential individuals (Ofilie, Giuliani) acting within institutions and bringing their power to bear to advance their own deeply held beliefs and conceptions of excellence.

Thus contemporary views of social change are deeply concerned with hegemony, that is, with the power of one group to impose its values on another group that is less powerful. It is important to be realistic, as well. Sometimes we endorse marginalization and endorse imposing social sanctions on those who are marginalized. Some individuals break fair legal contracts, or are violent criminals who gratify their selfish or pathological impulses at the expense of social order, or are mentally impaired and cannot fend for themselves. In all of these cases, we are glad to have a dominant group impose their decisions on those who are at the margins. Foucault (1979) reminded us this is the cultural power that we give to institutions like prisons and hospitals, whose aim is to maintain order or promote the public good.

RECONCILING PROGRESS AND POWER

The genius, artist, and dissident are all agents of cultural change. Acknowledging these different sources of change serves to highlight the difference between early modern and recent perspectives on cultural transformation. Today we are less likely to believe wholeheartedly in Locke and the Enlightenment thinkers in the pursuit of excellence through an ever greater grasp of objective truth (despite the call by Wilson, 1998, for greater consilience between the sciences). We are more likely to share the concerns of Nietzsche and Foucault about the use and possible abuse of power.

But progress is an idea that dies hard, perhaps because it contains a grain of truth. It is morally suspect to allow widespread access to technology that would allow "designer babies" that have a certain gender, a certain appearance, and a greater chance of acquiring a certain temperament or IQ (as in Huxley's distopia, *Brave New World*). Indeed, Ian Wilmut (creator of Dolly, the first mammal cloned from an adult cell) said that he could think of no legitimate reason to allow human cloning and a lot of reasons to legislate against it for the sake of any children produced by this method.

But an equally eminent biologist, James Watson (1999), has been deeply involved with the Human Genome project, a project with the express aim of mapping the human genome in order to help eradicate individual genetic defects that cause so much human suffering, and ultimately, one suspects, to "improve mankind." And if there is a way to eradicate Down syndrome, or congenital blindness, or any number of genetically related causes of human suffering, who but the most zealous would object? Like atomic power, technology can be used for good or evil. Indeed, Watson (1999) explicitly made this point in a recent talk to the Joint Center for Biomedical Ethics. But in this jaded age, after so many wars, we have little faith that the good will necessarily outweigh the evil in the final balance.

Still, I think that local progress is possible within existing disciplines and their established ways of making sense of the world. Our understanding of the atom allows us to build an atom bomb or a nuclear reactor when our ancestors could not. And we have deepened our understanding of genetics to the point where we can now map the human genome, or develop genetically altered plants that produce their own insecticide, or (more startling) pigs that might grow human organs to be used for transplants. We are perhaps on the brink of designing entire new organisms (Hopkin, 1999). Technological power has advanced far beyond our ancestors' simple tools: but is that progress? The unequivocal "yes" that used to be the answer is much more hesitant after this warring century. Now we are much more sensitive to the value systems that lead us to want this sort of technological power, and have concerns for alternative values and a more ecologically oriented concern with balance of power (Capra, 1996).

But whether technological advance does or doesn't represent progress in an absolute sense, I think it is local progress. Such progress echoes Bourdieu's idea of amassing *cultural capital* by drawing distinctions; within a discipline, we admire exceptional individuals (geniuses) who make finer distinctions or more interesting distinctions about the disciplinary content we value. This applies across cultures, if the issue under study is the same (Eco, 1998; Taylor, 1995). Thus, having studied karate for over 15 years, I can state with some confidence that karate (and other Oriental martial arts), as performed by the best practitioners, is simply more elegant and effective than any boxing I have witnessed. These Oriental martial arts grow out of a tradition that is richer, older, and designed for use in life-and-death situations, so this is perhaps not surprising. What is important here is that learning the Oriental martial arts requires making the same distinctions that boxing does, and more; it is this more that makes them more excellent. Some might argue with my assessment, but objections can be decided by results (Taylor, 1995). Consider the scene from Kurosawa's 1954 film *The Seven Samurai*. An inferior swordsman and a braggart refuses to let the results of a simulated fight stand and insists that he won the contest. He foolishly challenges the master to a true test of their abilities and is sliced in half by the better swordsman.

Thus, ever more subtle distinctions within a discipline lead to measurable local progress. This requires accumulating expertise, both within disciplines in society and within individual practitioners of those disciplines. Such progress represents excellence within the discipline, but its background assumptions can always be challenged. For practitioners of aikido, it is never ethically justifiable to kill another, even in self-defense, and so the actions of the master samurai would never be considered excellent, no matter how skilled.

RECONCILING COMPETING TRADITIONS AND CRITERIA FOR EXCELLENCE

A difficult question to answer is how to categorize things when confronted with competing categories (Taylor, 1995). This problem of indexing with regard to excellence is particularly interesting, especially if one considers that what is excellent for one category or construal is poor for another. For example, the excellence of a legal decision such as that put forward in *Prigg v. Pennsylvania*, in which a bounty hunter captures a runaway slave now living in the free state of Pennsylvania (see Amsterdam & Bruner, 2000, for a riveting account of this case), depends on whether the case is categorized as concerning the excellence of individuals (i.e., their right to freedom) versus those of the functioning of institutions (i.e., the smooth functioning of the U.S. legal system). Thus how one categorizes the problem seems to make all the difference in how specific decisions will seem to uphold standards of excellence.

Two systems of thought in a culture may be incommensurate, but MacIntyre (1990; also Taylor, 1995) reminded us that sometimes it is in developing a new synthesis between traditions (e.g., as Aquinas integrated the ideas of Aristotle and Augustine) that one generates the most interesting forms of progress.

Competing traditions are reconciled by posing questions that neither can solve, but that both acknowledge as important. This, I believe, is a critical challenge for modern times: to continue to pursue excellence, not merely within existing structures, or by replacing one set of values with another—through force or attrition—but also through the creative integration of the best elements of various cultural traditions that have so far developed largely independent of one another (Taylor, 1995). Such integration can lead to more deeply considered and universally shared views on excellence. We can see interesting inroads into this kind of integration, for example, in the use of modern medicine and acupuncture to foster individual health, two systems of medicine that are at one level incommensurate (Thagard & Zhu, in press). Other examples include the chemical analysis of traditional medicines that are then mass marketed, or used in traditional medical settings to help promote health or cure disease. Such creative syntheses of knowledge from different traditions require a very subtle negotiation between practitioners and experts from these alternative traditions, perhaps similar to the kind Amsterdam and Bruner (2000) describe occurring in Reggio Emilia between local religious and political institutions.

Talk of global perspectives on excellence that support global institutions like the United Nations or the World Trade Organization to foster negotiated superorganic world values, like diversity and community, is utopian. But Ricoeur (1986) reminded us that consideration of utopias are inevitable when discussing excellence because they necessarily point out a noncongruence with current states of society and culture. Utopias can be cautionary, even deeply misguided, as we now consider Baldwin's views on eugenics and we need to approach such a task with humor, given its enormity (Wells, 1904). Indeed, consider the powerful humor of More's (1518/ 1989) *Utopia*, of Tarde's (1896/1904) *Underground Man*, and more recently of works like Okri's (1995) *Astonishing the Gods*. These books, and even television shows like *Star Trek*, at least ask us to consider what sort of institutions we should strive toward and what kind of world we should work to create and defend.

Finally, utopias are not only to be sought in some final ideal individual or social system. Rather, I agree entirely with Amsterdam and Bruner (2000) who suggested that ideally a culture is populated with people who "appreciates [culture's] integrity as a composite—as a system in tension unique to a people not in perpetuity but at a time and place" (p. 231). This seems like an important aspect of excellence, as it is manifested in culture broadly construed and in specific institutions like courts, schools, hospitals, or other institutions.

What is central to this entire approach toward excellence is the need to consider actual cases in all their messy detail to really have anything relevant to say in evaluating them. True, none of us can "stand above the battle" (Amsterdam & Bruner, 2000) but we can choose where we will fight and what we will fight for. This seems the heart of a real treatment of excellence as it is lived and applied, not theorized from an ivory tower.

A striking point that comes out of considering actual U.S. Supreme Court decisions, is that evaluations of excellence are ongoing, and require considering the specific circumstances of each case (and how that case relates to other cases). Thus cultural—and personal—excellence is never final, but rather requires a shifting and subtle negotiation within a developing situation. Indeed, different judges read the same body of previous decisions and decide how to best further what they see to be the excellence that the courts are meant to uphold in light of how they frame the case under consideration.

This emphasis on the need to consider excellence in light of the circumstances of specific cases is reminiscent of Jonsen and Toulmin's (1988) discussion of casuistry which emphasizes the need for a case-by-case consideration of the specific circumstances at work in any ethical dilemma, and not an appeal to abstract principles. In this sense, excellence might be reflected in how well one is able to categorize new cases in light of old ones, and to adapt one's categories as times and circumstances and canonical narratives change.

IMPORTANCE OF RHETORIC

Rhetoric seems critical in explaining how we structure what is possible and imaginable, and hence in establishing the framework for considering what excellence is, and what is ideally to be expected as excellence in this situation. It sets the "presumed background" for excellence. Indeed, the rhetoric surrounding attributions of excellence seem as important as narrative or categorization in determining what is an excellent legal decision and why (Amsterdam & Bruner, 2000; Brooks, 2000). There are rhetorical narratives of excellence, in which one pleads that someone do the right thing. And such pleading can only be done by tailoring what one says to a particular audience, by entering into a dialogue with them and establishing shared subjectivity; otherwise, why would they listen? Presumably, they will listen better if what is said to them fits with what they feel is the natural or expected or legitimate state of affairs to strive for. And whether the entreaty is thought to be sincere depends on what we consider the presumed relation between actors and what responsibilities and rights that relation entails. We see throughout the cases discussed by Amsterdam and Bruner (2000) how different aspects of legal decisions are held up as an excellence to be maintained against perceived threat. Rhetorically we set up certain interpretations of what counts as excellence (or lack of it) in a particular case.

But this does not imply that there exists no objective meaning of excellence, just subjective ones—to the self and to the community. Consider Socrates and Plato in their criticism of the Sophists. As I take it, this criticism amounts to saying that one might be great at convincing others, but perfectly wrong in what one says. The Sophists imply that excellence is to be sought in the way in which one uses rhetoric to pursue one's ends; so, for example, Grice's maxims set standards of excellence for speaking, regardless of what one says. This is especially true when one considers that contested events can be organized into more than one narrative and that a choice between them depends on one's perspective, circumstances, or interpretive frameworks. However, for Plato and Socrates (and more recently Popper, 1990) excellence is sought in a correspondence to the truth.

Metacognition is perhaps associated with rhetoric, because it has much to do with how one frames and reframes experience. Lacking metacognition, we are sometimes fooled by our own rhetoric into self-delusion (Amsterdam & Bruner, 2000). This provides a brilliant insight into how we can end up acting in ways that we originally thought excellent, but later repudiate, as was the case for Justice Powell's appraisal of his judgment in the case of *McCleskey v. Kemp*.

The role of rhetoric in the interplay between established law and cultural imagination is wonderfully expressed in America's dialectic of legal decisions about race (Amsterdam & Bruner, 2000). This dynamic shows the difficult struggle to maintain or attain ideals of excellence in the face of powerful and widespread narratives (and individual voices) that seek to undermine any advances made. But it also shows the power of changes to the noetic space, as exemplified in the decision to desegregate the American public school system in *Brown v. The Board of Education*. Even those who seek to undermine noetic advances toward a new standard of excellence pay tribute to those advances, in word if not in spirit. Thus, even those who wish to undermine the advances made in the *Brown* decision speak highly of it.

And the negotiation between religious and political authorities in Reggio Emilia over hundreds of years seems like an especially powerful model for this sort of historically situated expression of excellence (Amsterdam & Bruner, 2000). It is striking to compare this dynamic to the case of the former Yugoslavia, held together by Tito, only to be torn apart by the inflammatory rhetoric of Milosovic that rent the delicate political balance in place there, and hardened each side against any form of negotiation. How can one negotiate after such atrocities as have been committed under his name? Is there a way to circumvent this dynamic and replace it with a more harmonious one? In other words, given existing tensions, can a cultural dialectic exemplified in the "Reggio approach" be copied? I hope the answer is, "Yes, if someone has sufficient noetic imagination to adapt that dialectic to the particular historical and cultural circumstances at play."

REFERENCES

Amsterdam, A., & Bruner, J. (2000). *Minding the law: Culture, cognition, and the courts.* New York: Harvard University Press.

Aristotle. (1984). Politics. In J. Barnes (Ed.), *The complete works of Aristotle* (Vol. II, pp. 1986–2129). Princeton, NJ: Princeton University Press.

Augustine, St. (1998). *The confessions* (M. Boulding, Trans.). (1st ed.). New York: Vintage Books.

Baldwin, J. M. (1896). The genius and his environment. *Popular Science Monthly, 49,* 312–320, 522–534.

Baldwin, J. M. (1899). *Social and ethical interpretations in mental development: A study in social psychology.* (2nd ed.; reprint edition 1973 by Arno Press). New York: Macmillan.

Baldwin, J. M. (1911). *The individual and society or psychology and sociology.* (reprint edition 1974 by Arno Press), New York: Macmillan.

Baldwin, J. M. (1913a). *History of psychology* (Vol. I). London: Watts.

Baldwin, J. M. (1913b). *History of psychology* (Vol. II). London: Watts.

Baldwin, J. M. (1916). *The super-state and the "eternal values."* London: Oxford University Press.

Baldwin, J. M. (1930). James Mark Baldwin. In C. Murchison (Ed.), *A history of psychology in autobiography* (pp. 1–30). New York: Russell & Russell.

Becker, E. (1974). *The denial of death.* New York: Simon & Schuster.

Blackmore, S. (1999). *The meme machine.* New York: Oxford University Press.

Bourdieu, P. (1994). *Raisons pratiques* [Practical reasons]. Paris: Seuil.

Bourdieu, P. (1997). *Méditiations pascaliennes* [Pascalian meditations]. Paris: Seuil.

Brooks, P. (2000). *Troubling confessions: Speaking guilt in law and literature.* Chicago: The University of Chicago Press.

Bruner, J. (1986). *Actual minds, possible worlds.* Cambridge, MA: Harvard University Press.

Bruner, J. (1990). *Acts of meaning.* Cambridge, MA: Harvard University Press.

Bruner, J. (1996). *The culture of education.* Cambridge, MA: Harvard University Press.

Bruner, J., & Kalmar, D. A. (1998). Narrative and metanarrative in the construction of self. In M. Ferrari & R. J. Sternberg (Eds.), *Self-awareness: Its nature and development* (pp. 308–331). New York: Guilford.

Capra, F. (1996). *The web of life.* New York: Doubleday.

Cohen, L. (1991). *Beautiful losers.* Toronto: McLelland & Stewart.

Cole, M. (1996). *Cultural psychology: A once and future discipline.* Cambridge, MA: Belknap Press of Harvard University Press.

Csordas, T. J. (Ed.). (1994). *Embodiment and experience: The existential ground of culture and self.* New York: Cambridge University Press.

Daniel, E. V. (1994). The individual in terror. In T. J. Csordas (Ed.), *Embodiment and experience: The existential ground of culture and self* (pp. 229–247). New York: Cambridge University Press.

Dennett, D. C. (1991). *Consciousness explained.* Cambridge, MA: Bradford/MIT.

Dennett, D. C. (1996). *Kinds of minds: Toward an understanding of consciousness*. New York: Basic Books.

Eco, U. (1998). *Serendipities: Language and lunacy*. New York: Columbia University Press.

Ericsson, A. (1996). The acquisition of expert performance: An introduction to some of the issues. In K. A. Ericsson (Ed.), *The road to excellence: The acquisition of expert performance in the arts and sciences, sports and games* (pp. 1–50). Mahwah, NJ: Lawrence Erlbaum Associates.

Ferrari, M., & Mahalingam, R. (1998). Personal cognitive development and its implications for teaching and learning. *Educational Psychologist, 33*, 35–44.

Foucault, M. (1979). Omnes et singulatim: Towards a criticism of "political reason." In G. B. Peterson (Ed.), *The Tanner lectures on human values* (pp. 223–254). Salt Lake City: University of Utah Press.

Foucault, M. (1997). On the genealogy of ethics: An overview of work in progress. In P. Rabinow (Ed.), *Ethics: Subjectivity and truth* (Vol. I, pp. 253–280). New York: The New Press. (Original work published 1994, interview given 1984)

Freeman, M., & Brockmeier, J. (2000). *Narrative integrity: Autobiographical identity and the meaning of the "good life."* Unpublished manuscript.

Gandhi, M. K. (1957). *An autobiography: The story of my experiments with truth*. Boston: Beacon Press.

Gardner, H. (1993). *Frames of mind* (10th anniversary edition). New York: Basic Books.

Gardner, H. (1997). *Extraordinary minds*. New York: Basic Books.

Gardner, H. (1999). *The disciplined mind: What all students should understand*. New York: Simon & Schuster.

Gould, S. J. (1999, August 23). Dorothy, it's really oz. *Time*, 39.

Hamilton, E., & Cairns, H. (Eds.). (1961). *The collected dialogues*. Princeton, NJ: Princeton University Press.

Hegel, G. W. F. (1967). *The phenomenology of mind* (J. B. Baillie, Trans.). New York: Harper & Row. (Original work published 1807)

Hopkin, K. (1999). Designer genomes. *Extreme Engineering, 10*(4), 78–81.

Jonsen, A. R., & Toulmin, S. (1988). *The abuse of casuistry*. New York: Cambridge University Press.

Kuhn, T. (1970). *Structure of scientific revolutions* (2nd ed.). Chicago: University of Chicago Press.

Kuhn, T. (1993). Afterwords. In P. Horwich (Ed.), *World changes* (pp. 311–342). Cambridge, MA: MIT Press.

Lamolinara, G. (1999). "Frontiers of the mind" symposium looks to the future. *The Library of Congress Information Bulletin*, July (Part I). University Press.

Lorenz, K. (1965). *Evolution and modification of behavior*. Chicago & London: University of Chicago Press.

MacIntyre, A. (1990). *Three rival versions of moral enquiry*. Notre Dame, IN: University of Notre Dame Press.

Marrus, M. R. (2000, March 1). *Invoking the Nazis in bioethics*. Sixth annual University of Toronto Joint Centre for Bioethics Jus Lecture, Toronto, Canada.

Matthews, G. (1999). Augustine and Descartes on the souls of animals. In M. J. C. Crabbe (Ed.), *From soul to self* (pp. 89–107). New York: Routledge.

Meyerson, I. (1948). *Les fonctions psychologiques et les oeuvres* [Psychological functions and works]. Paris: Vrin.

More, T. (1989). Utopia. In G. M. Logan & R. M. Adams (Eds.), *Cambridge texts in the history of political thought* (series). New York: Cambridge University Press. (Original work published 1518)

Nietzsche, F. W. (1949). *The use and abuse of history* (A. Collins, Trans.). Indianapolis, IN: Bobbs-Merrill. (Original work published 1874)

Okri, B. (1995). *Astonishing the gods*. Boston: Little, Brown.

Pinsky, R. (1999, October). Poetry and American memory. *The Atlantic Monthly*, 60–70.

Popper, K. R. (1990). *A world of propensities*. Bristol: Thoemmes.

Propp, V. (1984). *Theory and history of folklore*. Minneapolis: University of Minnesota Press.

Ricoeur, P. (1986). *Lectures on ideology and utopia* (G. H. Taylor, Ed.). New York: Columbia University Press.

Rushdie, S. (1999, September 2). Locking out that disruptive Darwin fellow. *The Globe and Mail*, p. A13.

Schorske, C. E. (1971). *Fin de siècle Vienna: Politics and culture*. New York: Vintage Books.

Searle, J. R. (1998). *Mind, language and society: Philosophy in the real world*. New York: Basic Books.

Shore, B. (1996). *Culture in mind: Cognition, culture, and the problem of meaning*. New York: Oxford University Press.

Sperber, D. (1985). Anthropology and psychology: Toward an epidemiology of representations (Malinowski Memorial Lecture, 1984). *Man (N.S.)*, *20*(1), 73–89.

Stanley, A. (1999, October 31). Correspondence/Italy: It looks like the lunch menu. It's really your child's report card. *The New York Times*, p. WK-7.

Sternberg, R. J., & Davidson, J. E. (Eds.). (1995). *The nature of insight*. Cambridge, MA: MIT Press.

Tarde, G. (1904). *Underground man* (C. Brereton, Trans.). Westport, CT: Hyperion Press. (Original work published 1896)

Taylor, C. (1989). *Sources of the self: The making of modern identity*. Cambridge, MA: Harvard University Press.

Taylor, C. (1995). *Philosophical arguments*. Cambridge, MA: Harvard University Press.

Thagard, P., & Zhu, J. (in press). *Acupuncture and incommensurability*. Unpublished manuscript.

Watson, J. D. (1999, May). *DNA and politics*. Fifth annual University of Toronto Joint Centre for Bioethics Jus Lecture, Toronto, Canada.

Wells, H. G. (1904). Preface. In G. Tarde, *Underground man* (C. Brereton, Trans.). Westport, CT: Hyperion Press. (Original work published 1896)

Wilson, E. O. (1998). *Consilience: The unity of knowledge*. New York: Knopf.

Chapter 9

Conclusion: What Is Excellence and How to Study it?

Michel Ferrari
University of Toronto

This final chapter sets out some themes that are common to the various chapters in the volume. It will immediately become apparent that the themes chosen are somewhat idiosyncratic, and certainly do not pretend to capture the depth of thought that went into each of the original chapters. That said, I found it striking that a common theme, on which authors divide, concerns how to study excellence empirically. This is the topic of the next section.

METHODS OF EMPIRICALLY STUDYING EXCELLENCE

We need a science of psychology and education that is comprehensive, and hence that has something to say about how to develop and foster the most excellent members of different disciplines. Echoing Allport (1942) writing many years earlier, Gardner[1] notes that science should be ruled by phenomena, and not be a slave to past methods or hobbled by a lack of imagination about how to study important phenomena. But what phenomena is involved in a study of excellence?

---

[1]Authors are named without specific citation in reference to their chapters in the present volume. To avoid very unwieldy sentences, in cases of multiple authors, only the first author of each chapter is referred to (with my apologies to co-authors, who are of course included in intent).

Several authors define excellence as synonymous with expertise and the phenomena under study as consistently reproducible superior performance. Ericsson laments that much of our knowledge of experts' development and early performances is anecdotal. He implies that such accounts of experts may be altered (perhaps unintentionally) to suit canonical narrative forms (e.g., that of heroic or tragic tales). Hence Ericsson's worry that many of our accounts of experts or geniuses in different fields are suspect when written by people themselves in old age, or by others who hold up their biographies as examples to novices in specific fields. In light of this potential problem, Ericsson and Smith (1991) suggested three key steps to any scientific study of excellence: (a) capture the essence of standardized performance under laboratory conditions of representative tasks as they occur in the discipline (e.g., organized competitions such as the Olympics); (b) provide detailed analysis of superior performances on these tasks; and finally, (c) account for the acquisition of the characteristic cognitive structures and processes that mediate or support experts' superior performance. Studying expertise in this way requires developing some representative and reproducible tasks that are useful in real life and transportable to the lab.

Gardner agrees that a nomothetic approach to the study of excellence can involve searching for quantitative correlates between variables and some authors such as Sternberg and colleagues focus uniquely on nomothetic relations between variables in explaining excellence. Likewise, Mascolo's chapter suggests that Fischer's dynamic skill theory provides a framework for charting nomothetic *trajectories* toward culturally valued endpoints in both academic and emotional skill development.

Gardner notes, though, that studies of excellence may also be interpretative, involving idiographic studies of extraordinary individuals and the subjective meanings that exceptional people themselves attribute to their life work. Gardner himself has set out to collect a sufficient number of idiographic accounts by artists, scientists, and political/religious individuals (through biographic and historical data) to allow a nomothetic understanding of excellence to emerge. Pinkus and Ferrari also emphasize historical and biographical approaches that rely on narratives. Zimmerman clearly aims to coordinate both quantitative and qualitative approaches in his account of excellence.

The tension between idiograpic and nomothetic approaches to excellence is found throughout the volume and supports Taylor's (1985) comment that psychology, like other social sciences, seems to be torn between a wish to follow the natural sciences in seeking objective correlates to experience, and a wish to explore hermeneutic approaches to analyzing experience that are the hallmark of the idiographic methods of study.

Not surprisingly, given these differences, authors diverge on how excellence is acquired, although all agree that excellence involves both a technical and an affective dimension.

HOW IS INDIVIDUAL EXCELLENCE ACQUIRED?

Individual excellence has a *technical dimension* that includes the knowledge and strategies needed to address prototypic and novel situations; this technical dimension is what is commonly considered to constitute individual expertise. How does one acquire such expertise?

Despite their very different data and methods, Gardner and Ericsson both agree that no immediate signs of greatness (e.g., an exceptionally high IQ, or performance on some standardized test) are typically indicative of children who later become extraordinary members of their profession. Furthermore, no quantum leaps forward are observed in the way these children learn (not even for prodigies). Instead, technical excellence is typically acquired by mastering traditional practices through extended engagement in domain-related activities. Several authors point out that at least 10 years of learning and dedicated practice are needed to achieve the highest levels of expertise in any given domain, no matter how gifted the individual. True, some extraordinary individuals manifest talent early in life, but this talent must always be shepherded by an adult who introduces them to the discipline. And most extraordinary individuals were not prodigies; in fact, many showed a strong and rebellious personality that marginalized them (because such individuals often see things in a new way, they may feel isolated/alienated). Once they do achieve a breakthrough in knowledge, they continue to do so every 10 years.

Gardner and Zimmerman point to important individual differences in the training practices of exceptional individuals. In all cases, such individuals explicitly credit their exceptional achievements to learning processes that allow them to monitor and control their learning and performances. For Ericsson, a particularly important training technique needed to develop individual expertise is to practice with the deliberate aim to improve specific aspects of performance during learning by attending to feedback that indicates progress and improvement.

Ericsson calls this sort of individual effort deliberate practice, and has conducted several studies to show that expertise is tied to the quality and amount of deliberate practice (Charness, Krampe, & Mayr, 1996; Ericsson, Krampe, & Tesch-Römer, 1993; Starkes, Deakin, Allard, Hodges, & Hayes, 1996). Such practice is very different from mindless repetition; rather, it is effortful and can be sustained only for short periods (about an hour at a time, 4 to 5 hours a day). This sort of focused and paced practice allows maximum gain while avoiding "burnout." According to Ericsson, and many other contributors would certainly agree, improvements in training methods within specific disciplines are the key reason why serious contemporary amateurs today can beat Olympic scores of the early century. Analogous progress is found in music (Lehmann & Ericsson, 1998); for instance, Tchaikovsky's first violin concerto was considered too difficult to play by the best violinists of his day, but is now part of the standard repertoire. Ericsson argues that not only is mental ability improved through practice, but even exceptional physical capacity to engage in domain activities is often acquired through practice. So, for example, exceptional runners develop greater lung capacity through extensive physical training in running.

Zimmerman refines Ericsson's general claim by providing a very fine-grained look at the self-regulatory processes that underlie efficient deliberate practice. Zimmerman makes the interesting point that there may be different types of self-regulatory practice, some of which are prerequisites to what Ericsson calls deliberate practice. First, students may *observe* a model. Second, they *emulate* expert practice that is modeled for them. Third, students engage in *self-control* based on specific memories of the expert model that serve to refine one's own performance. Only after one has acquired sufficient expertise in a domain is it reasonable to expect that individuals will be able to create and evaluate their own standards, and use these to *self-regulate* their performance.

Self-regulation leads one to develop more sophisticated mental representations through study and practice in the domain. Self-regulatory processes (e.g., self-monitoring, self-instruction, goal-directed attention, systematic use of feedback, time management, environmental structuring, seeking help from other experts) systematize learning and performance and play a greater role in developing expertise than does innate talent. Likewise, Sternberg and Simon note that expert knowledge is not enough; one must also make expert use of knowledge through an efficient use of strategic and metastrategic processes such as planning, monitoring, and evaluating specific performances (Sternberg, 1998).[2]

According to Zimmerman, self-regulation has three key components: forethought, performance, and self-reflection (which may serve as forethought for the next phase of self-regulated learning). All three of these components are different moments in an overarching self-evaluation that

---

[2]Note that monitoring and control may occur at different levels of consciousness; monitoring one's balance as one does constantly, is not the same as monitoring the accuracy of a mental image of a golf shot, for example, or of the coherence of a logical argument (Parilla, Das, & Dash, 1996).

is intrinsic to effective self-regulation. Self-evaluation is also essential to what Gardner calls metacognitive reflection, a stance toward learning that he considers essential to developing extraordinary ability, but Gardner also emphasizes the importance of leveraging one's strongest abilities to help one succeed at any given task. Like Sternberg, Gardner notes that individuals often fail to excel at certain aspects of complex tasks no matter how hard they try. Extraordinary individuals do not try to be good at everything, instead they capitalize on their strengths and find ways to remediate their weaknesses (which often may mean finding or hiring someone to help overcome those weaknesses). This is exactly what was seen for those extraordinary individuals described by Fink (1998) who overcame basic reading disabilities to become outstanding in their chosen fields. What this fact suggests is that deliberate practice and self-regulation considered in the abstract are not sufficient to assure individual excellence. Rather, what is key is to be critically self-aware of one's own strengths and weaknesses and to find a way to make extraordinary contributions by leveraging the first and minimizing the liability of the second.

Thus, many authors converge to say that innate ability is not the sole determinant of who will become excellent in a domain. For example, Sternberg and his colleagues present evidence suggesting that whereas basic abilities in a domain are not alone in determining who will achieve exceptional performances, it is certainly exaggerated to suggest that such abilities play no role whatsoever in who will achieve preeminence in a domain. Both quality of practice and genetically inborn potential to acquire specific abilities (which will vary in individuals as do all biological distinctions) are important to achieving excellence. As Gould (1996) points out, too, there are certainly biological limits to improvement of any physical activity, which is one of the reasons that the rules of baseball have been systematically adjusted to assure that advantages gained from improvements in, say, pitching, are balanced against the ability of batters, to assure the continued smooth functioning of the game.

Finally, there is an important link to be made between the ethical aspects of becoming excellent and the role of deliberate practice in developing expertise, as training in any knowledge domain necessarily involves mistakes; mistakes are inherent in all learning. As Pinkus and Sauder point out, the mistakes of advanced students and of practicing experts—who are not infallible—must be distinguished from incompetence. Mistakes that are acknowledged and serve for self-improvement or that advance domain-specific knowledge are a very different thing than are the mistakes of those who fail to meet the necessary standards of excellence in a domain. This distinction is important, not merely to maintain professional standards of practice, but also to maintain public confidence in the profession as a whole.

However, it is interesting to note different stances taken toward this reality of fallibility by different leaders in a field such as neurosurgery. Unlike Cushing, who held himself accountable for both his own errors and for those of students in his charge, Dandy held his students accountable for their own actions. Rather than asking all his students to adopt the same set of standard procedures, the techniques Dandy developed were innovative ones that he could perform along with a few selected others, but that he admitted were dangerous in the hands of amateurs. Like the exceptional individuals described by Gardner and Zimmerman, Dandy seems to advocate a more metacognitive approach to excellence in which students and other practitioners were required to evaluate their own capabilities and act accordingly. Dandy performed all operations and took full responsibility for all operations at which he was the most skilled surgeon present; when his students established their own practices, they were then equally accountable for their own actions. By contrast, Cushing aimed to establish professional norms and practices that would set a standard of excellence for the field as a whole.

As this example illustrates, a key tension in any discussion of excellence is whether excellence is defined as the ability to develop and guarantee tried and true procedures for success in a practice such as neurosurgery, or whether excellence requires developing innovative (and perhaps initially risky) procedures that advance knowledge in a domain. This is what Pinkus and Sauder, following Kuhn, call the essential tension between innovation and replication. Ericsson and Gardner both seem to assume that the best practitioners will necessarily advance the entire field to a higher standard than it had achieved when they entered it. This view implies that the most important task for any field is to develop and promote a small number of exceptional individuals (who constitute the leading edge in the noetic space of the field as a whole) able to draw new distinctions and imagine new possibilities that later become standard practice.

As mentioned earlier, both Zimmerman and Gardner consider self-evaluation a key aspect of metacognitive reflection. Zimmerman further notes that evaluation is necessarily made in light of the goals that one has set. However, one's goals are not merely a reflection of one's abilities, they also depend on *affective aspects* of performance, such as one's interest, pride, fears, estimated chance of success, and attributions about the cause of personal success or failure. For example, forethought is influenced by motivational beliefs, especially beliefs about self-efficacy and outcome expectations that affect one's interest, goal orientations, and process attributions. Self-efficacy is also reciprocally related to the long-term development of strategies and other forms of self-regulation. Self-evaluative judgments produce various emotional self-reactions (self-satisfaction or adaptive inferences). All of these reactions are fed into the next cycle that begins again with forethought.[3]

Mascolo and his associates point out that learning math is more effective when individuals are affectively as well as cognitively involved (e.g., when skill is acquired and employed in the context of a game and one wants to win). Their chapter also notes that the likelihood of adopting particular motivational and attributional beliefs is heavily influenced by one's culture and perhaps by the sort of narrative that one tells about the personal or social value of one's performance (culturally significant stories of exemplary or blameworthy individuals and how they acted under comparable circumstances).

EXCELLENCE INVOLVES AN INTERACTION BETWEEN INDIVIDUAL, DOMAIN, AND FIELD

The authors of the volume are unanimous in stating that excellence does not reside uniquely in the individual, but depends on an interaction between the individual and the context in which they are called on to act. This context involves both the current state of knowledge in a domain and the institutions, practices and individuals that are currently in place to instantiate that knowledge in society. Indeed, any determination of excellence must consider the interaction between the exceptional person, the current state of knowledge in a domain, and the current field of endeavor.

Mascolo and his colleagues are helpful in identifying four broad sets of processes within the organism–environmental system that are addressed by many other contributors to the volume. *Biogenetic processes* involve subpersonal processes—like lung capacity, cardiovascular activity—that can either be expressions of the genome or the result of special training. *Individual-agentive processes* involve the production of meaningful action, thought, experience, within the individual agents. *Social-relational processes* involve coregulated actions of two or more people. Finally, *cultural-symbolic processes* involve socially shared practices, institutions, and artifacts— physical and symbolic (e.g., language, math)—that have social meanings for individuals.

These four sets of processes, that some may consider to involve increasingly complex levels of functioning, mutually inform and regulate each other. So, for example, whereas individual deliberate practice or self-regulation will certainly improve one's skills, the ability to even engage

---

[3]According to researchers adopting a dynamic systems approach, this interaction between cognition and affect may be nonlinear (Lewis, 2000).

such individual practices will be bounded by biogenetic limits. For example, one would imagine that no amount of practice will allow an infant to create complex sentences in the first 6 months of his or her life. Furthermore, brain damage may make certain forms of learning impossible. Likewise, effective self-regulation is only possible to the extent that social support is provided in the form of best practices and representational structures that help develop individual expertise, and will often make use of symbol systems and knowledge that has been accumulated by cultural institutions over generations. Excellence thus is always situated at the interaction between individual capabilities, both inborn potentials and acquired skills that are considered relative to standards that are set by a field. And new fields are often linked to the emergence of new institutions to house experts and to organize their activities.

As one important form of interaction between levels, many contributors to the volume emphasize the need (at least initially) for individuals to engage in socially structured practice, if they are to achieve the highest levels of excellence in a domain. Such practice is organized by parents or teachers, the teachers often employed by learning institutions (or hired as tutors to prepare students to become eligible to join reputable learning institutions). Coaches or teachers are expected to orient and set up conditions that allow for optimal levels of practice and performance until the individual learns to create such conditions on their own. Thus the focus of individual deliberate practice is itself the product of extended engagement of students in traditions that have very definite ideas about how best to train the most promising individuals to participate in particular domains, fields, and institutions. Furthermore, as Simon points out, individual excellence sometimes involves creating new institutions that fill an important gap in existing fields. For example, creating an institution to conduct research into the now well-accepted reciprocal connections between practice and theory was a radical innovation when Robert Glaser founded the Learning Research and Development Center and began exploring these connections in the 1960s.

Pinkus and Sauder provide another good example of the power of institutional settings, in their discussion of the emergence of neurosurgery as a subspecialty of medicine along with the modern hospital. Established around 1900, by 1920 hospitals already had achieved their characteristic modern look (in which their internal spaces are defined by their functions and support a heavy administrative bureaucracy). Originally championed as a laboratory for scientific inquiry, critics by 1920 had already pointed out that they tended to treat the patient in isolation and attend to cure rather than prevention. Still, the very existence of this new institution was intimately tied to the development of current medical specializations like neurosurgery.

COMMUNITIES PROVIDE NORMS
FOR EXCELLENCE

Excellence is more than just technical expertise, considered in isolation; it involves expertise as embedded in a social context of cultural institutions and practices that impose normative expectations on the categories and stories by which one trains and evaluates individuals (children or novices in general). It is precisely by means of such norms that cultures maintain and foster their identity over time, and reward those judged most excellent. Cultures impose normative expectations on their members as embodied in our understanding of accepted practice, or in judges, executives, and other key representatives of cultural institutions.[4]

Such norms define the parameters of what Ferrari—following Amsterdam and Bruner (2000)—calls a culture's noetic space. A culture's noetic space includes those possibilities that represent the "cultural imagination" or possible worlds in which individuals imagine that they can live and act, and what I understand Bourdieu (1997) to mean by cultural capital. It is against these expectations that individuals measure their performance, whether the culture is that of school or the basketball court or the music hall. Ferrari proposes that excellence may represent an upper bound of canonical normativity, one that points the way to the further enrichment of the canon. In this view, as Mascolo and colleagues point out, excellence only makes sense in light of culturally posited developmental outcomes or endpoints, as judgments of excellence imply an implicit or explicit comparison of one's specific performances to some idealized fully developed form.

If this is so, then excellence necessarily deals with culturally determined *narratives*, like stories of heroes, saints, or utopian tales (including everyday transient utopias like a "perfect day" at the beach), or the contrast case of narratives about evil people and scoundrels that any self-respecting person should not emulate. All such narratives have to do with considering the best ways that events should unfold, and are necessarily tied to views of what people ought to do and value (Taylor, 1989, 1995).

Stories often valorize the lives of exemplary individuals (experts, heroes, and saints), with narratives exemplifying excellence sometimes acquiring canonical forms with certain stock features, such as the hero tale (Bruner & Kalmar, 1998; Propp, 1984). Narratives exemplifying excellence require surpassing expectations and are necessarily bound up with implicit praxic knowledge—knowledge of what should happen in particular circumstances. In fact, stories about excellence are often distorted to make them fit the genre and we resist attempts to introduce real-world complexities into

---

[4]Although little mention is made of this point, the noetic space in which the authors of the volume imagine experts' acting is a very different one than, say, that of an expert at Shamanistic practices of the Malay (Laderman, 1994) or of some Amazon tribes (Rivière, 1999).

them (e.g., complexities about the personal lives of scientific heroes like Einstein). Although narratives about excellent individuals do not necessarily go unchallenged, they are essential to engaging that *noetic* space in which everyday individuals imagine how the world might be different.

Judgments of excellence are also bound up with *categories* relevant to particular reference groups—what is good in one time or place is not necessarily valued in another. Such categorical notions of excellence are tied to prototypes and organized into category systems; they allow one to identify particular people as, for example, heroes or saints (categories that only exist in a field of contrasts that includes cowards and evildoers). Whether events and individuals are considered excellent depends crucially on how they are categorized, and the problem of what to do when confronted by competing categories and standards of excellence is still very much with us today.

Excellence as Involving Personal Commitment to Particular Communal Values

While many of the authors in the volume emphasize excellence in terms of technical skill, many also point out the importance of ethical dimensions of excellence. Excellence presupposes value judgments, and is evaluated by ourselves and significant others in terms of how ably we navigate cultural value systems. Indeed, some authors like Pinkus and Sauder and Mascolo and colleagues define excellence in terms of values, skills, and outcomes that people need to function well in a particular community.

This reflects a deep point made by Taylor (1989, 1995) that might be paraphrased in two key questions that one might ask about excellence: "How can we explain exceptional performance?" (critical for science), and "How should we act in order to be a good person?"(critical for ethics and morality). Both of these questions are embraced by the authors in the volume as essential to any deep understanding of excellence and how it might be fostered through education.

For example, Pinkus and Sauder note that Harvey Cushing aimed to address both technical expertise and the ethical aspects of excellence in neurosurgery when training medical interns and residents. He expressed this synthesis in his professional maxims or rules for becoming a good physician.[5] Recent research by Benner, Tanner, and Chesla (1996) shows

---

[5]Sometimes such maxims are not as obvious in people's published work, but can be an important aspect of their thinking. At his 1998 retirement party, Robert Glaser read a list of maxims to the assembly, many of which had a deeply ethical (and humorous) character. One of the most memorable, for me, was the following: "People who are all wrapped up in themselves make very small bundles." A deep truth that I am sure reflects some of the spirit behind fostering an institution as complex as Pittsburgh's Learning Research and Development Center.

that this ethical stance toward medical practice is very much a part of excellent nurses' perspective on what is essential to their practice. Benner and colleagues' study of expert and inexpert nurses' narratives about critical cases shows that expert nurses were able to recall not only their technical actions (e.g., the amount of medicine they administered), but also their ethical reasoning surrounding those decisions. These ethical judgments sometimes led them to question or even rebel against decisions by others on the medical team (e.g., less-experienced residents) when they felt the decision was unethical or simply unwise. Inexpert nurses, with equivalent years of experience, were unable to do either. The key point is that for these nurses, excellence is not merely a matter of technical expertise, but is essentially bound up in their interpretations of their ethical responsibility to provide quality care and to deal with patients compassionately.

Individuals Endorse Communal Norms in Interpreting Personal Excellence

Personal appraisals of excellence are intimately tied to cultural expectations of what it means to be a good person (Freeman & Brockmeir, in press; Taylor, 1989). Self-interpretation is thus bound up in communal values that we cannot help but endorse if we are to have a personal identity within a particular society (Bruner & Kalmar, 1998; Taylor, 1989). We judge others and ourselves as excellent or the opposite in terms of how we measure up to these norms. Thus, excellence is intimately tied up with narrative, categories, and rhetoric about what is excellent that are provided by our community; ideas that we must interpret and endorse in light of our own experience.

Indeed, we generate our own synthesis of cultural narratives and categories by selecting those that we wish to endorse and pursue and those that we wish to fight against or merely ignore (Ferrari & Mahalingam, 1998). And sometimes we search for a way to *transcend* cultural expectations, and look for narratives of those who have transcended the limitations of society (Bloom, 1996). A cross-cultural example of transcendence is seen in the Mahabharata (Vyasa, 1970), one of the oldest and most widely read epic poems from ancient India. One episode in the epic (section 134) tells the story of an excellent student, Ekalaivya. According to the story, this student was an untouchable, who wanted to learn archery from the greatest Brahmin instructor, but was refused because that teacher had promised to instruct royal princes to be the best. But by contemplating a clay statue of the teacher and training diligently using his methods for years, Ekalaivya became the greatest archer in the land. When this was discovered, the teacher demanded a payment of his choice, as was the custom: He asked for Ekalaivya's right thumb. Without hesitation Ekalaivya cut off his thumb and handed it to his teacher. This story, disturbing to a modern Western reader like me, has a powerful resonance in India. Like the story of *Uncle Tom's Cabin* for American slaves years ago, the story of Ekalaivya remains an inspiration to the moral imagination. It strikes an emotional and an ideological chord in which excellence is an act of resistance, and where sacrificing physical/technical ability is a sign of an excellent character.

Strength in Numbers: Organizations and Fields as Enhancing the Potential for Social Excellence

Simon points out that human beings have only a bounded rationality and so our judgments of excellence refer to attempts at seeking acceptable solutions, not optimal ones. Furthermore, we band together with others to increase our individual agency. A very effective way to go beyond individual limitations is to found organizations in which to share our knowledge and experience. Many, if not most, major cultural achievements are accomplished within organizations, not by individuals working in isolation. Thus, Simon insists that we need excellent organizations, not a world without organizations.

However, the excellence of an organization's vision is defined in light of the environment to which it must adapt or the population it must serve. Organizations are considered good when they lead to the development of intellectual and political alliances; they are considered bad when they inflame ethnic or national loyalties at the expense of justice, as seen in the recent histories of Serbia, Rwanda, and Cambodia.

Institutional excellence depends on the excellence of the individuals who populate them, if not in isolation, then in their work as part of an excellent team. According to Simon, not much systematic research has been done on entrepreneurs, but they are critical to developing excellent institutions. Simon suggests that entrepreneurs not only lead and manage institutions, but they also create and nurture them to promote excellence. Entrepreneurs are innovators, but not necessarily inventors. Shaping the future, for them, requires not a utopian dream, but rather an understanding of what is feasible at the time. For example, George Leland Bach was in a position to design the sort of business school he thought ideal, because he was essentially starting from scratch. But he was careful to maintain a balance of new and old in the new school to assure that the innovative aspects of the curriculum would be accepted by students, potential employers, and other learning institutions. In other words, he wanted graduates who would be accepted by others in the field and by their clients. The key for Bach and other entrepreneurs, according to Simon, is to forego following a fixed plan and instead to develop the organization step by step, adapting as prevailing conditions demand. Such an approach is characteristic of what Sternberg (1998, 1999) calls practical or successful intelligence, or what in applied ethics is called casuistry, in which one considers the specific circumstances of particular cases when deciding upon the wisest course of action (Jonsen & Toulmin, 1988; Kuczewski, 1997).

Importance of Individuals for Organizational Self-Definition

Some individuals' contribution to the organization is to enhance the excellence of the organization itself; these are individuals who come to typify the ideals of a local culture or a "local moral ecology" (French, 1994). For Simon, Allen Newell exemplified the virtue of acting according to the "Reasonable Person Principle," which reflected an ethical stance as much as any technical or knowledge-based approach to his profession; this principle became the "ethos" of the Psychology Department at Carnegie Mellon University.

Gardner and Simon add that excellence rarely develops without a deep commitment to goals, even in the face of discouraging or threatening circumstances. Key to promoting institutional excellence is a shared vision and shared goals for the new institution. This requires both dedicated leaders and loyal followers. Sometimes leaders are technical experts, as Cushing was in neurosurgery or like Glaser in psychology. But, sometimes leaders are those who are able to gather the right team of people together, or lead indirectly by their own example, as in the case of Newell.

Sometimes leaders found an entirely new discipline, as did Cushing with neurosurgery. However, Cushing and Dandy were both key in establishing criteria (standards of excellence) that would assure quality control for excellent or at least highly competent practice and struggled precisely over how to improve neurosurgery.

As this struggle between Cushing and Dandy shows, fields like medicine are not unified and monolithic within a culture, and thus do not necessarily share a single interpretation of how to strive toward excellence. Even without the appearance of new subspecialties, medicine was not an organized professional field at the turn of the century, nor is it today. As always, minority fractions among medical practitioners (homeopathy, acupuncture, etc.) remain an important influence on how the field as a whole continues to develop and change. Likewise, Pinkus and Sauder note that at Shouldice Hospital outside Toronto, surgeons perform only hernia-repair operations; being specialized, they are able to successfully complete these operations in half the time and at half the cost. This excellent result occurs even if they have not completed the certification that would allow them to be hired as surgeons by American hospitals.

CULTURES ARE NOT MONOLITHIC, NOR ARE THE
NORMATIVE EXPECTATIONS THEY GENERATE

Different institutions like schools or churches that are a gateway into culture (Bruner, 1996) strive to promote different sorts of valued endpoints in their constituent members, and this may cause their goals and their proposed pathways toward those goals to diverge. In other words, one can be excellent according to one set of cultural standards and ordinary, or even deviant, according to another. This is true in small ways when a student is an excellent musician but a mediocre scholar, or in ways as large as Salman Rushdie being considered an excellent writer by his Western readers and a dangerous religious heretic by many fundamentalist Muslims around the world.

Furthermore, just as different constituencies within or between cultures may value different forms of expertise as excellent, so may different educational institutions strive to foster different skills considered necessary to become an excellent student. For example, Li (1997) examined Chinese and American conceptions of ideal learners and found that Western schools focus on "achievement motivation" whereas Chinese schools focus on "passion for learning." The Chinese conception of *hao-xue-xin* (literally, "heart and mind for wanting to learn," or passion for learning) is held to differ substantially from the North American ideal of personally excelling relative to peers. Although neither culture is monolithic, Li suggests that the aim of American education centers around ability (which individuals may think is fixed, or that it can be developed; Chiu, Hong, & Dweck, 1994; Nicholls, 1984); as such, people feel pride at success, and guilt at failure. For the Chinese, key educational values include effort and positive regard for school. Parents in China praise attempts to learn or perform for their own sake, independently of one's success; the emphasis is on learning itself, rather than on achievement. Further, the goal of learning is "to perfect oneself"; that is to develop one's moral character, rather than to learn specific disciplinary knowledge or skills. Thus, for the Chinese children, shame and guilt are associated with poor attempts at learning, not poor achievement. Not only that, shame is shame before one's family, and achievement is attributed to family.

Still, despite the important differences in the educational system of China and America identified by Li, I think it is important not to overexaggerate them. Many North Americans will readily grant that their success is due to social opportunities. I certainly believe that my current situation in life has very much to do with family, and I imagine that many North Americans share this view. Even popular maxims about education in both cultures, despite surface differences, may share a very similar spirit. For example, the Chinese maxim, "No obstacle doesn't fear a wanting heart" for me has an English near equivalent in, "If at first you don't succeed, try and try again." Furthermore, in a deep sense, excellence in learning in American education is increasingly thought to involve students' hearts (i.e., through provoking an emotional resonance in the learner) as well as their minds (i.e., through generating an abstract conceptual understanding) (Jackson, Doster, Meadows, & Wood, 1995). Indeed, this idea of engaging "the heart" as foundational to learning has a long history in Western theology and philosophy of education (Ware, 1999).

Be that as it may, North American schools, as cultural institutions, are certainly designed to teach students a variety of knowledge domains (although as Egan, 1997, noted they sometimes have competing aims of explaining what is true, fostering personal development, and social preparation that sometimes pull in competing directions). However, schools are not alone as institutions of learning. Many other institutions like music academies, art schools, or karate and chess clubs, are set up specifically to train promising candidates in knowledge domains that reflect different aspects of culture.[6]

Finally, standards of educational excellence are not always uniquely generated within a particular type of institution. Many political and cultural institutions interact and fight over the right to set standards. This is true when one considers cases of malpractice in medicine that are brought to trial, or the right for schools to teach scientific theories (like the theories of evolution or the big bang) that contradict literal religious interpretations of the Bible, a case that has repeatedly been before the courts (Gould, 1999).

The very idea that there exist different canons and constituencies in any given culture means that any discussion of excellence is intimately bound up to issues of power and rhetoric. Excellence thus necessarily involves a dynamic process that negotiates the best balance between many competing ideals. Rhetoric is critical to the outcome of such negotiations, as the person who has the most convincing rhetoric will often carry the day (and not always for the best reasons, as cases of self-delusion clearly show; Amsterdam & Bruner, 2000; Taylor, 1995).

LESSONS LEARNED FROM CONSIDERING EXCELLENCE THROUGH EDUCATION

Some individuals or institutions are not seen as excellent in a given domain because they achieve a minimum level of competence and are satis-

---

[6]Less formally, many individuals may become sophisticated movie critics, skiers, or well versed in a host of other skills by participating with interested others who are themselves excellent at these special skills.

fied. Thus individuals may engage in activity for fun (play) with no aim to improve, or they may engage in it competitively (work) and not feel able to risk failure on the chance of improving. Although some may see this as unfortunate, it is important to acknowledge that achieving excellence in any given domain is rarely without its cost in other aspects of one's life. A life in pursuit of excellence is demanding, may be harsh on others, and is certainly not for everyone. Nevertheless, important lessons can be learned for education generally from considering excellent practitioners and institutions.

Gardner states that an important lesson from considering extraordinary individuals is that detailed studies of such individuals show that they are not born different; they achieved what they did by working hard, often against the odds. Such people give us vivid examples to emulate, as long as we realize that they are multidimensional, with strengths and weaknesses. Students need to be trained in ways that let them truly emulate extraordinary individuals, and not merely admire them. Also, studies suggest that it is worth treating all students as potentially extraordinary, as we can't at present know who will really become extraordinary. Another important lesson was summed up by Kuhn (1977) who said that scientists require a thorough commitment to the tradition with which if they are completely successful, they will break. In other words, what begins as a quantitative difference between individuals becomes a difference in kind.

However, it is also important to remind students, with Eco (1998), that although knowledge and training methods are certainly important to achieving excellence, one must never underestimate the importance of serendipity as an unexpected path to excellence. A wonderful example is the story of Christopher Columbus. Had he not miscalculated the circumference of the earth, he would never have dreamed of setting sail for India in three small ships, with limited provisions—but he still ended up discovering America.

Gardner notes three key attitudes adopted by extraordinary individuals that are important precepts for all students, and that make allowance for bounded rationality and serendipity:

1. *Reflecting*, which includes setting goals, monitoring progress, and keeping some sort of record. Naturally, effective self-regulation may be substantially different in different individuals. For example, different excellent writers like Proust and Hemingway organized their time and efforts very differently. One ended up writing voluminously and the other more sparingly, but both had a great impact on their field; determining which strategies work best for a given individual requires individual reflection.

2. *Leveraging*, which involves identifying one's strengths and weaknesses in intelligence, temperament, and personality, and promoting the

strengths while overcoming one's weaknesses. This allows one to carve a niche that capitalizes on one's strengths. Mascolo and his colleagues' chapter points out that there are many paths to excellence, with development better thought of as a web than a ladder. This metaphor suggests that there are multiple pathways to excellence in any given field, although presumably not an infinite number. Thus some people achieve excellence in their careers, even with an inability to excel at certain component skills of basic tasks such as reading (Fink, 1998). This study provides a great example of what Gardner means by being reflective and leveraging existing skills to compensate for weaknesses.

3. *Framing*, in which individuals ponder their defeats and learn from them. Of course, in situations where one is the target of injustice, as in the story of Ekalaivya, excellence can sometimes require a framing that transcends the limitations of one's current situation (Bloom, 1996) and demonstrates one's moral superiority.

Gichen Funakoshi (1975), considered the father of modern karate, illustrates these points nicely in the closing paragraphs of his autobiography, written in his ninth decade of life:

> One thing I often say to my young pupils they find confusing. "You must," I tell them, "become not strong but weak." Then they want to know what I mean, [. . .]. It is hardly necessary, they tell me, to train in order to become weak. Then I reply that what I am saying is indeed difficult to understand. "I want you to find the answer within yourselves," I tell them. [And] I am convinced that if young people practice [. . .] with all their heart and all their soul, they will eventually arrive at an understanding of my words. He who is aware of his own weaknesses will remain master of himself in any situation; only a true weakling is capable of true courage. Naturally, a real [. . .] adept must refine his technique through training, but he must never forget that only through training will he be able to recognize his own weaknesses. (pp. 114–115)

REFERENCES

Allport, G. W. (1942). *The use of personal documents in psychological science* (Prepared for the Committee on Appraisal of Research). New York: Social Science Research Council.

Amsterdam, A., & Bruner, J. (2000). *Minding the law*. New York: Harvard University Press.

Baldwin, J. M. (1930). James Mark Baldwin. In C. Murchison (Ed.), *A history of psychology in autobiography* (pp. 1–30). New York: Russell & Russell.

Benner, P., Tanner, C. A., & Chesla, C. A. (1996). *Expertise in nursing practice: Caring, clinical judgment, and ethics*. New York: Springer.

Bloom, H. (1996). *Omens of millennium. The gnosis of angels, dreams, and resurrection*. New York: Riverhead Books.

Bourdieu, P. (1997). *Méditiations pascaliennes* [Pascalian meditations]. Paris: Seuil.

Bruner, J. (1996). *The culture of education.* Cambridge, MA: Harvard University Press.

Bruner, J., & Kalmar, D. A. (1998). Narrative and metanarrative in the construction of self. In M. Ferrari & R. J. Sternberg (Eds.), *Self-awareness: Its nature and development* (pp. 308–331). New York: Guilford.

Charness, N., Krampe, R., & Mayr, U. (1996). The role of practice and coaching in entrepreneurial skill domains: An international comparison of life-span chess skill acquisition. In K. A. Ericsson (Ed.), *The road to excellence: The acquisition of expert performance in the arts and sciences, sports, and games* (pp. 51–80). Mahwah, NJ: Lawrence Erlbaum Associates.

Chiu, C., Hong, Y., & Dweck, C. S. (1994). Toward an integrative model of personality and intelligence: A general framework and some preliminary steps. In R. J. Sternberg & P. Ruzgis (Eds.), *Personality and intelligence* (pp. 104–136). New York: Cambridge University Press.

Eco, U. (1998). *Serendipities: Language and lunacy* (W. Weaver, Trans.). New York: Harcourt Brace.

Egan, K. (1997). *The educated mind. How cognitive tools shape our understanding.* Chicago: University of Chicago Press.

Ericsson, K. A., Krampe, R. T., & Tesch-Römer, C. (1993). The role of deliberate practice in the acquisition of expert performance. *Psychological Review, 100,* 363–406.

Ericsson, K. A., & Smith, J. (1991). Prospects and limits in the empirical study of expertise: An introduction. In K. A. Ericsson & J. Smith (Eds.), *Toward a general theory of expertise: Prospects and limits* (pp. 1–38). Cambridge, England: Cambridge University Press.

Ferrari, M., & Mahalingam, R. (1998). Personal cognitive development and its implications for teaching and learning. *Educational Psychologist, 33,* 35–44.

Fink, R. P. (1998). Literacy development in successful men and women with dyslexia. *Annals of Dyslexia, 48,* 311–346.

Freeman, M., & Brockmeier, J. (in press). Narrative integrity: Autobiographical identity and the meaning of the "good life." In J. Brockmeier & D. Carbaugh (Eds.), *Narrative and identity: Studies in autobiography, self, and culture.* Amsterdam & Philadelphia: John Benjamins.

French, L. (1994). The political economy of injury and compassion: Amputees on the Thai-Cambodia border. In T. J. Csordas (Ed.), *Embodiment and experience: The existential ground of culture and self* (pp. 69–99). New York: Cambridge University Press.

Funakoshi, G. (1975). *Karate-do: My way of life.* New York: Kodansha International. (Original work published in Japanese 1956)

Gould, S. J. (1996). *Full house: The spread of excellence from Plato to Darwin.* New York: Harmony Books.

Gould, S. J. (1999). *Rocks of ages: Science and religion in the fullness of life.* New York: Ballantine.

Jackson, D. F., Doster, E. C., Meadows, L., & Wood, T. (1995). Hearts and minds in the science classroom: The education of a confirmed evolutionist. *Journal of Research in Science Teaching, 32*(6), 585–611.

Jonsen, A. R., & Toulmin, S. (1988). *The abuse of casuistry.* New York: Cambridge University Press.

Kuczewski, M. G. (1997*). Fragmentation and consensus: Communitarian and casuist bioethics.* Washington, DC: Georgetown University Press.

Kuhn, T. (1977). *The essential tension: Selected studies in scientific tradition and change.* Chicago: University of Chicago Press.

Laderman, C. (1994). The embodiment of symbols and the acculturation of the anthropologist. In T. J. Csordas (Ed.), *Embodiment and experience: The existential ground of culture and self* (pp. 183–197). New York: Cambridge University Press.

Lehmann, A. C., & Ericsson, K. A. (1998). The historical development of domains of expertise: Performance standards and innovations in music. In A. Steptoe (Ed.), *Genius and the mind* (pp. 67–94). Oxford, England: Oxford University Press.

Lewis, M. (2000). The promise of dynamic systems approaches for an integrated account of human development. *Child Development, 71*(1), 36–43.

Li, J. (1997). *The Chinese "heart and mind for wanting to learn" (hao-xue-xin): A culturally based learning model*. Unpublished doctoral dissertation, Harvard University, Cambridge, MA.

Nicholls, J. G. (1984). Achievement motivation: Conceptions of ability, subjective experience, task choice, and performance. *Psychological Review, 91*, 328–346.

Parrila, R. K., Das, J. P., & Dash, U. N. (1996). Development of planning and its relation to other cognitive processes. *Journal of Applied Developmental Psychology, 17*, 597–624.

Propp, V. (1984). *Theory and history of folklore*. Minneapolis: University of Minnesota Press.

Rivière, P. (1999). Shamanism and the unconfined soul. In M. J. C. Crabbe (Ed.), *From soul to self* (pp. 70–88). New York: Routledge.

Starkes, J. L., Deakin, J., Allard, F., Hodges, N. J., & Hayes, A. (1996). Deliberate practice in sports: What is it anyway? In K. A. Ericsson (Ed.), *The road to excellence: The acquisition of expert performance in the arts and sciences, sports, and games* (pp. 81–106). Mahwah, NJ: Lawrence Erlbaum Associates.

Sternberg, R. J. (1998). Metacognition, abilites, and developing expertise: What makes an expert student? *Instructional Science, 26*, 127–140.

Sternberg, R. J. (Ed.). (1999). *Handbook of creativity*. New York: Cambridge University Press.

Taylor, C. (1985). *Philosophy and the human sciences: Philosophical papers 2*. New York: Cambridge University Press.

Taylor, C. (1989). *Sources of the self: The making of modern identity*. Cambridge, MA: Harvard University Press.

Taylor, C. (1995). *Philosophical arguments*. Cambridge, MA: Harvard University Press.

Vyasa (1970). *Mahabharata* (Vol.17) (P. Lāl, Trans.). Calcutta: Writers Workshop.

Ware, K. (1999). The soul in Greek Christianity. In M. J. C. Crabbe (Ed.), *From soul to self* (pp. 49–69). New York: Routledge.

Author Index

Subject Index